"With vigorous, purposeful prose and a killer knack for building suspense . . . Mnookin crisply captures the tit-for-tat tenor of the Gray Lady's newsroom, describing how its historically significant foundation of trust was nearly obliterated."

—*Entertainment Weekly*

"In *Hard News*, a con man is the center of attention, but the ideal of 'getting it right' is the book's true heart—a juicy morality tale for the information age."

—Sarah Vowell

One of "The 50 Best Books on Media."

—*The Independent* (U.K.)

"Seth Mnookin has done the improbable: Written a book about a newspaper's personnel problems that not only reads like a crime thriller but says some important things about American culture. How did he do it? The old-fashioned way—through painstaking reporting and engaging writing. . . . It's a hell of a story, even for those who don't spend their days inside a newsroom or read the *Times* each day as if it were the Dead Sea Scrolls. . . . Mnookin finds the drama, sees the story arc, and delivers it beautifully. Vision, narrative thrust, and telling detail: It's all here."

—*The Buffalo News*

"This is an enthralling tale that's part soap opera, part Greek tragedy, and part detective story. . . . *Hard News* is not only a good book, it's also a good read."

—*San Antonio Express-News*

"This is two terrific books in one: a riveting thriller, starring a heroic Dirty Dozen team of reporters risking their careers to unearth dangerous truths; and a Shakespearean tragedy about hubris and race and good intentions and self-destruction featuring a pathetic, half-mad villain and a noble, deluded king. Seth Mnookin has written the definitive chronicle of this extraordinary upheaval."

—Kurt Andersen

"An important new book . . . In the end the good guys prevailed, but Mnookin rightly is less interested in the *Times*'s individual winners and losers than in the powerfully cautionary lesson his riveting account offers to all journalists. . . . *Hard News* is a memorable warning that reporters and editors worldwide should heed."

—*Financial Times*

"A fascinating book . . . suspenseful and Shakespearean . . . You don't have to be a newsroom employee or media geek to enjoy *Hard News*. Mnookin's story reads like a taut thriller, and in Raines it even has a tragic hero."

—*Omaha World-Herald*

"A heck of a good yarn . . . Mnookin sets the stage with a brief summary of the *Times*'s history, enough to give the story context, and then plunges ahead with a rip-roaring tale about audacious deception and how the *Times* let it happen by failing to enforce its traditional high standards."

—*The Hartford Courant*

"[A] gripping account of the Jayson Blair scandal and the brief, disastrous reign of former *New York Times* executive editor Howell Raines . . . Mnookin provides an admirably full account of this ultimate crash-reporting assignment and the foxhole mentality it bred among the investigative team. . . . It's compulsive bedside reading."

—Salon.com

"An edge-of-your-seat thriller that details the fall of both a mighty institution and its leader, the cocky Howell Raines."

—*The Palm Beach Post*

"A juicy, fly-on-the-wall account of the upheaval that engulfed America's preeminent newspaper."

—*The Boston Globe*

"[Mnookin's] new book . . . is a thorough and riveting examination of the institution that is *The New York Times*, and how the Jayson Blair scandal and its aftermath nearly brought that institution to its knees."

—*The Boston Phoenix*

"*Hard News* is a finely scripted tale that should appeal not only to journalists and news junkies, but also to anyone in corporate America interested in what happens when an egocentric manager abandons meritocracy for favoritism and is driven by a specious ideology."

—*The Columbus Dispatch*

"Mnookin . . . has written a book that is definitive, balanced and as gripping as a detective novel."

—*Tucson Citizen*

"If the book has an aspect of a classic mythic tale of hubris, it also reads in parts like a thriller. . . . For newspaper junkies, this is a seductive book, but even for those who don't make their lives in the newspaper world, it's a gripping read."

—*The Charleston Gazette* (West Virginia)

"A comprehensive, well-argued, humanizing narrative . . . [Mnookin's] conclusions about the Blair incident show a deeper understanding of how newspapers work and fail."

—*The Village Voice*

"Full of insight and valuable information."

—*New York Post*

"Seth Mnookin is one of the hardest working, most ambitious, and most talented reporters of his generation. . . . [*Hard News* is] a gripping, fast-moving tale. Mr. Mnookin has all the insider tick-tock of the story . . . and he's a smooth writer. . . . A significant feat of nonfiction narrative writing."

—*The New York Sun*

"Eminently readable . . . One of the most inspiring stories about journalism since *All the President's Men*."

—*The News Tribune* (Tacoma, Washington)

HARD NEWS

C.2

HARD NEWS

Twenty-one Brutal Months
at *The New York Times* and
How They Changed the
American Media

SETH MNOOKIN

RANDOM HOUSE TRADE PAPERBACKS
New York

2005 Random House Trade Paperback Edition

Published in the United States by Random House Trade
Paperbacks, an imprint of The Random House Publishing
Group, a division of Random House, Inc., New York.

RANDOM HOUSE TRADE PAPERBACKS and colophon are
trademarks of Random House, Inc.

Originally published in hardcover in the United States
by Random House, an imprint of The Random House
Publishing Group, a division of Random House, Inc.,
in 2004.

LIBRARY OF CONGRESS CATALOGING-
IN-PUBLICATION DATA

Mnookin, Seth.
Hard news : Twenty-one brutal months at *The New York Times*
and how they changed the American media / Seth Mnookin.
p.   cm.
Includes bibliographical references and index.
ISBN 0-8129-7251-1 (alk. paper)
1. New York times.   2. Press—United States—History—
21st century.   3. Journalism—United States—History—
21st century.   I. Title.
PN4899.N42M66 2004
071'.471—dc22
2004051250

Printed in the United States of America

www.atrandom.com

2   4   6   8   9   7   5   3

Book design by Dana Leigh Blanchette

For my parents

and

Dedicated to the memory
of Hunter S. Thompson

Were it left to me to decide whether we should have a government without newspapers, or newspapers without a government, I should not hesitate a moment to prefer the latter.
　　　　　—*Thomas Jefferson,*
　　Letter to Colonel Edward Carrington, 1787

This was not exactly the truth, but then, what is, exactly?
　　　　　—*Howell Raines,*
　　Whiskey Man, *1977*

Contents

INTRODUCTION

The first newspaper printed in America lasted only one issue. *Publick Occurences, Both Foreign and Domestick*, was printed in Boston on September 25, 1690, but it wasn't until a century later that newspapering in this country truly got going. By 1783, at the end of the American Revolution, there were 43 papers, and by 1787 the young American government had formally recognized how important a healthy press was to a healthy democracy: The First Amendment to the republic's new Constitution famously promised that "Congress shall make no law . . . abridging the freedom of speech, or of the press." Encouraged, the press mushroomed. By 1814, there were 346 domestic newspapers; by 1880, there were 11,314.

While America has always enjoyed a more or less free and healthy press, the commonly accepted practices of journalism have undergone a radical transformation between its beginnings and the present day. For the first century of the country's existence, the notion of a uniformly "objective" press seemed quaint and naïve. While some papers strove to be fair-minded and accurate, many others chose sensationalism, or political expediency, or tawdry slander. By the end of the nineteenth century, a pair of irascible (and incorrigible) press barons, Joseph Pulitzer and William Randolph Hearst, had turned their bitter newspaper rivalry into a lesson in warmongering and dishonest reportage, creating scandals for the express purpose of embarrassing the competition and disseminating jingoistic propaganda. (Hearst, in his inimitable way, would later brag that he had all but started the Spanish-American War. He wasn't far off.)

It was into this world that the modern-day *New York Times* was born. In the late 1800s, the *Times* was a small, struggling broadsheet, minuscule in comparison with Hearst's *Journal* or Pulitzer's *World*. The paper made a name for itself by seizing an underrepresented market niche. By emphasizing judicious reporting (and official proclamations), the *Times* transformed itself into a true paper of record, one avowedly uninfluenced by public opinion and dedicated to reporting the truth. Over generations, the paper earned a hard-won and much-cherished reputation for being fair and impartial. Readers, in turn, came to trust and rely on the *Times* with an almost religious fervor and, in doing so, helped to make the *Times*, and the sort of journalism it had created, the standard to which all other newspapers would have to compare themselves. More than any other single source, the *Times* would come to represent the closest journalism could get to unvarnished truth.

———

TODAY, *The New York Times* is the most important newspaper in America. That's not to say it's always the best. *The Wall Street Journal* is frequently more eloquent. *The Washington Post* often leads the pack on political stories and of late has been both nimbler and more authoritative. For the last several years, the *Los Angeles Times* has produced a more purposeful news report, and in 2004 it thoroughly dominated the Pulitzer Prizes. But *The New York Times*—by dint of the talent of its staff, its location in the world's media capital, and its decades-long position as the bible of the American elite—is the institution that represents the pinnacle of its field.

Whether or not it will remain so is an open question. In an increasingly fractured media landscape that is characterized by declining newspaper readership, a proliferation of cable news networks and weblogs, and a blurring of the lines between entertainment and journalism, the *Times* is fighting to maintain the grip it has had on America's collective consciousness for more than half a century. Ironically, that fracturing is as responsible for the *Times*'s lingering dominance as is its journalistic excellence—these days, the number of media options is so overwhelming that there almost needs to be a default standard-bearer. The rest of the media world, from broadcast news to cable outlets to other newspapers to glossy magazines, still looks to the *Times* to tell it what's important, what each day's conventional wisdom will be. Every evening, when the *Times* sends out the next day's story list on its newswire, it sets the agenda for hundreds of other daily papers across the country. Every morning, the *Times*'s front page comes closer than any other single source of information to determining what will count as major news for the next twenty-four hours. *The New York Times* continues to serve as a beacon for the rest of the media world, and it continues to set the standard to which all other media outlets must aspire or against which they must rebel. The *Times* is like Harvard or the New York Yankees. It so dominates our imagination that it has become an archetype of what it means to be a journalistic enterprise.

That's not to say the *Times* can, or indeed does, take its position for granted. Aside from the fact that consumers are less likely to read a daily paper today than at any time in the last hundred years, it is also easier to get instant access to news from almost anywhere in the world. A 2004 Project for Excellence in Journalism study on the state of the country's news media found that "journalism is in the midst of an epochal transformation, as momentous probably as the invention of the telegraph or television." That five-hundred-page study also spent considerable space addressing how "major news institutions have changed their product in a way that costs less to produce while still attracting an audience." To continue to dominate the field, Arthur Sulzberger Jr., the publicly held Times Company's uniquely powerful chairman and the *The New York Times*'s publisher, has had to try to reimagine what it means to be both a topflight newspaper company and a news-gathering operation. Sulzberger is keenly aware that he sits at the head of a company that his family—and the country—regards more as a public trust than as anything so prosaic as a business concern. For more than a hundred years, the Sulzbergers and the Times Company have operated on the principle that they know how to do one thing well: run a big-city broadsheet. Their dedication to this mission has demanded that they pass up some plum investment opportunities. At the turn of the twentieth century, the Times Company declined an opportunity to invest in Coca-Cola because the soft-drink firm was too far removed from the company's core business. Just after World War II, it turned down an offer from the government to create a television station in New York City for next to nothing, so that it could focus on newspapering. (The Hearst Corporation, by contrast, eagerly launched television stations when given the opportunity and today is one of the country's largest media combines.) As media companies were becoming media conglomerates, as family papers like the *Los Angeles Times* were gobbled up by corporations like the Tribune Company, *The New York Times* remained relatively small and enormously successful.

Despite the efficacy of the *Times*'s historic single-mindedness, Arthur Sulzberger has become convinced this conservative road will eventually lead to ruin, a concern that has made him determined to broaden the *Times*'s audience while simultaneously increasing its revenues. Sulzberger considers himself a visionary with a single mission: to ensure that in ten and twenty and fifty years, *The New York Times* will still be the brightest star in the world's information firmament. He is trying to achieve this goal both by expanding the newspaper's reach—today almost half the paper's daily circulation comes from outside the New York City metropolitan area—and by striving to make the Times Company "platform agnostic." "TV, the Internet, all of that is integral to the growth of *The New York Times*'s brand," Sulzberger told me in early 2004. "That's how we're going to reach more like-minded readers. That's how we're going to remain profitable in the years ahead. If print starts to become less of a growth area—which is not happening right now, but if and when it does—we need to be ready. We're thinking long range here. . . . That means you have to invest in the future even as you're managing a brand."

This path of expansion has been, as often as not, tumultuous. Some Wall Street analysts question whether or not, in aggressively chasing after national readers and advertisers, the *Times* has neglected its extremely profitable New York base. Some wonder if it wouldn't have made more sense to build a national network of premier newspapers instead of trying to force the *Times* on a national audience. (This has been the path of the Tribune Company, which today owns the Baltimore *Sun*, the *Los Angeles Times*, south Florida's *Sun-Sentinel*, *The Hartford Courant*, the *Orlando Sentinel*, and Long Island's *Newsday*—many of which the *Times* itself has, at one time or another, had the opportunity to buy.) Journalists at the *Times* wonder why the company is investing so many millions of dollars in television ventures and the Internet while the newspaper is under what some feel are prohibitory budget constraints. What's more, Sulzberger's early efforts to expand the Times Company's reach have produced decidedly mixed results. In 1999, the New York Times Company acquired Abuzz.com, an online information-swapping portal, for $30 million. In 2001, it closed the company's offices and took a $22.7 million charge related to the site. In April 2002, the Times Company invested $100 million in the Discovery Times Channel, a digital TV station it co-owns with the Discovery Channel, which thus far has produced a string of well-reviewed programs that relatively few people have seen. Even investments that have been more obviously in tune with the *Times*'s core business have not always unfolded smoothly. In October 2002, Arthur Sulzberger forced *The Washington Post* to sell its 50 percent stake in the *International Herald Tribune* (*IHT*) for $70 million by threatening to start an overseas edition of the *Times*. Sulzberger maintains the *IHT* is needed to expand the *Times*'s global reach, although Europe has historically been a sinkhole for American newspaper companies trying to establish an international presence—the audience can be difficult to define, and the cost of doing business is often prohibitively high. What's more, the Graham family, which owns *The Washington Post*, was insulted by what they viewed as Sulzberger's heavy-handed ways.*†

Whether in agreement or not with his manner or his business decisions, no one disputes that Sulzberger does have a vision. In the late 1990s, just as Sulzberger was reimagining what a newspaper company should look like, he was also thinking about what his newspaper should look like—and searching for an equally visionary editor to help implement his plans. He found Howell Raines. Raines, who had spent much of his twenty-three-year career at the *Times* cultivating Sulzberger's attentions and affections, was named the paper's executive editor in May 2001. (He started his new post on September 5 of that year.) The plan was that while Sulzberger was remaking the company, Raines would remake the paper into a true national daily. That meant the *Times* would dominate on every story, regardless of where it was breaking. Pop culture and college sports would get just as prominent play as presidential campaigns and foreign wars. Raines would train *Times* reporters to "flood the zone," overwhelming the competition with the paper's supreme firepower and resources. They'd do more quick-hit reports on the hot topic of the week and invest in fewer laborious, time-consuming projects, and they'd do it all with the same number of staffers and without a significant budget increase.‡ In his well-strategized campaign to become executive editor—a campaign that included battle plans, rehearsed speeches, one-on-one sessions with *Times* business executives, and a dedicated courtship of Sulzberger—Raines had argued that the *Times* was becoming bloated, lazy, and complacent and that he was the only man capable of fixing it.

Before Raines had a chance to begin implementing his vision, though, the world was transformed. In the days after September 11,

---

* The *Post* and the *Times* had co-owned the *IHT* since the 1960s.
† In 2003, Sulzberger made an offhand offer to buy *The Wall Street Journal* from its owners, the Bancroft family, which shocked even executives at his own company, who worried that he hadn't run the numbers.
‡ The *Times* has approximately one thousand editorial employees (editors, reporters, photographers, designers, and so on) on its payroll and another two hundred nonprofessional staffers, including news clerks.

2001, when for the first time in a generation the country viscerally realized the importance of being well informed, the *Times* found itself suddenly and urgently necessary in a way it had not been in years. While shrill pundits on both the left and the right were making a mockery of the notion of an objective press, the *Times* proudly demonstrated to the world why it is still crucially important to give equal stories equal weight, to base coverage on news judgments and not personal vendettas or convictions, to never let a compelling story get in the way of the true story. The *Times*'s coverage of the crisis was exemplary, and the paper received overwhelming accolades for its work. This praise was gratifying, but it must also have been confusing to Raines. If, as he had argued, the *Times* had for years been falling asleep on the job, how could he explain its tremendous achievements? For Raines, the answer was simple: The *Times* could not have performed as well had he not been at the helm.

"Howell seemed to think that if the September 11 attacks had occurred one week earlier, we'd all have been sitting at our desks with our thumbs up our asses," veteran *Times* foreign correspondent and columnist Clyde Haberman told me in 2004. In the months following September 11, Raines received so much affirmation that many of his underlings feared he had begun to see anyone who questioned him as an impediment to his vision. He embraced his authoritative nature and began editing the paper according to his whims and predilections, in the process embarrassing and marginalizing people who disagreed with him. Although departing members of the staff voiced their complaints, Sulzberger continued to pledge his unequivocal support.

Over the next year, *The New York Times* became an increasingly unhappy place to work, and that unhappiness began to be reflected in the pages of the newspaper. Key editors stopped talking to one another and, worse, stopped expressing their concerns about the paper's missteps and problems. In late 2002, Raines was ridiculed for launching a relentless crusade against Augusta National, a Georgia golf course that hosts the Masters Tournament and doesn't admit women as members, and was publicly embarrassed when two sports columns that disagreed with the *Times*'s stance were killed by editors fearful of Raines's anger.

That summer, the paper's coverage of the buildup to the war in Iraq alternated between flat-out wrong and woefully disorganized. The paper's reporting on the hunt for weapons of mass destruction (WMD) in Iraq proved to be an embarrassment, as *Times* reporter Judith Miller, with Raines's active encouragement, bullied her way onto the paper's front page with a series of "exclusives," many of which were later revealed to be either incomplete or incorrect. In its own sorry way, the *Times* came to reinforce the public's perceptions of the media as another special-interest group, one more concerned with profits and its own agendas than the truth. According to one recent study, Americans today think journalists are "sloppier, less professional, less moral, less caring, more biased, less honest about their mistakes, and generally more harmful to democracy" than they did just twenty years ago. Even the paper's own employees took offense: More and more staffers who had clawed their way into a job at the *Times*—long the serious print journalist's brass ring—began defecting to other papers, including more than half a dozen of the paper's highly regarded national correspondents in 2002 alone. Raines, for his part, seemed not to care about reporters' bruised egos, the petty concerns of weak-willed editors, or a public that wanted desperately to be shown why it should have faith in its institutions. He was focused instead on his legacy, and he wanted to put his distinctive stamp on the most revered newspaper in the world. *Times* policy dictated that he would have to retire before February 5, 2009, his sixty-sixth birthday, and he surely heard the clock ticking every day.

All this turmoil might have been of little interest to anyone but journalism junkies and ivory tower academics. Howell Raines might have ridden out the storms of his first years. He might have realized the damage he was inflicting on the paper and recalibrated his leadership style accordingly. Arthur Sulzberger might have finally understood the extent of the mess in the newsroom and moved to fix it. But before any of this could happen, a journalistic suicide bomb detonated in *The New York Times* with the May 1, 2003, resignation of Jayson Blair, a twenty-seven-year-old reporter. An internal investigation turned up three dozen stories that Blair had fabricated or plagiarized in one six-month period. Following the investigation, the *Times* devoted four full pages of its Sunday paper—more space than it gave to coverage and analysis of President Bush's State of the Union address—to an astonishing report about the incident that was part mea culpa, part journalistic tour de force, and wholly unprecedented. In true form, the rest of the media world fell into line, dedicating endless pages of newsprint and hundreds of hours of airtime to the paper's dysfunction. Jayson Blair's story became an indictment of Howell Raines's leadership, and Raines's leadership became emblematic of every poor decision Arthur Sulzberger had ever made. The *Times*'s policy and track record on affirmative action came under scrutiny (Blair is African American), and minority staffers felt the unwelcome glare of suspicion as white staffers muttered privately that they always suspected black reporters were given more slack. *The New York Times*, the reserved newspaper where reporters and editors traditionally toiled in relative obscurity, became the subject of open ridicule, of demeaning and humiliating news reports by lesser competitors around the country, even of late-night talk-show quips. ("You know the old slogan of *The New York Times*, 'All the news that's fit to print'?" David Letterman deadpanned one night in his opening monologue. "They've changed it. The new slogan is, 'We make it up.' ")* Eventually, the clamor became an open staff rebellion, and Sulzberger was forced to fire Howell Raines, less than a month after announcing he wouldn't accept Raines's resignation even if it was offered and less than two years after he had appointed Raines to lead the *Times* into its bright future.

———

In HINDSIGHT, every august institution can point to the years in which it was forced to change in fundamental ways. For the *Times*, the twenty-one months of Howell Raines's tenure as executive editor will surely be those years. Raines wanted to go down in history as a revolu-

---

* A full year later, the *Times*'s travails had so infused popular culture, they were the subject of an offhand joke in a May 2004 episode of *The Simpsons*, in which an elementary school reporter gets in trouble for datelining a dispatch from Baghdad when he was actually in Basra.

tionary editor. The changes his tenure resulted in will indeed be revolutionary, but history will not look kindly on his leadership. Arthur Sulzberger, meanwhile, has been trying his entire life to prove he deserves the post he received by an accident of birth. The verdict is still out on whether he will be seen as the publisher who led the *Times* into a new era or the publisher who, by tinkering with what the *Times* does best, permanently damaged the company he's in charge of.

The New York Times's struggles—with the electronic age, with race, with the increasingly porous wall between editorial and business operations—have come to illustrate the challenges facing all news organizations, and they've affected the way we conceive of information itself. The story of the *Times* is also the story of how media institutions have had to adapt to the public's tastes as they also shape them. It is no longer enough to serve as "the paper of record"; today, consumers want "value added," just as with any other product. They want analysis and attitude and star power. Media companies need to maximize profits, and the *Times* may be one of the few institutions that believes that high-quality journalism and the impressive margins that come with more popular fare can be had simultaneously.

Howell Raines convinced Sulzberger—and initially his staff—that he was the only leader who would be able to accomplish this. In the process, he made the fatal mistake of many talented men and women who allow their rise to the top to be defined by ego and blind determination: He confused his own identity with that of the company he led. In the end, this self-created man was done in by his need to see himself at the center of every story. By claiming the paper (and its successes) as his own, he also found himself ultimately responsible for its failures.

Part One

BEFORE

April 8, 2002

The third-floor newsroom of *The New York Times*, located about one hundred yards west of Times Square, can be a grim place. The exposed ventilation system, the humming fluorescent lights, the claustrophobic cubicles, and the standard-issue off-white paint job make the newsroom feel simultaneously retro and futuristic, as if the *Times*'s nerve center were designed as a contemporary interpretation of the stereotypical city room of old. For many of the hundred-plus metro, national, and business reporters whose desks are on the third floor, the newsroom is an intensely stressful place to work, a place where career-long reputations can be badly dented by one deadline-induced mistake, a place where staffers fight ruthlessly over bylines and credit. One metro reporter described the newsroom as a simulacrum of a bitterly competitive premed program, where success is strictly relative and no one can achieve without someone else failing. Reporters, especially those lower on the slippery newsroom totem pole, carry with them a jangling fear of looking dumb in front of their editors, of falling out of favor, of failing to deliver. Max Frankel, the retired executive editor of the *Times*, once quipped that he enjoyed the paper only when he was away from the office, reading it.

The newsroom's uninspiring décor and its vaguely Hobbesian feel contrasts mightily with, say, the minimalist sophistication and noblesse-oblige ethos that pervade the Condé Nast building, located a block from the *Times*'s headquarters. Condé Nast, home to high-end magazines like *The New Yorker*, *Vanity Fair*, *Vogue*, and *GQ*, has a Frank Gehry–designed cafeteria and special guest chefs from Hong Kong and Tuscany. The *Times* has a commissary furnished with plastic ferns and Formica tables. Condé Nast writers get generous expense accounts, flexible deadlines, and private offices with frosted-glass doors and wood-paneled bookshelves. *Times* reporters get embittered copy editors and off-beige desk dividers. What's more, *Times* reporters and editors are, on average, paid less and work more than their colleagues in the glossy magazine world.

But *Times*men, of course, get an immeasurable level of prestige and an inexorable sense of purpose. They get the recurring adrenaline rush of knowing that they have the power to move markets, to influence elections, to shape world affairs. They get their fingerprints (and their bylines) on the first rough drafts of history. In this regard, at least, not much has changed since the 1960s. In his fascinating 1969 bestseller, *The Kingdom and the Power*, author and former *Times* reporter Gay Talese described how the political and cultural elite looked to the paper he worked at for more than a decade as "necessary proof of the world's existence, a barometer of its pressure, an assessor of its sanity."

On most days, this power is barely acknowledged. Reporters push their way in through the *Times*'s revolving doors on the north side of West Forty-third Street around ten in the morning. Soon after, section editors begin working the floor, checking for scoops or updates or new angles on old stories. By noon, reporters write up "sked lines," one- or two-sentence summaries that their editors can use at the daily page-one meeting to pitch their stories. A couple of hours later, if a reporter has picked up a breaking news story, as opposed to a feature or an off-news color piece, there's the familiar ritual of canceled dinner plans, apologetic phone calls to frustrated spouses, thrice-postponed drinks dates postponed one more time. By 8:00 or 9:00 p.m., after circling back to this or that source for a juicier quote or a flashier anecdote, when it's finally time to stumble out into Times Square's neon-lit frenzy, there's still an hour or two of cellphone queries from copy editors to look forward to. *Isn't there anyone who'd go on the record about the mayor's new parking initiative? Would you mind if we changed your lead around?*

Such a schedule leaves very little time for self-congratulation, but the afternoon of April 8, 2002, was a break from the numbing daily slog, a time to pause and celebrate *The New York Times*'s unique role in American society. The seven months since the September 11 terrorist attacks had been defined by balls-out reporting, seven months in which countless staffers worked without a single day off, seven months in which reporters were relocated from local government beats to war zones throughout the Middle East and in Afghanistan.

As the day stretched toward 3:00 p.m., a space was cleared in front of the spiral staircase that connects the third and fourth floors of the *Times*'s newsroom. *The New York Times* was about to win seven Pulitzer Prizes, half of all the Pulitzers awarded for journalism and four more than the previous one-year record the *Times* shared with two other newspapers.* Six of the awards that year recognized the paper's coverage of the September 11 attacks on America. It was as if the Pulitzer board were affirming the *Times*'s place as the center of the journalistic universe.

After Sig Gissler, the administrator of the Pulitzer Prizes, made the official announcement from Columbia University, Raines, a short, bow-legged Alabamian with brushy gray hair and a bulbous nose, strode up to a small wooden platform underneath the staircase. Reporters and editors snaked up the stairs and jammed the hallways. For the first time in *The New York Times*'s storied and celebrated history, all of the paper's

---

* In 2004, the *Los Angeles Times* won five Pulitzer Prizes.

living executive editors had gathered in one room. A. M. Rosenthal, who hadn't been inside the *Times*'s West Forty-third Street building since his rambling Op-Ed page column had been canceled two and a half years earlier, was there. Rosenthal's successor, Max Frankel, one of the few men who inspired fear in Raines (and who was said to have re-signed early to block the possibility of Raines's ascension in the early 1990s), was there. Joe Lelyveld, Raines's immediate predecessor, was there, along with the man Lelyveld had openly campaigned for as his successor, former managing editor Bill Keller, now a biweekly Op-Ed page columnist and *Times Magazine* writer. Assembling these five men in one room was a major undertaking of its own. Rosenthal's and Frankel's mutual disdain was legendary. Frankel had been particularly insulting to Rosenthal in his memoir, in which he referred to himself approvingly as "the not-Abe." And Lelyveld, who since leaving the *Times* had been working on lengthy pieces for *The New Yorker* and *The New York Review of Books*, made no secret of how happy he was to have moved on to the next phase of his life.

Off to the side of the wooden platform, a stooped and frail old man overshadowed even this summit of journalistic lions. Arthur Ochs Sulz-berger, known both inside and outside the paper simply as "Punch," was making one of his increasingly rare trips to the newsroom. Punch had handed over the publisher's title to his son in 1992 and had given Arthur Ochs Sulzberger Jr.—or "Young Arthur," as he was sometimes known—the title of chairman of the New York Times Company in 1997. (Behind his back, Sulzberger Jr. was occasionally referred to as "Pinch," a moniker he found demeaning. "A man deserves his own nickname," he once said.) Punch leaned in to speak quietly with Lely-veld, two legends of American journalism watching a new generation eclipse their accomplishments.

To a round of applause, Raines stepped onto the platform. "I was re-minded today of the words of Mississippi's greatest moral philosopher, Dizzy Dean," Raines, a proud southerner leading the most elite of northern institutions, told the throng of journalists. " 'It ain't bragging if you really done it.' Ladies and gentlemen of *The New York Times*, you've really done it." On that day, Raines was eloquent and forceful, humble and proud. "We are ever mindful of the shattering events it was our task to record in our city, nation, and world community," he said. It was also important to realize, he added, that the *Times*'s September 11 journalism "will be studied and taught as long as journalism is studied and practiced. . . . We have a right to celebrate these days of legend at *The New York Times*." Raines made a point of acknowledging and thanking Lelyveld and Keller—it was, after all, the staff they had assembled and trained that won all those Pulitzers—before handing over the microphone to Arthur Sulzberger Jr., whom he called "a great publisher."

Punch, a shy and private man, was probably just as happy that Raines hadn't singled him out. Raines later told Ken Auletta, the *New Yorker* media writer whom he had invited into the newsroom to record the scene, that he intentionally didn't mention the elder Sulzberger so that his son would have a chance to pay homage to the family patriarch. But to some in the newsroom, it was a noticeable and telling slight, a sign that Raines's humility and graciousness were nothing but lip service. "Howell mentioned a lot of folks on whose shoulders we stand, but he forgot one," Arthur Sulzberger told the crowd. "And I'm grateful that he did, and that is my father."

THE SULZBERGER FAMILY

Every company likes to refer to itself—at least publicly—as a family. Most of the time, that's a specious metaphor. But in the case of *The New York Times*, the analogy is nearly accurate. It's true that *The New York Times* existed before Adolph Ochs came on the scene—it was founded in 1851 as a daily broadsheet. But the modern incarnation of the *Times* was born in 1896, when a virtually bankrupt thirty-eight-year-old first-generation American named Adolph Ochs (his parents were German-Jewish immigrants) was able to acquire notes worth $75,000 of credit to gain control of the financially struggling daily known then as *The New-York Times*. Today, the New York Times Company has a book value of some $1.4 billion, and its market capitalization is $6.9 billion. (Annual revenues in 2003 were $3.23 billion.)

Ochs was intensely dedicated to two things in his life: his family and *The New York Times*. He passed on those values to three successive generations, and since 1896, the paper has had only five publishers, all of them family members. After

Ochs retired in 1935, the husband of his only child, Iphigene, inherited the position. Arthur Hays Sulzberger led the paper from 1935 until 1961, when Orvil Dryfoos, the husband of Arthur and Iphigene Sulzberger's oldest daughter, Marian, was named publisher. When Dryfoos died unexpectedly in 1963, Arthur "Punch" Ochs Sulzberger, the thirty-seven-year-old only son of Arthur and Iphigene Sulzberger, rose to the top of the *Times*'s masthead. And in 1992, Punch's son, Arthur Ochs Sulzberger Jr., took over. "They're a monarchy," Max Frankel said in 1994. "I thank God for that monarchy because every other newspaper that has lost its family control has gone to seed."

Understanding the *Times* means, to some extent, understanding the Sulzberger clan. For most of the *Times*'s existence, the family has run the paper more or less the same way: by pouring money back into the paper's editorial operation and then getting out of the way. And the family has remained remarkably united—the *Times*, it has always agreed, outweighs any individual agendas or concerns. In 1996, on the occasion of the Sulzbergers' one hundredth anniversary of owning the *Times*, Harold Evans, the former editor of London's *Sunday Times*, wrote in *The New Yorker*, "Great newspapers and great families rise (and fall) together—for a family, unlike a standard corporation, can take editorial and financial risks without incurring the wrath of stockholders bent upon maximizing return. Under the Sulzbergers, the *Times* has evolved into something more than a newspaper; it has become, over its century, nothing less than an ontological authority."

In order to recognize just how unique the *Times*'s situation is, it's useful to remember that most family-owned newspaper dynasties, like those of the Binghams in Kentucky, the Chandlers in Los Angeles, and the Taylors in Boston, have been either driven apart by internal squabbles or sold to corporate entities.* Once-great papers like *The Miami Herald* and *The Philadelphia Inquirer* have been bought by conglomerates like Knight Ridder and bled mercilessly in search of ever higher profit margins. But the Sulzbergers have remained resolutely committed to maintaining the *Times*'s excellence and its unique position in

---

* The Taylors sold *The Boston Globe* to the New York Times Company in 1993.

American society. Indeed, for some people, the Sulzbergers are the *Times*. Nearly forty years after leaving the paper, Gay Talese is still awed by the Sulzberger clan. "We don't have trust in government," Talese said. "The Wall Street world? Forget it. Where can people [go] who have values and a sense of right and wrong, of standards? . . . I think today the Sulzberger family and *The New York Times* [are] our only hope. And if they weren't there, I don't know where you would look."*

More than a decade after stepping down as publisher, Punch Sulzberger remains the current embodiment of this legacy. The last of four children, he was born in 1926, following Judith (1923), Ruth (1921), and Marian (1918).† Since Iphigene was the only child of Adolph Ochs and Effie Wise, her children provided the only direct blood ties to the family's patriarch, and Punch, as the only male child, faced no real competition from his sisters when it came time for someone from his generation to lead the paper.

Along with Punch's ascension came the birth of the modern-day *New York Times*. The paper, since Ochs's purchase more than half a century earlier, had been run as if "profit be considered desirable but somewhat beside the point," as Susan Tifft and Alex Jones wrote in *The Trust*, the definitive history of the Sulzbergers and the *Times*. But in the mid-1960s, crippling labor strikes and union unrest convinced Punch that for the paper to survive, it had to be more mindful of the bottom line. He began a path of haphazard diversification that would have been anathema to his father or grandfather, for the culture of the *Times* had always been predicated on focusing all of its attention on its core product. But the world had changed since 1896, and Punch wasn't able to carry out the sleight-of-hand machinations Adolph Ochs had performed to get the mysterious line of credit he used to gain control of the *Times*. If he wanted to diversify, he needed capital, and if he wanted

---

* Perhaps not coincidentally, two of the country's other three great newspapers, *The Washington Post* and *The Wall Street Journal*, are also family owned.

† Punch's lifelong nickname originated from a picture book his father made for him when Punch was an infant. Riffing on the fact that he followed three girls, the last one named Judy, his father wrote that, like the seventeenth-century English puppet, he was destined to "play the Punch to Judy's endless show."

capital, the only real option was to take his family's company public. So on January 14, 1969, New York Times Class A stock was made available on the American Stock Exchange for $42 a share.

Most public companies are governed by a board of directors that is answerable to shareholders. The directors, in turn, sign off on the major executive appointments—in the Times Company's case, the chairman of the board, the chief executive officer, and the publisher of the *Times*. The chairman's main responsibility is running the board meetings, the CEO oversees the actual day-to-day operations of the company, and the publisher dictates the budget and manages the newspaper. In 1969, Punch Sulzberger held all three roles. By taking the company public, he could have risked family control of the *Times:* If the shareholders elected directors who had plans for the company that differed from his, those directors could, in theory, oust Sulzberger from his role at the top of the company. Sulzberger may have wanted to modernize the paper, but not at the risk of losing family control.

The company solved this problem by creating a structure whereby the Sulzbergers would always retain ultimate authority. Class A stockholders would get to appoint three out of nine directors. The owners of the Class B stock—which was exclusively in the hands of the Sulzberger family—would appoint the remaining six members of the board. (Over time, that calculus became proportional, with Class A stockholders electing 30 percent of the board.) And Punch Sulzberger would remain publisher, chairman, and CEO.*

Ensuring family control, however, did not mean the *Times* could continue to rely on anachronistic business practices. The joke within the *Times* was that "God [was] our personnel manager" because people were never fired and positions were never left unfilled. The business side of the paper was sadly disorganized. "We didn't have a planning process, we didn't have any goals, we didn't have any of the things pub-

---

* In 1986, the Sulzbergers drafted a covenant that ensured the *Times* would remain in family control virtually until the end of the twenty-first century. Under the agreement, Iphigene's four children and thirteen grandchildren agreed not to sell their Class B stock to anyone outside the family; if they wanted to convert their Class B shares to cash, they could sell them only within the family or to the New York Times Company. This agreement is binding until twenty-one years after the death of the longest-living descendant of Iphigene's who was alive in 1986. Pamela Dryfoos, Marian Sulzberger Dryfoos's granddaughter, was born in 1984.

lic companies usually [have]," James Goodale, a former *Times* in-house counsel and executive vice president, told Tifft and Jones. Amazingly, until 1964, the paper had never even been required to work within a predetermined budget.

Wall Street quickly became aware of the company's woefully out-of-date business practices. Between January 1969 and early 1971, *Times* stock dropped from $42 to $16 a share. The fortuitously timed 1971 acquisition of Cowles Communication, which owned *Family Circle* magazine, some newspapers in Florida, a CBS station in Memphis, and Cambridge Books, helped the earnings situation, but it would be years before the Times Company instituted anything close to the rigor and accountability financial analysts looked for when rating companies worthy of investment. But while the progress toward modernization might have been slow, it was successful, and under Punch's stewardship the *Times* not only survived what might have been crippling financial downturns, it emerged stronger than ever.

Punch also dramatically changed the scope of the newspaper during his time as publisher. When he took over, the *Times* was a two-section daily, short on pictures and long on tedious official pronouncements and rote coverage of press conferences. In a move typical of his tenure, Punch decided during the financial crises of the 1970s that he would bulk up the paper instead of paring it back. "My father, Walter Mattson, Abe Rosenthal—that was the generation that said, 'One, our readers are leaving the city. They're moving to the suburbs. And two, our paper needs to be rejuvenated,' " says Arthur Sulzberger. The *Times* responded to its financial difficulties by adding the Living and Home sections and later by transforming itself to a four-section daily. Purists roundly criticized the new sections, but they increased both the newspaper's reach and ad revenues while also boosting circulation. "Instead of putting more water in the soup," A. M. Rosenthal said of the decision to add heft to the paper during a difficult period, "we put in more tomatoes." Also in the 1970s, the *Times* invented something called the Op-Ed page,* a section in the paper in which *Times* columnists and

---

* Op-Ed stands for "opposite the editorial page," not "opinions and editorials," as many people think.

outside writers would have a venue to make their voices heard. Today, daily newspapers around the country almost universally include both those specialty sections and an Op-Ed page.

Punch made another lasting contribution to the culture of the *Times* by creating the post of executive editor. It was a job his father, Arthur Hays Sulzberger, had liked to perform himself, but Punch had neither the inclination nor the temperament to resolve editorial disputes or make snap news judgments. Like Orvil Dryfoos before him, Punch wanted to find a way to unite the Sunday and daily papers, thereby replacing the existing system in which news decisions on Mondays through Saturdays were made by the *Times*'s managing editor but on the seventh day by Lester Markel, the increasingly intractable Sunday editor. In 1964, Punch appointed managing editor Turner Catledge to the newly created executive-editor position. In 1967, when Catledge retired, James "Scotty" Reston, the paper's longtime Washington bureau chief and columnist, took over on a temporary basis. From 1969 to 1976, the post remained unfilled: A. M. Rosenthal was the paper's managing editor* but was deemed unready to rise to the top spot. In 1976, Rosenthal finally assumed the role and served until 1986, when Max Frankel was installed; he in turn remained until Joe Lelyveld took over in 1994.

Catledge, Rosenthal, and Frankel all had close personal relationships with Punch, and all three men were careful to court the publisher's affections. They were given great authority but always were expected to remember that it was the Sulzbergers, and not any individual editor, who made *The New York Times* special. In turn, the executive editors were treated as more than simply the editorial stewards of the newspaper: Punch consulted with them about strategic decisions involving the *Times*'s future and relied upon them to help steer the company.

While Punch was a forceful leader, he was not an overbearing one.

---

* When Rosenthal was named managing editor in 1969, it marked the first time a Jew had sat atop the *Times*'s editorial hierarchy. The Sulzbergers, and Adolph Ochs before them, had always been concerned that if a Jew was running a Jewish-owned paper, readers would wonder about the religious influence on the news pages.

He preferred to operate behind the scenes and only rarely exercised his prerogative to overrule the paper's editorial-page editor.* (More commonly, he voiced disagreement by writing letters to the paper, which he signed A. Sock, a play on his nickname.)† "Unpretentiousness is his greatest gift," said Max Frankel, who served as editorial-page editor and was the executive editor when Punch stepped down as publisher. "He was remarkably serene about letting his subordinates do their work. His interventions were extremely polite."

In 1971, in what would become one of the defining moments of his career—and a defining moment for American journalism—Punch authorized the *Times*'s publication of the Pentagon Papers, a secret government history of the Vietnam War. After the paper's outside law firm, Lord, Day & Lord, said it wouldn't defend the *Times* if it published the report, Punch retained new lawyers. The *Times*'s decision to publish, and the Nixon administration's efforts to halt that publication, led to a landmark Supreme Court ruling that upheld the right of a newspaper to publish free of government's "prior restraint."

BY THE EARLY 1990s, Punch, who would turn seventy in 1996, began preparations to cede his title to the next generation of the family. His only son, Arthur Sulzberger Jr., was the obvious leading candidate, although Michael Golden, the second son of Punch's sister Ruth, was also ambitious and active in the company. Arthur Sulzberger had undergone an apprenticeship that went far beyond that of any of the previous publishers at the paper—he had served as a reporter and editor, worked in the paper's ad department, done nights in the production department, and helped his father as the assistant and deputy publisher. Punch had known he wanted his son to succeed him since

---

* One of Punch's interventions was credited with helping to change the course of modern American political life: In 1976, he insisted that the *Times* endorse Daniel Patrick Moynihan over Bella Abzug in the Democratic primary for U.S. senator. In a close race, that endorsement was seen as being a deciding factor, and Moynihan went on to serve as senator from New York until his retirement in 2000.
† With some rare exceptions, Punch ended that practice in 1979, when Gail Gregg, his daughter-in-law, wrote a rebuttal to one of his letters that concluded, "Mr. Sock deserves a punch." Sulzberger was convinced his cover had been blown.

the mid-1980s, and in 1986, when he appointed Max Frankel executive editor, Punch told Frankel he had three requests. As Frankel recounted in his 1999 memoir, *The Times of My Life and My Life at* The Times, Punch told him: "Make a great paper even greater. Help to break in my son Arthur as the next publisher. Make the newsroom a happy place again." Also, in the mid-1980s, Punch had formed what was termed the Futures Committee, a group that Arthur Sulzberger sat on with Frankel and Lance Primis, the paper's new general manager. "It was . . . a vehicle to force Arthur Jr. to confront the competing demands of news and business from a management point of view," wrote Tifft and Jones.

In late 1991, Punch floated the idea of naming Arthur publisher. The company's board of directors was surprisingly tepid to the idea and asked for more time to learn about the younger Sulzberger. One of the board's concerns, they told Punch, was that Arthur Sulzberger's appointment would be seen as a de facto coronation and that it would only be a matter of time before he became the company's CEO as well.

By January 1992, after more face time with Arthur—and after being assured by Punch that just because Arthur was taking one of his titles didn't mean he'd eventually get all three—the board was placated, and the forty-year-old Sulzberger became the fifth member of his family to run the newspaper. But Arthur Sulzberger's ascension was far more complicated than his father's had been. At the same time that he was charting his rise within the *Times*, the twelve other sons and daughters (known as the cousins) of the four children of Arthur Hays Sulzberger and Iphigene Ochs (known as the siblings) were struggling with their own roles in the future of the Times Company. The same year Arthur Sulzberger Jr. became publisher, the cousins, five of whom were actively involved in the *Times*'s operations in one way or another, invited the siblings to dinner and said they wanted to formalize how the company, and the family, would be run in the future. When the four children of Iphigene Sulzberger passed on, there would be a much larger group of family members who could claim the *Times* as part of their inheritance. The family hired Craig Aronoff, the head of Kennesaw State University's Family Enterprise Center, to serve as a moderator and facilitator. The result of Aronoff's work with the cousins was a fifty-page bound volume titled *Proposals for the Future: To the Third Generation of the Ochs-Sulzberger Family from the Fourth and Fifth Generations*. The preamble stated two goals: to maintain stewardship of the *Times* and to preserve the unity of the family. These were precisely the goals that had made the Sulzbergers such strong owners, and in the report, Adolph Ochs's great-grandchildren made it clear that they were just as intent on nurturing that philosophy as Ochs himself had been a hundred years earlier.

By the end of the 1990s, Arthur Sulzberger had solidified his position on the top of the *Times*'s hierarchy. In early 1997, he withstood a challenge from Lance Primis, the company president, who sought to become CEO, and on October 16 of that year, Sulzberger was elected to the *Times*'s board of directors and named chairman of the company. After the Times Company directors approved his new post, he was invited into the company's boardroom on the fourteenth floor of the *Times*'s headquarters. Punch got out of the chair at the head of the table and invited his son to take the seat.

"If you think I'm sitting in that chair, you're nuts," Sulzberger said. He made his first brief remarks as chairman while standing.

Sulzberger would not inherit his father's third title, that of chief executive officer. Instead, he and Punch worked to install a governing structure whereby the Times Company would hire a nonfamily member as CEO, but that person would report to the company's chairman instead of to the board. This was a reflection of how the company had actually been run when Punch had held all three titles; first Walter Mattson and then Primis had essentially served as CEOs, which had helped assuage the business community's fears about Punch's managerial bona fides. Sulzberger hired Russ Lewis, who had started his career at the *Times* as a copyboy before working in the legal department, as head of the circulation and production departments and as the president of the *Times*.

On the afternoon Punch passed the torch to his son, he was feted in an impromptu newsroom ceremony. Joseph Lelyveld, the paper's executive editor, noted that three things made that day, October 16, 1997, a landmark one. For the first time in its history, the *Times* had run color photos on its front page. Second, at 138 pages, that edition of the paper was the largest daily *Times* in history. And third, the paper had its first chairman emeritus.

Punch, from the sidelines, chimed in. "There are four things," he said. "The stock is at an all-time high." It was intended as a light-hearted comment, but it also hinted at the intense pressure on the company to prove to the business world that continued family owner-ship would result not only in a superior product but in sizable profits as well. Arthur Sulzberger Jr. made it clear that he too understood those pressures. "The most important partnership in this institution is the relationship between the family and the non-family management," he said in an interview that day. His ascension, he said, and the promotion of Russ Lewis to the chief executive's office, "continue on a corporate level the partnership that allows this institution to survive."

"This place doesn't run like a family fiefdom," says Lewis. "It's got the best of both worlds: the constancy of purpose that Arthur and the family have given it for over a hundred years, and the accountability of a public company."

The day after Punch stepped down, the *Times*'s two-thousand-word, front-page account of the passing of the generational torch made note of Sulzberger's unique place in American journalism. "His ac-tion," *Times* reporter Clyde Haberman wrote of Punch's decision to name his son chairman of the Times Company, "affirmed that in a troubled age for American newspapers, when many of them worry about their future and are increasingly governed by distant corporate boards, control of The Times would remain with the Sulzberger family, the paper's guiding force for 101 years."

THE PRINCE

If the Sulzbergers are, as some writers have noted, the closest thing America has to a royal family (when Prince Charles visited the country in 1988, he invited Arthur, along with Don Graham, the heir to *The Washington Post*, to dinner because he thought they'd best understand his position), then Arthur Ochs Sulzberger Jr. is its crown prince and one who has endured a lifetime of royal-level scrutiny. He's rarely addressed it publicly, but Sulzberger finds the examination of every aspect of his life intrusive. The few times he's spoken of the microscope under which he often finds himself, he's made his annoyance clear. Take one incident in 2000, when Sulzberger visited Harvard to speak at the Joan Shorenstein Center on the Press, Politics and Public Policy. The center is run by Alex Jones, who, in addition to co-authoring *The Trust*, wrote about the media for the *Times* from 1983 to 1992 and won a 1987 Pulitzer Prize for his reporting.

At the beginning of the talk, Sulzberger made a reference to his alma mater. "By the way, if you want a more full account of my days at Tufts, you can consult a book, *The Trust*, which was co-authored by our host, Alex Jones," he said, and then added dryly, "I do, however, wonder why anyone—other than my wife and children, perhaps my father—would have any interest in such an incredibly dull topic." This remark, a message of frustration cloaked in the guise of a quip, was typical of Sulzberger, who often tries for humor, only to sound either glib or slightly harsh. He had already complained about the book to his friends. *The Trust*, he said, delved too deeply into his family's personal history, their frustrated marriages and intergenerational tensions.

A lifelong New Yorker, Arthur Sulzberger is a boyish-looking fifty-three-year-old, an avid outdoorsman and frequent rock climber. He likes to take off on weekend motorcycle trips or self-styled "Rambo" excursions. He's infamous for speaking off-the-cuff and for making outrageous and inappropriate comments.* A child of the 1960s and 1970s, Sulzberger seems to have a mystical side, and, besides the *Times*, the organization with which he feels the most kinship is Outward Bound.

But for him, as with his father and great-grandfather, the *Times* has always come first. Indeed, Sulzberger has spent his entire life, in one way or another, auditioning to run the *Times*. After graduating from Tufts University in 1974, he went to North Carolina to work for *The Raleigh Times*. His apprenticeship at *The New York Times* can be traced back eight years before that, when he moved out of his mother's New York City apartment and in with his father. One reason for the move was Sulzberger's mother's tense second marriage. But "the more compelling motivation for Arthur Jr.'s decision," wrote Tifft and Jones, "was his desire to become better acquainted with his father and to claim his rightful place in the extended Sulzberger clan, in which he had begun to feel like an outsider."

Early on, Sulzberger yearned for validation from Punch, but that validation was slow in coming. He was an awkward and shy child. While working as a reporter at *The Raleigh Times*, he would send clips

---

* Soon after becoming publisher, Sulzberger told *The New Yorker*'s Ken Auletta that he didn't worry about those who thought he was pushing reform too quickly: "I'll outlive the bastards!" he said.

to Seymour Topping, a *Times* editor in New York, suggesting he could show the better ones to his father. In 1976, when Sulzberger and his wife, Gail Gregg, moved to London, Sulzberger secured a job at the Associated Press and Gregg applied for one at United Press International. Punch, in his recommendation for Gregg, initially wrote, "We think she is smarter than he is," before his secretary told him he couldn't possibly say such a thing.

Sulzberger's sense that he was never quite able to satisfy his father had led to his lifelong struggle to prove himself. Whereas Punch had been content to stay in the background, Arthur Sulzberger Jr. was the opposite—not only did he think his father was sometimes too passive, he seemed to need to remind people constantly how talented and important he himself was.

It became clear quite soon after Sulzberger assumed the position of publisher that he had a very different management style from his father's. To begin with, there was his personal approach: Punch is often painfully modest, even self-effacing. Arthur, it was quickly noted, wasn't nearly as demure about his ambitions or as shy about his accomplishments. He struck some as headstrong and impetuous, even offensive.

And unlike his father, Sulzberger wanted his presence to be felt. In December 1992, less than a year after he was appointed publisher, he immediately set about changing the working culture inside the newsroom. He has often professed to have a philosophical belief in teamwork and open communication, and he made it clear that he wanted the *Times* to be a more fluid organization. Sulzberger's attempts to make the newsroom less autocratic and hierarchical met with mixed results. During his first year, Sulzberger held retreats in which facilitators bandied around terms like "change agent." One series of management seminars was the subject of a lengthy and unflattering magazine story. "Sulzberger . . . is impatient with the resistance he sometimes encounters," Ken Auletta wrote in the June 28, 1993, issue of *The New Yorker*. "He wants more minority employees in executive positions. He wants more women in executive positions. He wants a less authoritarian newsroom and a business side that is more nimble. He wants each member of the staff to feel 'empowered' as part of a team." "Some would argue that fear is an inherent by-product of any structure based in hierarchy," Sulzberger told Auletta. "I can't swear that's true, but I suspect it is. And if it's true our course is clear. For *The New York Times* to become all it can be and for it to flourish in the years ahead, we must reduce our dependency on hierarchy in decision making of every sort." Needless to say, though, wishing your staff would feel "empowered" and actually having them feel so are two different things, and *The New York Times*'s senior staff was generally not impressed by Sulzberger's rhetoric.

In 1994, two years after becoming publisher, Sulzberger had to make his first big appointment, when Max Frankel, the paper's executive editor, retired. Sulzberger had little choice but to promote the fifty-seven-year-old managing editor, Joe Lelyveld, a cerebral man who also felt that Sulzberger's retreats were simplistic and belittling to Frankel.* Despite Lelyveld's deserved reputation for aloofness, he managed to improve morale during his tenure. Frankel, who had run the *Times*'s Sunday paper and editorial page before being named executive editor, had installed a tier of assistant managing editors—known as "the masthead," because these positions were listed on the editorial page under the executive and managing editors—between himself and the desk editors who ran the newsroom departments. "When you run a desk, you have real power," says Soma Golden Behr, who was the paper's national editor before being promoted to the masthead by Max Frankel. "When you go on the masthead, all your power is derivative. It all depends on the boss. Max gave each masthead editor a few departments to worry about, which means they would serve as a kind of rabbi." Lelyveld, by actively promoting strong desk editors, assembled a cadre of talented desk heads during his eight-year tenure, including Jon Landman on metro, Mike Oreskes in Washington, Bill Keller on foreign, Dean Baquet on national, and John Geddes and Glenn Kra-

---

* In a 1994 interview with Charlie Rose, Max Frankel described a conversation he had with Sulzberger in which he first brought up Lelyveld's ascension. "We've got to decide about Joe Lelyveld," Frankel said he told Sulzberger during a March 1993 train ride to Washington. "Because he's my choice and you're going to hear from me soon about how I want to step down . . . and he's my man. But if he's not your man, we got a hell of a problem."

mon on business. In returning authority to the desk editors, Lelyveld made the paper's reporters feel as if they were involved more intimately with shaping the daily report, but in the process he disenfranchised and alienated the masthead.

Lelyveld also coaxed Gene Roberts, the retired editor of *The Philadelphia Inquirer*, to serve as his managing editor for a couple of years, knowing he'd reach the paper's mandatory retirement age before Lelyveld and therefore wouldn't be in the running to be the paper's next editor. (Roberts is a newsroom legend: After a stint as national editor at the *Times*, he was named executive editor of the *Inquirer* in 1972. In his eighteen years at the helm of the paper, the *Inquirer* won seventeen Pulitzer Prizes; since he retired, it has won one.) Roberts in particular viewed the *Times*'s masthead as being basically worthless, and he made no secret about his views.

"Joe didn't use the masthead well," says Behr. "It was a very frustrating time." In 1997, Gene Roberts retired and returned to the University of Maryland to teach journalism. Lelyveld chose Bill Keller as Roberts's successor. Keller, who had been the paper's South African bureau chief when Lelyveld took over the *Times*, had been an editor for only two years, since Lelyveld and Roberts appointed him foreign editor in 1995. But Lelyveld felt Keller was a naturally gifted editor, responsive to reporters and skilled at sniffing out good stories.

As Lelyveld was reorganizing the newsroom, Sulzberger was imagining the *Times*'s future and was eager to move forward with his plan to make the *Times* "platform agnostic." As well as Arthur Sulzberger seemed to be settling into his new role, he was still missing something. Sulzberger wanted a partner. He wanted an executive editor who shared his vision, his ambition, his desire to shake off the cobwebs and make the *Times* a publication reborn. Sulzberger's relationship with Lelyveld was less than ideal—Sulzberger sometimes felt Lelyveld wasn't moving quickly enough, and Lelyveld and some of his top editors occasionally worried that Sulzberger's investments in new technologies were drawing needed resources from the newsroom. So when, in early 2001, Joe Lelyveld told Sulzberger he was planning on retiring in September, about a year ahead of schedule (he wouldn't turn sixty-six until

April 5, 2003), he did so hoping his protégé, Bill Keller, would replace him. Sulzberger, however, had other ideas. He had already found his editor, one who shared his bold vision and his conviction that the *Times* should be shaken up, and it was not the mild-mannered Keller. His name was Howell Raines.

The Making of
an Editor

As a teenager in Alabama, Howell Raines was captivated by the literary life, and for many years he hoped to become a great novelist. Instead, almost by accident, he became a newsman: In 1964, after graduating from Birmingham-Southern College, he landed a job as a reporter at the *Birmingham Post-Herald*, followed by a two-year stint at a local TV station. In the late 1960s, Raines shuttled between school, novel writing, and reporting; it wasn't until 1970 that he returned to journalism full-time, taking a job as a reporter at *The Birmingham News*. He soon distinguished himself and before the year was out had landed at *The Atlanta Constitution*, where he stayed for four years, working as a political reporter and movie reviewer during the week and as a novelist on the weekends. During his tenure there, he learned to project authority. John Huey, who first met Raines in the *Constitution*'s newsroom and is currently the editorial director of Time Inc.'s magazine division, told *The New Yorker*'s Ken Auletta of Raines, "He always had an air that he had been around—and he hadn't."

In 1974, Raines left journalism to write an oral history of the civil rights movement. That book, titled *My Soul Is Rested*, and a subsequent novel, *Whiskey Man*, were published to positive reviews in 1977, but by that time Raines was already back in the game, having been hired in 1976 as the political editor of the *St. Petersburg Times*. At the time, Raines was married to his first wife, Susan Woodley, whom he had met while in college, and the couple had two young sons. But he was restless.

In 1978, on the recommendation of Washington bureau chief Bill Kovach and national editor Dave Jones, Raines was hired by *The New York Times* as a national correspondent based in Atlanta, one of the paper's most prestigious national postings. "I was looking for a southern reporter with political skills," remembers Jones. "And I just thought he was a huge talent." During their interview, Jones explained to Raines that while he was being hired to cover Atlanta, he would need to start his career at the *Times* in New York. That has long been the paper's practice—it gives new reporters a chance to work with the top editors, to learn the system, to soak up some of the *Times*'s history and value system. Raines agreed. But by the time he got out of his interview with A. M. Rosenthal, then the paper's executive editor, Rosenthal was convinced that Raines was exactly what was needed in the paper's Atlanta bureau and wanted him to start there immediately. During Jones's fourteen years as national editor, Raines was one of only two correspondents who began their *Times* careers outside the paper's home office.

Howell Raines's rise through the ranks of *The New York Times* was impressive. After less than a year as a correspondent in Atlanta, he was named bureau chief. Less than a year after that, in 1980, the thirty-seven-year-old Raines was drafted by Kovach to cover the first Reagan campaign and then the White House. While in Washington, Raines met the thirtysomething Arthur Sulzberger, who was working as a reporter in the D.C. bureau. Raines immediately struck up a friendship with Sulzberger—some on the paper viewed it more as a courtship, with Raines the suitor—that lasted for the next twenty years. "Howell was a mentor to Arthur when Arthur was a young correspondent in the Washington bureau," says Jack Rosenthal, a former editorial-page and *Times Magazine* editor and currently the head of the Times Company's charitable foundation. "It always seemed to me from then that [Arthur] ordained Howell to climb the ladder." Both Raines and Sulzberger responded well to Bill Kovach, an editor who managed to be both respected and liked; Sulzberger, in particular, liked Kovach's open-door policy, in which all of the bureau's employees were encouraged to tell him if they had any concerns or problems.

But in a cutthroat industry where reporters constantly vie for the next, bigger assignment, Raines was questioning his place in the world. In his 1993 memoir, *Fly Fishing Through the Midlife Crisis*, Raines wrote of the frustration he experienced covering Reagan, a president he felt was "making life harder for citizens who were not born rich, white and healthy." He wrote of this time, "And I, as a boy wonder writer who had set out to create novels about the great struggles of our time, was a middle-aged man in a gray suit who trudged to the White House press room to write stories that began, 'President Reagan said today . . .' They call it journalism, but some days it felt like stenography."

This feeling of malaise, of intense introspection, came to permeate Raines's life for years. Anxious and depressed, he began browsing the self-help section of local bookstores. "Figure out what you really want to do and do it," one book told him. "Easy for you to say," Raines responded. There was, he would later say, a hole in his soul, an overwhelming feeling of hopelessness, a sense of time "being piddled away, by me, in the grind of daily newspapering."

Later in his fly-fishing memoir, Raines wrote, of himself and of humankind, "We are full of lust, and some of it has to get out." Howell Raines had no outlet for his lust. His marriage was struggling. It appeared he would never be known as a great novelist. Increasingly, he even seemed unsure he'd ever be known as a truly great reporter—it was the 1980s, he was in his forties, and he hadn't yet won a Pulitzer Prize. He'd had an impressive career, but neither his reportage nor his writing particularly stood out at the *Times*, a paper well staffed with talented wordsmiths and reporters. "So here is where I came out as I entered my fiftieth year," he wrote. "We are not on this earth for long. Part of what the midlife crisis is about is figuring out what gives you pleasure and doing more of that in the time you have left without asking for permission or financial or emotional subsidy from anyone else."

So Raines set his sights on the *Times* itself. Thwarted in his other ambitions, he'd instead become a great editor, perhaps even the greatest editor in the history of the paper. It was a job that traditionally went to men in their mid- to late fifties. Raines still had plenty of time to prepare.

In 1986, Max Frankel succeeded A. M. Rosenthal as executive editor of *The New York Times*. Bill Kovach, disappointed that he hadn't gotten the paper's top job, left to become editor of what had become *The Atlanta Journal-Constitution*. Raines lobbied to be named Kovach's successor as Washington bureau chief, but Frankel, according to "The Howell Doctrine," Ken Auletta's seventeen-thousand-word, June 10, 2002, *New Yorker* profile, didn't think he was up for that job, which required leading a largely autonomous office. Instead, Frankel offered Raines his choice of three postings: national editor, where he'd work in New York under the supervision of the paper's top editors, or London or Paris bureau chief, both positions that were really super-reporter jobs rather than supervisory editing ones. Mindful of the fact that the Sulzberger family often vacationed in London, Raines decided to move to England. Journalistically, his two-year stint there was unimpressive, devoid of any major scoops or memorable reporting. But Raines did deepen his already strong bond with Arthur Sulzberger Jr.

While Raines was in London, Craig Whitney, Kovach's replacement in Washington, was floundering. Whitney came to Washington without ever having worked in the capital, and he had tried to force out about half a dozen of the bureau's correspondents soon after his arrival. It soon became clear he had difficulty understanding the nuances of the culture. The D.C. bureau of the *Times* has a long tradition of struggling against the authority and control of New York, and Whitney wasn't attuned to that struggle. Within two years, he was forced out, the victim of a staff mutiny, and Raines was headed back from London—to take the job he had wanted in the first place.

———

RAINES DROVE his staff hard. In the 1980s, only a decade after Watergate, the *Times*'s D.C. bureau was still very much in the shadow of *The Washington Post*, and Raines worked furiously to make his troops more competitive. He told associates at the paper that the bureau was used to coming in on Monday, getting back in the swing of things for a day or so, and kicking into gear on Tuesday afternoon. Under his tutelage, it was clear working in Washington was a full-time job. "He was a damn good Washington bureau chief," says Soma Golden Behr, the paper's national editor in the late 1980s. "When he came on board my life got a lot easier, just because the stuff coming out of Washington was so much better."

But Raines wasn't making many friends in the process. While in Washington, he gained a reputation for being imperious—even cruel. His underlings coined a new verb—"to Raines," translated both as "to pretend not to own slaves" and "to have slaves and not admirers." Raines could be autocratic to the point of ridiculousness—he declared the bureau's reporters had to stack the books on their desks horizontally instead of vertically and once famously instructed a clerk to take his ficus plant out to a balcony so it could receive its nourishment from natural rainwater. He also was known for dividing the staff into a caste-like system whereby his favorites (and fishing buddies) would get the plum assignments and the rest would get the leftovers: At one point, he even told the staff he had mentally divided them into an A team and a B team.

"He could be very combative and arrogant," Behr says. "If one of my editors was involved in fixing something on a Washington story, he would get his back up." Raines, she felt, could be disrespectful: "There was an arrogance and this macho swagger, and I hated that." Behr would push back against Raines, and eventually he came to respect her judgment and that of her editors. "Over time we got rid of [his arrogance], to the point where we collaborated on stories and had a really good time."

It was during this time that Raines wrote the story that won him a Pulitzer Prize, practically a prerequisite for editors who hoped to run the *Times*'s newsroom. Raines's winning article, "Grady's Gift," which appeared in the December 1, 1991, *New York Times Magazine*, was a loving portrait of the African American housekeeper who had helped raise him. "She had been 'our maid,' but she taught me the most valuable lesson a writer can learn, which is to try to see—honestly and down to its very center—the world in which we live," Raines had written.* Later in the piece, Raines stressed that he didn't want to make Grady sound like "some 50's version of Whoopi Goldberg." "Grady had given me the most precious gift that could be received by a pampered white boy growing up in that time and place," he wrote. "It was the gift of a free and unhateful heart." Some black staffers found Raines's magazine piece condescending—and some referred to the article as "Driving Mr. Raines"—but the overall reaction was positive and further proof of Raines's fluid prose and literary flair. Still, reporters in the newsroom noted that Raines was forced to rely on a personal remembrance rather than gumshoe reporting or foreign correspondence to win his Pulitzer.

By the early 1990s, Raines was ready to move on to a new challenge. He knew he was a long shot to replace Frankel, who was to retire as executive editor in 1994, so he spoke with Sulzberger about an appointment as a politically liberal Op-Ed page columnist. Sulzberger, however, had a different idea. He wanted Raines to become the paper's editorial-page editor. It was a post, Sulzberger promised, where Raines would be considered part of the steering committee that debated issues concerning the future of the *Times*. Raines, along with the next executive editor and the newspaper's president, would meet once a week for lunch to discuss the paper's, and the company's, future. For Raines,

---

* It was this article that caused the formulation of "to pretend not to own slaves" as a definition for "to Raines."

it was, of course, a chance to further build his relationship with Sulz-berger.

Howell Raines took over as the editorial-page editor of *The New York Times* on January 1, 1993, one month before his fiftieth birthday.* The *Times*, like most daily American newspapers, maintains a Chinese wall between the paper's news-gathering organization and its editorial page, with the publisher of the paper serving as the only bridge be-tween the two operations. During the eight years that Raines ran the paper's editorial page, Sulzberger and Raines grew extremely close.

In replacing Jack Rosenthal, a more traditional-minded journalist, Raines inherited an editorial page that had long defined itself as sober and judicious. He made it clear from the start that he wasn't much in-terested in learning from those who came before him. "While we were still in transition, he declined my advice," Rosenthal says. "He was per-fectly polite about it, but I would have thought that, whether or not he wanted advice from me in journalistic terms, he would at least want to know what I thought of individuals and how to handle people."

Raines wasted no time transforming the tone and spirit of the page. One of his earliest editorials referred to Bill Clinton—who was inau-gurated as president on January 20, three weeks after Raines took over the page—as Slick Willie, a startling break from the page's historically high-minded tone:

> On the job training is a messy process, and when you're President everyone gets to watch. Bill Clinton's early moves on the budget have been a three-ring circus of novice mistakes. Before long—and sooner wouldn't hurt—he needs to show that he, not Slick Willie, is the ringmaster.

Raines's editorial page was an instant sensation. He quickly estab-lished himself as a maverick, someone who took obvious delight in throwing metaphoric grenades into crowds just to see what people's re-actions would be. Raines gleefully called Republicans "Dobermans"

---

* Raines was born on the same day—February 5—as Punch Sulzberger. Punch was born in 1926, Raines in 1943.

and wrote that the party's "intellectual cupboard" was "barer than at any time since the Goldwater implosion." He accused Clinton of being disingenuous: "Does he really care about the environment," one editorial asked, "or was that just something he told the voters?" Another piece accused the president of confusing "mere assertion with real accomplishment." Before spring was out, Raines had made the editorial page a must-read for Washington power brokers and the New York media elite alike. The page was feisty, provocative, fearless, and suddenly, startlingly relevant. Bob Dole, then the minority leader, denounced Raines from the floor of the Senate, complaining that the *Times*'s editorial page had abandoned the "traditional high road for the gutter." (Raines shot right back, "It's an unusual feeling to be called too tough by Bob Dole.")

Before the spring was out, *The Washington Post* had run a feature on Raines, which described how the *Times*'s "new chief pontificator is wielding a stiletto-sharp quill." Raines explained his seemingly strident editorials by quoting the aphorism about Harry Truman's search for a one-armed economist so he would no longer be presented with opinions that began, "On the one hand . . ." Raines also broke from *Times* tradition in another way: By the mid-1990s, he had become a visible figure in New York's social scene and gossip columns. He was dubbed "Howell on the Prowl" thanks to his penchant for squiring attractive women to parties (he and his wife, Susan, had divorced while Raines was still in Washington), and unlike the stereotypical *Times* editor, who shuttled from home to work outfitted in rumpled shirts and sagging trousers, Raines delighted in wearing bespoke shirts and elegant silk ties.

It wasn't long before some of the paper's veteran editorialists began (anonymously) denouncing their boss in the press. "When you spend a lot of paragraphs bashing people, you don't spend a lot of paragraphs making sound arguments," one said to *The Washington Post*. "You sort of dumb down the page." Another griped to the *National Journal*, "We sound like the *New York Post*, an editorial page of shrill braying as opposed to sound argumentation." Even his predecessors on the page, Jack Rosenthal and Max Frankel, criticized Raines. In his memoir,

Frankel wrote how Raines "did rattle the china for a while, but if he read more of yesteryear's papers, he'd have recognized that mere invective is no substitute for vigor and verve." And Rosenthal told *George* magazine, "I didn't want us to undermine our reporting staff in the way *The Wall Street Journal* editorial staff undermines its reporters."

Although the complaints ostensibly concerned Raines's philosophical approach to the editorial page, underlying them was a criticism of his managerial style. "He tended to lecture the board," says one longtime editorialist. "He saw us as a group of very intelligent people who didn't quite understand the importance of journalism or the positions of the paper as well as he did." The grumblings echoed what had been said in Washington: Raines was autocratic; he didn't have patience for anyone but his stars; he was unwilling to treat the board's twelve members as partners. Before long, editorialists started leaving.

In their place, Raines was able to install like-minded writers, and within a couple of years had assembled a close-knit group whose talents and careers he nurtured. "He made that editorial page so exciting," says Gail Collins, whom Raines recruited from *Newsday* in 1995, where she had been a political columnist. "I imagined it as everybody sitting around a table having very boring discussions. He was hugely into doing things on deadline, being up on the news, traveling on assignment.

"Howell had a vision of what the editorial page should be like," Collins continues. "It should create talk, encourage this national conversation about the issues of the day." The offices of the editorial page, located on the tenth floor of the *Times*, are some of the nicest in the building. There's an extensive library with wood paneling. The tops of the doors are framed with small stained-glass windows, and the walls are trimmed with gothic moldings. It's here that the fifty people involved in producing the two daily pages under the editorial-page editor's control spend their days. Working with a relatively small group of people enabled Raines to develop a personal relationship with every member of his staff. Despite his truculence, he had always been a hugely charismatic figure, and he used that charisma to mold the editorial page to his vision. "There was a desire to get Howell's attention, to convince him, to make him interested in your things," Collins says. "It's a very useful charisma. It drove things because you wanted him to dwell on you."

The press certainly dwelled on Raines, but their attention was often critical. In Slate, Timothy Noah wrote that Raines's editorials "routinely attempt to hide simpleminded logic behind lapidary prose and promiscuous contempt. Such elegant smugness! Such magnificent indifference to nuance!" And Michael Tomasky wrote in *The Nation*, "Raines would do well, once this is over, to give thought to the legacy he's left—extinguishing many of the *Times*' nobler traditions while using the country's most important newspaper as his personal soapbox." Some writers within the paper thought Raines's approach had more to do with marketing than conviction. "To me, it seemed like a business approach," says one editorial writer. "Like, 'Let's put the *Times* in a place where we'll be talked about.' It seemed like part of the business model Arthur [Sulzberger] and Howell understood."

Other people thought Raines's vitriolic tone—especially with respect to Bill Clinton—was fueled by nothing so much as personal rage. "That was a stormy time for the editorial page," says one writer whom Raines hired. "The relentlessness, the savagery of those editorials [about Clinton]. There was no other subject on which we were more passionate, and it would have been good to at least have been that passionate about genocide." Privately, Raines himself joked about the root of his animus for Clinton, riffing in conversation about a "certain type of person who reminds us of who we hated when we were kids." For Raines, he said, it was "the fat kid in the band."

There were times, everyone agreed, that Raines used the editorial page to great effect. In Raines's last eight months as editorial-page editor, the page ran thirty-six editorials on campaign finance reform, of which he was a fierce advocate. "[Campaign finance] is the most boring issue in the entire world," says Gail Collins. "It was just hell on wheels to try to make it interesting. I swear . . . if God had meant for campaign finance to be reformed, he wouldn't have made it so boring."

But Raines found a way to make it more exciting: by naming the senators and congressmen who were impeding passage. "He'd torture them," Collins says admiringly. "And to not be afraid to run that many [pieces] when you're the person who has this 'exciting' editorial page was sort of a great standard-bearing thing in itself."

In one two-week period between March and early April 2001, Raines ran nine campaign finance editorials, including two on the same day. That whole year, the headlines were similar to the point of redundancy: "The Battle to Save Shays-Meehan"; "The Battle for Shays-Meehan"; "New Peril for Campaign Reform"; "Perils for Campaign Reform"; "The Senate's Next Test"; "Next Test for Finance Reform"; and "An Impending Test for Reform." "He would not stop," Collins says. "He was totally and utterly committed." And Raines never worried about going overboard. "It wasn't the sort of thing Howell thought about," she says.

Raines's most famous editorial was written on the occasion of Robert McNamara's 1995 memoir, *In Retrospect*. McNamara, who had served as secretary of defense in the Kennedy and Johnson administrations, was one of the main architects of the Vietnam War. Twenty years after its conclusion, he finally admitted it was a mistake. On April 12, 1995, Raines unleashed his fury in a 742-word piece titled "Mr. McNamara's War."

Comes now Robert McNamara with the announcement that he has in the fullness of time grasped realities that seemed readily apparent to millions of Americans throughout the Vietnam War. At the time, he appeared to be helping an obsessed President prosecute a war of no real consequence to the security of the United States. Millions of loyal citizens concluded that the war was a militarily unnecessary and politically futile effort to prop up a corrupt Government that could neither reform nor defend itself.

Through all the bloody years, those were the facts as they appeared on the surface. Therefore, only one argument could be advanced to clear President Johnson and Mr. McNamara, his Secretary of Defense, of the charge of wasting lives atrociously. That was the theory that they possessed superior knowledge, not available to the public, that the collapse of South Vietnam would lead to regional and perhaps world domination by the Communists; and moreover, that their superior knowledge was so compelling it rendered unreliable and untrue the apparent facts available to even the most expert opponents of the war.

With a few throwaway lines in his new book, "In Retrospect," Mr. McNamara admits that such knowledge never existed.

Raines went on:

It is important to remember how fate dispensed rewards and punishment for Mr. McNamara's thousands of days of error. Three million Vietnamese died. Fifty-eight thousand Americans got to come home in body bags. Mr. McNamara, while tormented by his role in the war, got a sinecure at the World Bank and summers at the Vineyard.

In both the newsroom and the editorial board, the reaction to Raines's piece was mixed. Many felt it was just the kind of tough piece that the *Times* should be printing, that it behooved the most powerful paper in the country to take an impassioned stand. Others felt it unseemly. Editorial writer Leon Sigal, who at the time was writing on foreign policy for the page, thought the personal nature of the attack was beneath the *Times*. "It was simply beating up a guy," he said. Arthur Sulzberger, however, wasn't ambivalent about the piece: He nominated it for a Pulitzer and wrote a personal letter to the Pulitzer board. (Bob Semple, another *Times* editorial writer, ended up winning the award for editorial writing that year.)

Sulzberger's gesture on Howell Raines's behalf—and the intensely close relationship between the two men—did not go unnoticed by the staff. Indeed, some of the paper's top editors felt their relationship bordered on the sycophantic. In a rare joint appearance with Raines on C-SPAN in 1997, Sulzberger was asked how editorial policy at the paper was set. "Howell and I talk all too frequently," Sulzberger began.

"Not too frequently for me," Raines cut in, flashing a sly grin.

At times, Sulzberger seemed dependent on Raines to let him know what was going on. At one of the annual State of the *Times* talks Sulzberger holds for employees, Sulzberger was asked if the paper had been "objective and unbiased" in its coverage of the Monica Lewinsky scandal. "Howell and his editorial colleagues, and me as well, felt that nothing we already knew warranted impeachment," Sulzberger answered, before explaining that the *Times* had been an early advocate of . . . what? "I forgot the word," Sulzberger said, looking out into the audience to find Raines.

"Censure," Raines called back to him.

Raines, it became clear, was more than just a confidant of Sulzberger's. And soon he'd be more than just *The New York Times*'s editorial-page editor.

THE COMPETITION

In early 2001, shortly after Joe Lelyveld announced his pending retirement, Arthur Sulzberger approached Raines and managing editor Bill Keller and told the two men he wanted to speak with them, separately and over a series of dinners, about becoming the next leader of the *Times*. For Sulzberger, it would be a defining choice. When Max Frankel had retired, Sulzberger was relatively new on the job, and there was no obvious candidate except for Lelyveld. What's more, he remembered how A. M. Rosenthal had stymied his father's efforts to groom a successor. This time, Sulzberger made sure there were two viable candidates. The two men presented a stark contrast. Keller, a onetime foreign correspondent, is rangy and has a slightly patrician air. He had had a privileged childhood—his father was a former chairman of Chevron—and attended Pomona College in California. He has small, deep-set eyes and a reserved manner. Raines, in contrast, is short and expansive. His dark, fierce eyes intimidated subordinates even when he wasn't speaking, and his family and colleagues said he sometimes looked like an angry hawk.

Raines has written about how he had prepared for years for these job interviews. "I thought the paper was becoming duller, slower, and more uneven in quality with every passing day," he wrote in a May 2004 *Atlantic* cover article. In fact, the *Times* was coming off an overwhelming and fast-changing story—the 2000 presidential election and Florida recount—for which it had provided excellent coverage, an inspiring combination of daily reporting, and in-depth investigations and analyses. Late on Tuesday, November 7, as soon as it had become clear that Florida would decide the election, Lelyveld had dispatched the *Times*'s enormous resources into the state. On Thursday, the *Times* ran more than twenty stories about the recount, twice the number *The Washington Post* ran that day. The *Times* blanketed the story so completely that a special rubric—"Counting the Vote"—was adopted to guide readers through its coverage. Throughout November and into December, the paper's combination of breaking news and investigative reportage led the pack. On November 17, for instance, Raymond Bonner and Josh Barbanel broke a story about the disproportionately high number of ballots cast by African American voters in Duval County that had been invalidated. Several weeks later, on December 8, a front-page story by David Barstow and Somini Sengupta broke news about the controversial history of a judge in Leon County whose ruling crippled Al Gore's chances. Even *Washington Post* ombudsman Michael Getler noted how completely the *Times* dominated the story. In an internally circulated memo, Getler wrote how "our rivals up the road" had won the ground war. "It seems to me that what must have been a big and well-organized commitment of resources to Florida by the NYT paid off in some important and enterprising stories and in raising the profile of the paper's on the ground reporting," he wrote. During his tenure, Lelyveld had also reinvigorated the paper's metro and business staffs and created a top-notch investigative team.

Another of Lelyveld's lasting contributions to the *Times* was to break with a tradition in which those who hadn't spent their entire careers at the paper were looked on with distrust. Lelyveld, like Frankel and Rosenthal before him, was a *Times* lifer, but he fought to bring outsiders into the fold. To this end, he recruited John Geddes and Jill Abramson from *The Wall Street Journal* to help run the business and Washington desks, respectively, and snared Pulitzer Prize–winning investigative reporter Dean Baquet from the *Chicago Tribune*. He actively promoted longtime Washington reporter Gerald Boyd, who had begun his career at the *St. Louis Post-Dispatch*. He tapped Adam Moss, a pop culture–savvy editor who had cut his teeth on New York's magazine scene, to lead *The New York Times Magazine*, which Moss transformed into one of the best weekly publications in the country. "The period in which it became normal to have a paper run by people who knew how other folks did things, who had seen a competitive landscape from a variety of perspectives," says Bill Keller, "was the Joe regime."

But to make a plausible argument for his ascension, Raines had constructed a narrative in which he was needed to rescue the paper from editorial and financial ruin. For a decade, Raines had been quietly preparing a file of the paper's problems, so when he and Sulzberger sat down for the first of their dinner-cum-interviews, he was well prepared. Raines told Sulzberger that the paper was slow out of the gate, that the cultural coverage was in shambles, that the *Times* had ceded its traditional dominance by becoming lazy and moribund. He talked of wanting to dismantle the paper's "old-boy network." "The ingrained management habit of favoring seniority and networking skills over talent had its roots in a kind of Skull and Bones system in which people who came to the *Times* at an early age and advanced to high positions made sure that the guys with whom they had been clerks and cub reporters were taken care of," Raines would write in 2004.

This critique dovetailed nicely with what Raines knew was Sulzberger's strategic belief that for the *Times* not only to survive but to continue to serve as the country's, and the world's, dominant newsgathering organization, it had to undergo a major overhaul. For the past several years, Sulzberger and Janet Robinson, the paper's president and general manager,* and Russ Lewis, the Times Company's chief executive officer, had sought to focus the paper's growth on its national expansion. "We had to create a new newspaper for the next generation of readers and advertisers," says Sulzberger.

And Raines was prepared to argue that the *Times* was failing in exactly this endeavor. "Whether we liked it or not, *USA Today* and *The Wall Street Journal* were better than the *Times* at editing for a national audience that was, for example, interested in both foreign policy and the Super Bowl, both Medicare funding and the constantly shifting American youth culture," he wrote, describing the *Times* at the turn of the century. It's difficult to determine which newspapers Raines was reading. Under Lelyveld, the *Times* certainly dominated on all these topics, especially when compared with *USA Today* and the *Journal*. Even the *Journal*'s traditional domination of business stories had grown less secure. If there was an area in which *USA Today* beat the *Times*, it was in college and national sports—but amping up the *Times*'s sports coverage to make it truly a national page would be a hugely costly proposition. The *Times* did well with the resources it had. There was, of course, room for improvement, especially in the paper's often stodgy culture coverage, and there were entire departments that could have been made more efficient. But any major overhaul would require a similarly major investment, and the advertising downturn of the early twenty-first century precluded that.

Keller, on the other hand, refused to articulate a vision for the paper that included a denigration of Joe Lelyveld's work, despite the fact that he sensed Sulzberger was looking for just such a critique. And while Lelyveld was vocal in his praise of Keller, he refused to knock Raines. As the quiet, closed-door selection process progressed, it was becoming increasingly clear that Howell Raines had the upper hand. Significantly, Raines's personality seemed more suited both to Arthur Sulzberger's outgoing nature and to leading a large institution. Raines

---

* In February 2001, Robinson was named senior vice president in charge of newspaper operations, and in February 2004, she was named the company's chief operating officer and executive vice president. At the end of 2004, she will take over as the company's chief executive officer.

loved people. He loved socializing and was skilled at circulating through a room, glad-handing and making small talk. Keller, by contrast, gravitated to the corners of parties. Raines always seemed to say just the right thing in large gatherings; Keller was the opposite, famous for cracking jokes that made people feel awkward. "My wife sometimes refers to me as socially autistic," he would say later.

At the time, even some of Lelyveld's deputies felt that Raines might be the right choice to lead the paper. Raines is a dynamic and forceful presence—he can "fill a room," as Dean Baquet, a *Times* national editor under Lelyveld, says. When Baquet left New York in 2000 to become managing editor of the *Los Angeles Times*, Sulzberger asked him who he thought should be the next editor of the paper. "Raines," said Baquet, and after Sulzberger told some of the paper's executives what Baquet's answer had been, it was repeated, sotto voce, around the newsroom. Raines's leadership of the paper's editorial page, Baquet thought, proved he could be an energetic steward. Besides, Baquet said, Raines would need to retire in 2009, before he turned sixty-six. Keller would be only sixty and would still have almost six years to lead the paper on his own. What's more, Raines had made it a point, while editorial-page editor, to invite to lunch members of the *Times*'s increasingly frustrated masthead. If he was in power, he assured them implicitly, things would be different. "Under Joe, I felt really marginalized," says Al Siegal, a *Times* assistant managing editor. "Howell at the time was the editor of the editorial page. We would have lunch twice a year or so, and he was very understanding about how I felt in my working life. He was empathetic."

"There was a feeling on the masthead that Howell was a good idea," says Soma Golden Behr. "Bill was fine, but he seemed kind of quiet and subdued. Howell seemed exciting and daring. He took risks. I thought we could use a little of that."

Sulzberger agreed, and on Monday, May 21, 2001, he announced that Howell Raines would be *The New York Times*'s next executive editor. "Howell will continue to improve the news report of the *Times* and build on Joe's outstanding accomplishments," Sulzberger said in a public announcement, praising Lelyveld for "shepherd[ing] The Times through one of the most momentous periods in its 150-year history."

Raines, for his part, publicly disavowed much of what he had been saying privately in his conversations with Sulzberger. "My first and foremost responsibility will be to protect and build upon The Times's tradition of quality journalism," he said after being appointed. "I also feel great joy at the prospect of working again with my talented colleagues in the newsroom and our bureaus." The newsroom greeted the announcement with a mixture of apprehension and excitement. Keller was known and respected, but he was not considered a particularly warm leader. Raines, on the other hand, was a mystery. There was concern about Raines's reputation as an autocrat and a tyrant: Written in an open comment book in the *Times*'s newsroom on the day of Raines's appointment were two telling entries. Under the heading of "I would like to see in the new building" (into which the *Times* was planning to move later that decade) were scrawled two anonymous comments: "No tyrannical executive editors," someone had jotted down. "No Howell Raines," wrote another. But for the most part, *Times* staffers were ready to be optimistic—maybe Raines would be a pleasant surprise.

Over the next several months (Raines wouldn't take over the newsroom until September), Raines went on a listening tour, getting acquainted with a 1,200-person news operation he had been removed from for almost a decade. Some staffers appreciated the gesture—Raines spent a shift with each section's copy desk, sometimes sitting with them until midnight, when the pages closed. Other times, Raines seemed to be doing more shouting than listening. He was vocal in expressing the low regard in which he held the business report and publicly criticized Glenn Kramon, the section's editor. He was outspoken in his criticism of the paper's culture department. And he was dismissive of the paper's sports coverage, which he deemed parochial.

"The first lesson of management should always be, it's a mistake for the new administration to come in trashing the old administration," says Baquet, who arrived at the *Los Angeles Times* in 2000, at the tail end of a period in which the paper had been rocked by scandal and then sold to the Chicago-based Tribune Company. "The reality of a newsroom is that it's the same population from editor to editor, especially at a place like *The New York Times*. The new administration shouldn't spend too much time dwelling on what the predecessors did, because eventually the reporters and editors will start thinking you're talking about them."

Raines, though, was in too much of a hurry for such niceties, and he began to lay out a vaguely defined vision: The paper would have a "higher competitive metabolism"; business would push harder on breaking stories; sports coverage would trend more national. Meanwhile, Joe Lelyveld was still running the newsroom. The tension between the two men grew. In August, when invitations were sent out for a gala fete celebrating Lelyveld's career, the gatefold invite featured dozens of datelines that Lelyveld had filed from, including Kashmir, South Africa, London, Nairobi, Geneva, and Burma. Some thought the design was intended as a barb to Raines, who, with the possible exception of Scotty Reston, was the least-traveled executive editor in the history of *The New York Times*.

THE DEPUTY

On July 26, 2001, Raines made his first, and most significant, appointment, naming as his managing editor the fifty-one-year-old Gerald Boyd, the paper's deputy managing editor for news. Boyd's elevation to the newsroom's second in command was not a surprise: Raines had made Boyd's ascension, which would make him the highest-ranking African American in the history of the paper, part of his campaign to win the executive editorship. But it did little to soothe those looking for a counterbalance to Raines's imperious ways. Boyd had a reputation for being cold and caustic—"No more Mr. Gruff," he told the newsroom after his appointment was announced. Boyd had worked with Raines in Washington and had been at the *Times* since 1983, when he was hired from the *St. Louis Post-Dispatch* as a political reporter. After a period spent covering the White House, Boyd had been an editor in Washington and had served time on the national and metro desks as well. He also did a stint as metro editor in the early 1990s.

Gerald Boyd grew up in St. Louis, Missouri. His early life was diffi-cult. His mother died when he was five, and he was raised by his grand-mother, whose only income was her pension. During high school, he worked full-time bagging groceries and won a University of Missouri scholarship sponsored by the *St. Louis Post-Dispatch*. At the university, he helped found and edit *Blackout*, a black student newspaper. He began reporting for the *Post-Dispatch* after graduating in 1973, working his way up from the city desk to land in Washington during Ronald Reagan's first term as president. From 1983 until 1990, he covered the White House for the *Times*, where he soon earned a reputation for being contentious, even with his sources. "He was extremely aggressive in the way he handled politicians," said Andrew Rosenthal, a *Times* re-porter and editor who worked with Boyd in both Washington and New York. "He was famous for calling the White House and getting [former presidential spokesman] Marlin Fitzwater or whoever on the phone and starting out the conversation, 'What in the hell is going on over there?' He had this idea that aggressive behavior was useful in dealing with the White House."

"Gerald is not your biggest book-learned guy," says Soma Golden Behr, who was one of Boyd's closest friends on the paper. "He's not like all the card-carrying Ivy League liberals that run around *The New York Times*. He's had a different life, and he has a way of zigging and zag-ging. He's not always going to tell you what he thinks. He might kid you. He might razz you."

Sometimes, Boyd seemed not to know exactly what it was he was looking for from his reporters, which made getting assignments from him a notoriously dicey process—he'd gather reporters around his desk, and they'd speak to fill in his awkward silences, trying to discern what it was he wanted. But although Gerald Boyd was never a widely beloved figure in the newsroom, there were those staffers in whom he inspired a fierce respect. He was loyal to his troops and had a deep love for the *Times*. "He was very proud to be a part of *The New York Times*," says Deborah Sontag, a *Times Magazine* writer who worked for Boyd as a reporter on the metro desk. "He had a huge belief in its power, its im-portance. In those days, he was charming and very avuncular." Early in her career, Sontag was mugged coming out of a subway station in Brooklyn. She was knocked down and bloodied in the process, and Boyd came to the hospital to see her that same night. "He treated it like it was a moral thing to do: 'These are my people, I'm responsible for them.' And he wanted to make sure the authorities knew how important this was, that the metro editor of the *Times* was coming out." At one point, as Sontag was in her hospital bed, she heard two cops talking. "Who's the black guy in the suit?" one asked. When told it was the metro editor of the *Times*, the response was, "No shit."

"I realized that must be what he hears and feels all the time," Sontag says.

Boyd's best work was on large projects that needed extensive coordination. He guided the *Times* staff on its coverage of the 1993 World Trade Center bombing, which won a Pulitzer Prize, and in 2000 worked with Behr to lead a team of reporters on a fifteen-part, Pulitzer Prize–winning project on race relations in America. "He's got incredible journalistic sensibilities," says Behr. "These projects would not have been half of what they were without him."[*]

"Gerald really showed me a lot during the race project," says former *Times* reporter Kevin Sack, whose story about an integrated Pentecostal church in Decatur, Georgia, led off the series. "That was a massive undertaking, and he made very good decisions."

As he rose up the paper's masthead, Boyd seemed to pride himself on adopting the *Times*'s hard-nosed swagger. When prospective reporters came in to meet with Boyd during their extensive job interviews (all candidates for positions at the *Times* go through a battery of one-on-one interviews), Boyd was famous for staring down the new recruit from across his desk and booming out, "So what makes you think you deserve to work at *The New York Times*?" According to people who worked for and with him, Boyd became increasingly thin-skinned the higher up the ladder he climbed.

In 1993, Gerald Boyd was promoted to assistant managing editor. His time as assistant, and then deputy, managing editor was frustrat-

---

[*] The race project, Behr says, was born out of her and Boyd's frustration with the lack of responsibility they were given on the masthead under Joe Lelyveld. "We both felt wasted," she says.

ing. In 1997, when Gene Roberts retired from the managing editor post, Joe Lelyveld spent a series of dinners and weekends with Boyd as he tried to decide whom he should appoint as Roberts's replacement. When, over dinner one night, Lelyveld told Boyd he had decided on Bill Keller, Boyd was so angry that he almost left the restaurant.

If on paper Gerald Boyd seemed a questionable fit for the second most powerful and important editorial position at the paper, he was also in some ways a smart choice, and Raines knew it. Boyd may have had a mixed record as a manager, but Raines knew full well of Sulzberger's deep commitment to diversity, of how much he wanted to be known as a publisher who aggressively diversified the *Times*. Raines quite explicitly made Boyd part of his pitch for the job during the interviewing process. "I wanted to see, as Arthur himself needed to, what Gerald Boyd could do in a high-demand situation," Raines would later write. It was a condescending slap. Boyd, Raines implied, hadn't been chosen as his deputy on the merits; instead, the managing editor's job would serve as a sort of audition, one that would determine for Sulzberger whether one day Boyd might be able to become *The New York Times*'s first nonwhite executive editor.

Over the years, Boyd came to keep his opinions on race in the newsroom more to himself; a lot of time had passed since the days in Missouri when he sported an Afro and an array of dashikis and sometimes affected the pseudonym Uganda X. What's more, Boyd had, as a friend noted when he was named managing editor, spent a career as a "first black."* On the day he was promoted, he told a *Times* reporter, "I hope tomorrow, when some kid of color picks up The New York Times and reads about the new managing editor, that kid will smile a little and maybe dream just a little bigger dream. That's all I'll say about firsts."

---

* Years earlier, Boyd did note that his status as one of the few nonwhite reporters covering Reagan didn't hurt his career. "There were just two minority reporters covering the White House back then," he said. "So that brought me to Reagan's attention. I got far more attention than I deserved, and I would always be called on by Reagan at press conferences."

Race in the Newsroom

For the media world, the industry's sorry record on diversity has been cause for embarrassment going back for decades, ever since the Lyndon Johnson administration's 1968 Kerner Report described how "the journalistic profession has been shockingly backward in seeking out, hiring, training, and promoting Negroes."* Ten years later, in 1978, the American Society of Newspaper Editors (ASNE) would propose an ambitious goal: By 2000, the percentage of minorities in newsrooms, it announced, should mirror the diversity of the general population. At the time, minorities made up only 4 percent of newsroom staffs around the country. By 2003, that number had risen to 12.9 percent—still far short of the 31 percent of the American population that is nonwhite. (ASNE recast its goals and is now aiming for parity in American newsrooms by 2025.)

---

* The Kerner Report was the result of President Johnson's National Advisory Commission on Civil Disorders, which was convened in 1967 to explain the riots that had plagued American cities every summer since 1964. The report concluded that the country was "moving toward two societies, one black, one white—separate and unequal."

There are many theories as to why minorities are underrepresented in American newsrooms, most common among them the pervasiveness of an old-boy network.* For decades, the *Times* has fought to diversify its reporting ranks, with mixed results. Too often, the paper's efforts to hire minority staffers have come across as tokenism to those being wooed and as clumsy quota-filling to the rest of the newsroom. "The culture is such that a lot of people feel in their guts that when they see a minority colleague, they feel a little jolt of unfamiliarity, and some may even feel that the person doesn't really belong," says Roger Wilkins, who worked for the *Times* in the 1970s and early 1980s as an editorial writer and columnist.† "I know that greeted me when I joined the editorial board in 1974. We're geniuses at reading white people's faces."

A semiformalized effort in the early 1990s to increase minority representation in the newsroom didn't help matters. That year, Max Frankel instituted a one-to-one quota for newsroom hiring: For every white reporter who was hired, a non-white reporter had to be hired as well. It was a crude and inelegant solution and fostered complaints from both whites and African Americans. Whites, of course, felt they were suffering from reverse discrimination, and African Americans who were hired complained that they were looked at askance. What's worse, some of the hires that resulted were journalists whose talents were not up to the *Times*'s standards.

Frankel would later speak of the problems that resulted from his campaign. He wrote in his memoir of a "senior black editor" who was promoted above his abilities and ended up suing the *Times* for discrimination. And in 1994, just after stepping down as executive editor, he spoke to Charlie Rose about the troubles he had encountered when he tried to diversify the staff: "There was a real problem, and the word was getting out that this was not a place that was entirely hospitable to blacks because they weren't [being promoted] fast enough." Attempts

---

* Another theory—that there are fewer minorities enrolling in journalism programs—is demonstrably false. Twenty-nine percent of students in American journalism programs in 2002 were minorities, and half of those were African American, according to University of Georgia journalism professor Lee Becker's Annual Survey of Mass Communication and Journalism Enrollments.

† In 1979, Roger Wilkins took part in a class-action suit against the *Times* alleging that black, Hispanic, and Asian American employees were paid less than their white counterparts. The suit was settled before trial without any admission of wrongdoing by the *Times*.

to counter that perception, Frankel said, "created some mistakes": "In the years when we were all practicing affirmative action on the first round and looking very hard to diversify, we grabbed at some people so fast that they were not always the right people. . . . At a certain point, you cannot compromise just for the sake of appearances with the quality of the people you bring in. So those failures, those disappointments, created a certain disillusionment, and they were confused with racism or inhospitality."

Sulzberger hadn't been publisher when Frankel instituted his one-for-one hiring quota, but he was a vocal champion of the need to alter quickly the makeup of the *Times*'s newsroom. In Lelyveld, however, he found an executive editor who questioned what he viewed as simplistic solutions to intractable and complex problems. "Joe was all for Arthur Jr.'s efforts to promote blacks, gays, and women," Tifft and Jones wrote in *The Trust*, "but was slow to release money in the newsroom budget earmarked for diversity training because he thought the approach naïve and vaguely degrading."

Raines, the author of an oral history of the civil rights era, had no such qualms. If anything, he took the opposite approach. He spoke often about the need to further diversify the *Times*'s ranks, and he served as a sympathetic sounding board when Gerald Boyd complained about Lelyveld.

The industry's and the *Times*'s well-documented history with affirmative action, coupled with Raines's and Sulzberger's public pronouncements on increasing the paper's diversity, must have made Boyd's position a little uncomfortable. His own impressive record at the *Times* was understood to be at least partially the result of the paper's in-house affirmative-action program: At several steps in his career, his superiors had made it clear that he was being promoted in part because there was such a dearth of qualified minority candidates. To take one example, at the same time that Frankel laid down his newsroom edict on hiring, he set out what he described as a "special, fast-track training program" by which Boyd "could prove himself capable of leading a department, and perhaps more."

In public, Boyd was careful to not be seen as giving black reporters special treatment, but behind the scenes he fought to make sure they were considered for top postings. Often, Boyd's private lobbying ended well for his protégés, who were sometimes unaware of his efforts. But occasionally the results were disastrous. In the summer of 1994, a black reporter named Kenneth Noble returned from his stint as West African bureau chief. At the time, Linda Mathews was a year into her difficult tenure as the paper's national editor; she had joined the *Times* from ABC News and never quite gained traction at the paper. Noble's return to the United States coincided with the opening of the paper's prestigious Los Angeles bureau chief job. From Africa, Noble had expressed interest in the job, but he had a reputation in New York for being an uninspiring correspondent, and Mathews wanted instead to assign him to San Francisco's one-person bureau. "But Gerald went and visited Ken in Africa and offered him the job in L.A. without even consulting me," says Mathews. "And when I complained, [Boyd] said the paper had a responsibility to bring along young, talented blacks."

According to Mathews, other *Times* senior editors, the L.A. bureau's other reporters, and reporters from other news organizations based in Los Angeles at the time, Noble had great difficulty from the moment he arrived in California. He came to the office infrequently. When he did appear, he was often dressed inappropriately, in sweatpants and T-shirts. He had trouble meeting the *Times*'s East Coast deadlines, and instead of attending the O. J. Simpson criminal trial, he occasionally wrote his copy off of Associated Press reports. Several times, copy editors noticed that stories Noble had filed seemed to contain multiple paragraphs lifted verbatim from the AP or a local California paper. "We had a couple of incidents," says Mathews. "It became clear to the editing staff that we had to be alert to the possibility that he was filching stuff." (Mathews says she didn't tell Boyd or the masthead about these incidents, because she assumed they didn't want to hear it.)

"Ken couldn't hack it," says a reporter who was in the Los Angeles bureau at the time. "There was a bizarreness to his behavior. Sometimes he'd show up, and sometimes he wouldn't. And this went on and on and on. Eventually I wondered why the *Times* was keeping him there. It was such a high-profile job, and it wasn't just O.J.—there was all this other stuff going on." Reporters from the dozens of news organizations covering the Simpson saga became close as the trial stretched on, and Noble's behavior—and his absences and overreliance on stringers to do his reporting—was spoken of openly. Soon after Noble arrived in Los Angeles, the *Times* brought in David Margolick, whom Boyd had rejected for the Los Angeles bureau chief job and instead installed in San Francisco, to cover the trial. He remained in Los Angeles for the duration of the Simpson case. "What struck me was the notion that Gerald saw [promoting black reporters] as his mission," says Mathews. "He was determined. I can't argue with that as an objective, but I think Ken was really just the wrong person."

By the end of 1996, Noble had been recalled from Los Angeles after an investigation into the bureau revealed rampant mismanagement. The next year, he left the paper for good.*

Noble's experience was obviously unique, and there were numerous African American reporters and editors who excelled at the *Times*. But the paper's very public efforts at diversification, coupled with clumsy promotion of reporters like Noble, meant that those within the newsroom who were inclined to see the *Times*'s efforts at affirmative action as producing nothing but negative results had examples to which they could point. In the years to come, they'd have even more ammunition.

---

* Noble is currently an assistant professor at the University of Southern California's School of Journalism. He did not respond to more than half a dozen e-mails and phone messages requesting comment for this book.

THE AGENDA

It didn't take long for Raines and Boyd to start planning how they would remake the *Times*'s staff. In August 2001, a month before they were to take over the paper, the two editors, joined by national editor Katy Roberts, flew down to Atlanta in the Times Company's corporate jet to meet with about half a dozen of the paper's national correspondents. Kevin Sack, the paper's Atlanta bureau chief, was the host of the event.

Sack had been hired by *The New York Times* in 1989, and during his twelve years at the paper, he'd had some experience working with both Raines and Boyd. After a brief stint in New York on the paper's metro staff when Boyd was editor there, he was moved up to Albany. By 1992, Sack had been covering the state capital—and New York governor Mario Cuomo—for more than two years. The previous December, Cuomo had finally decided against joining the presidential race, and he was slated to deliver the keynote address at that summer's Democratic convention. In his waning days as the paper's Washington bureau chief, Raines had asked Sack to help cover the rest of that year's presidential campaign. Looking for a story Sack could use to establish himself on the campaign, the reporter suggested he write about how Cuomo's speech had developed.

At the same time, Raines's staff was preparing a profile of Bill Clinton. The day before it was set to run, Raines decided he didn't like the story's lead, and he pulled a bunch of reporters off their assignments to dig for better anecdotes. Sack was one of those reporters, and he grumbled to colleagues about how he thought it would be a better use of his time to finish his story about Cuomo's speech.

One of the Washington bureau's senior reporters told Raines about Sack's complaint. Raines never said anything to Sack, but before the end of the convention, Gerald Boyd—with whom Sack was on good terms—pulled the reporter aside. "You need to be careful about this," Boyd said. "Howell heard you were complaining about him." Sack was soon pulled off of covering Bill Clinton.* Little did Sack know that his offhand complaint during the 1992 convention would follow him for years.

In 1995, after five years in New York's capital, Sack's wife said she wanted to return to her hometown of Atlanta. Atlanta appealed to Sack as well. "Her family is there, she wanted our newborn to be around her family, and she had spent some cold winters in Albany," says Sack. "Furthermore . . . as something of a student of the region, covering the South for the *Times* had always been a dream." Sack, knowing that the paper had hoped to use him as a political writer based out of Washington, asked Joe Lelyveld if he could cover the South for the paper instead, and Lelyveld agreed. That year, he moved to Georgia.

The *Times* has a long tradition of rotating national correspondents out of their domestic bureaus every four to five years. There are exceptions— Fox Butterfield has a seemingly permanent posting in Boston, and Rick Bragg was allowed to open his own one-person bureau in New Orleans—but the paper has a philosophical belief that it can get the

---

* Sack lost his post on the campaign trail when Ross Perot dropped out of the race, and Michael Kelly, one of his generation's best political writers, was assigned to cover Bill Clinton, effectively bumping Sack.

best out of its bureaus by having fresh eyes on the scene. Besides, the national posts are plum positions, something for reporters to strive toward. Sack, of course, was well aware of this. But in 2000, when Sack should have been preparing to transfer to another bureau, he found himself unable to contemplate leaving Atlanta. His marriage was disintegrating, and his wife was determined to stay in Atlanta with the couple's young daughter. Sack wanted to remain an active part of his only child's life, which meant he was determined to stay as well. Over the five years he had been in Atlanta, Sack was an integral part of the 2000 series on race in America that Boyd and Soma Golden Behr had coordinated, and he spent much of the rest of that year on the road covering Al Gore's presidential campaign. In May 2001, when Sack was in New York for that year's Pulitzer luncheon, he spoke to Raines about his predicament.

"I explained the situation, and I said, 'I know this puts you in a tough position,'" Sack says. "And he told me not to worry about it, that there was no need to discuss it yet."

Raines's tone had changed dramatically by the time he arrived in Atlanta for the August correspondents' dinner. Upon arriving, he and Sack had a one-on-one meeting. It was then that he told Sack that he thought Lelyveld had mismanaged the paper by allowing people to stay in domestic bureaus for too long.

"I had made a decision that I had to stay in Atlanta," says Sack. "I offered to cover any number of beats—race, immigration, religion, investigations. I tried to think of ways I could stay there without remaining on as bureau chief. He basically shot them all down at once. He just dismissed all of them. And I said, 'What do you think about a contract, where I'd leave the staff but write a certain number of stories a year?' He shot that down, too." Sack was confused—and upset—by Raines's stubbornness.

That night, the assembled correspondents and editors gathered in a room at 103 West, a rococo private restaurant in Atlanta's fashionable Buckhead neighborhood. At the dinner, Raines laid out his vision for the national staff. He said he wanted three or four bylines a week from each correspondent, all from different places around the country. He wanted more breaking news and fewer analytical "thumb suckers" and trend pieces. National reporters, he said, shouldn't expect to see much of their families.

The reporters were stunned. Not only was the leadership of Joe Lelyveld—who was still officially the executive editor of the paper—being dismissed, but the reporters' work was being disparaged as well. "We thought our metabolism was pretty fucking high," says one reporter who was at the meeting. "This asshole comes in after spending a decade sitting in his wood-paneled office on the editorial board and tells us we're not moving fast enough?" Sack, who had essentially been on the road for the last half of 2000—first on the campaign, then on the Florida recount story—remembers feeling as if he'd entered a parallel universe. Two years later, Katy Roberts still finds the memories of the meeting too painful to discuss. "Please don't make me relive those horrible two days," she wrote in an e-mail to me when asked about the Atlanta meeting.

Worse was still to come. Kevin Sack was one of the most respected reporters at the *Times*. He was always willing to push harder for a story, always willing to travel for a good scene. He was the type of reporter Raines should have coveted. But the incoming executive editor was treating Sack as if he were deadweight, destined to be pushed overboard. Raines seemed to have made his mind up about Sack, perhaps on the basis of one long-ago incident that was reported to him secondhand—at least, that was the only explanation anyone could think of. Howell Raines's era at *The New York Times* hadn't yet begun, but already, fears about the way he would run the newsroom were being stoked.

A New Era

On September 5, 2001—the day Howell Raines officially began his tenure as executive editor of *The New York Times*—the *Times* was in the middle of a slow news period. The Florida election fiasco was well in the past, the business scandals that would grip the country had yet to be uncovered, and the biggest local story concerned the upcoming New York City mayoral primary, in which none of the candidates inspired even a fraction of the excitement that the outgoing mayor, Rudy Giuliani, had prompted in his allies and enemies alike. The flagging economy was the story of the day: The *Times*'s front page on September 5 featured one story on an agreement between President Bush and Senate Democratic leader Tom Daschle not to use Social Security funds to pay government bills and another on New York's jobless centers.

Howell Raines moved into the executive editor's corner office that morning, the first time in his twenty-three-year career at the *Times* that he had worked in the paper's third-floor newsroom.

In one of his first official acts, he spoke to the staff in the newsroom and sent out a welcome letter and in the process took some not-so-subtle swipes at Joe Lelyveld. Raines promised the *Times* would no longer be outhustled by its competition and told the staff to stay hungry. He also said there wouldn't be any "imminent" changes in the newsroom, before pausing for a beat and continuing: "This week." Raines was followed by Boyd, who—alluding to the complaint that Lelyveld and Keller had often been hard to read—promised staffers they wouldn't have to "wonder what Howell and Gerald" wanted.

Soon, Raines lined the walls of his office with a series of photographs of Lyndon Johnson in his years as Senate majority leader. In the pictures, Johnson towers over Senator Theodore Green of Rhode Island; in each successive picture, Johnson moves in closer and closer, until Green seems to be almost doubled over. For Raines, a man who disdained Johnson's leadership during the Vietnam War and couldn't stand dishonesty in politicians, the selection of photographs of Johnson bullying a colleague was an interesting choice, one that many visitors to his office felt sent a pointed message.

Other changes came quickly. Raines tapped foreign editor Andrew Rosenthal, the son of former *Times* executive editor A. M. Rosenthal, to be an assistant managing editor; Rosenthal, along with Gerald Boyd, would be in charge of assembling the daily news report. Raines also instituted a 10:30 a.m. meeting of the paper's masthead in which the top newsroom executives would map out the major stories of the day. That was followed by the preexisting noon meeting, where the masthead and the department heads met to discuss that day's coverage. Then at 4:30 p.m. was the page-one meeting. In the first week of his tenure, Raines had established a pattern in which he'd spend half of his day in meetings with a select group of top editors. Most of his remaining time was spent back in his office in the northeast corner of the newsroom, where it was almost impossible, by virtue of geography, for him to see his reporters or have his reporters see him. The days of Raines's gregarious office meet-and-greets were over.

The 10:30 a.m. meeting was a sharp and purposeful departure from how Joe Lelyveld had run the newsroom. For decades, the editorial management of the *Times* has swung back and forth as if on a pendulum, as authority and power were either taken away from or bestowed upon the masthead and decisions either centralized or decentralized. Lelyveld, who empowered his desk editors, considered the *Times*'s reporters its most essential assets and wanted to create a system in which ideas trickled up. Raines disdained Lelyveld's approach, which he thought resulted in a group of highly paid editors at the top ranks of the paper who did little but burn in frustration. He wanted ideas to flow downward, from the executive editor to the masthead to the desk editors to the reporters.

In addition to instituting a top-down management style, Raines didn't seem much concerned with familiarizing himself with the newsroom's assorted factions. "I used to spend most of my day prowling the office," says Ben Bradlee, the former executive editor of *The Washington Post*. Bradlee is a legendary newsroom figure—the archetypal newsman, he led the *Post* in its Watergate coverage and is still stopped on the street by people who thank him for his contribution to the country. "I could stand two people talking in the newsroom, but suddenly if there were three people talking together, I want to know what the hell it's about," he continues. "And if it's good, I want a piece of it. I had glass walls in my office so I could see what was going on, and if there was something I didn't know about, it would drive me crazy."

Raines, tucked away either in his office or in high-level meetings, seemed content not to know. Privately, he would later reveal, he thought the newsroom was filled with lazy, occasionally incompetent staffers. The paper's "indifference to competition and its chronic slowness in anticipating the news" had dulled its journalistic wits and largely negated the advantage of the paper's superior resources, according to Raines's May 2004 *Atlantic* essay. Instead of taking the pulse of the newsroom, he barked out orders. He instituted pieces he called "all-known thoughts," weighty, multi-thousand-word exposés that ran on the front page of the Sunday paper. The stories were meant to distill authoritatively the hot news topic of the moment, but in practice the pieces often seemed larded with extraneous, recycled detail at the expense of actual news. He seemed to want buzzy, snappy pieces, regardless of whether any buzzy, snappy news was happening at any given time.

By Friday, September 7, just two days into Raines's tenure, the newsroom already felt as if it were under the gun, and staffers speculated openly about whose necks were on the chopping block. Word was out that Raines thought business editor Glenn Kramon was underperforming. In fact, Howell was said to be putting all his top editors on notice that they had better shape up. He'd called Washington bureau chief Jill Abramson at her vacation home in Madison, Connecticut, and told her he wanted "something to pop" from her for Sunday's edition. He'd moved Rosenthal off the foreign desk but hadn't yet officially tapped a successor: Roger Cohen would need to do the job with the word "acting" preceding his "foreign editor" title. Boyd, though at least well-known in the newsroom, was no comfort, either; he'd already begun to emulate the arrogant swagger of his executive editor.

The first weekend after Raines took office was unseasonably warm in New York City. Central Park was filled with people in shorts and T-shirts. Up in the Bronx, the Yankees took three straight from their archrivals, the Boston Red Sox. On Monday, September 10, the city was drenched in a torrential late afternoon downpour. The rain tapered off overnight, and Tuesday, September 11, was an impossibly clear, cloudless fall day.

Howell Raines lives in Manhattan's Greenwich Village, about midway between the World Trade Center towers and the *Times*'s headquarters. His four-story townhouse sits across the street from St. Vincent's Hospital. On the morning of September 11, he was sitting at his computer, not yet dressed, when American Airlines Flight 11 crashed into the north tower of the World Trade Center at 8:45 a.m. The impact was clearly audible in the Village; it sounded like a fireball exploding. Raines took a call from Arthur Sulzberger and rushed outside. United Airlines Flight 175 struck the south tower at 9:03 a.m. Raines arrived at the *Times* around ten o'clock, just as the south tower was collapsing. The Pentagon had also been hit. All local bridges and tunnels were shut down, as were all of the country's flight operations.

By the time Raines and the paper's top editors made their way to the paper, dozens of reporters had swarmed toward the World Trade Center. A handful of the paper's metro staffers were already downtown—September 11 was the scheduled primary day for November's mayoral election. Some of them would remain at ground zero for weeks.

That day, ultimately, *The New York Times* would dispatch three hundred reporters, thirty staff photographers, and twenty-four freelance photographers. Seventy-four staffers got bylines, and thirty-three pages of the next morning's paper were devoted to the attacks. According to a 2002 article in *The New Yorker,* on September 12 the *Times* devoted 82,500 words to coverage of the attack, almost as many as the number that make up the text of this book.

The *Times*'s coverage of the attacks and their aftermath was remarkable. Raines, whose first wife had been a photographer, made extraordinary use of the paper's photographers and produced a visually arresting paper that was more handsome and gripping than ever before. The paper's coverage was comprehensive and humane; the "Portraits of Grief," thumbnail-sketch biographies of the victims of the attacks, became one of the most profoundly moving components of the paper's daily reports. Even the solutions that had been conceived to manage the volume of coverage were daring and unique: Because the paper wanted to dedicate a daily, stand-alone section to coverage of the attacks, the paper's editors had to come up with a way to collapse two sections into one. Instead of beginning one halfway through another, they decided to run sports on the back of the daily metro section, flipped upside down, so readers could read each section with its own front page. In many ways, the *Times*'s robust coverage of September 11 played to Raines's greatest strengths: his vigor, his editorial ingenuity, his love of all-consuming stories, and his keen aesthetic sense.

Immediately after September 11, the *Times,* like many New York–based newspapers, made counseling available for staffers who felt emotionally overwhelmed, but the vast majority of reporters and editors were too busy, or felt too proud, to avail themselves of help. Over the months, the demands on the newsroom and the stresses of working at a potential target for terrorist attacks only grew. The *Times* wrote about how Times Square—its home—was a largely unprotected magnet for suicide bombers. "There was the enormous stress of September 11 as a news story, and then there was also the enormous stress of September 11 as a horrifying tragedy in your hometown," says assistant managing editor Mike Oreskes.

Oreskes himself says he didn't fully realize the pressure the newsroom was under until it was brought home by his young son. A couple of weeks after the World Trade Center attacks, his son was speaking with a counselor in school, and he said that he had never before realized that his parents had jobs that required them to rush toward danger. (Oreskes's wife is a New York–based columnist for the *Los Angeles Times*.) "[The events surrounding September 11] affected us individually as human beings in ways I don't think we quite realized," Oreskes says. "We had an anthrax scare in the newsroom. The enormous stress of the story was unlike anything our generation has ever dealt with.

"At some level, I think we accepted the idea that some of the problems we were wrestling with in the newsroom were about the multiple traumas of September 11," he says. "I thought we would recover. Things would get better—we would act to *make* them better."

As stressful as September 11 was to the staff, not all the tensions in the newsroom were attributable to the disaster. Editors and reporters alike became increasingly dismayed by what they felt was Raines's self-centeredness. The week of the September 11 attacks, Raines met with investigative editor Stephen Engelberg and reporter Ethan Bronner in a conference room on the fourth floor to strategize about the best ways to pursue the unfolding story. Engelberg tried to talk to Raines about a three-part series he'd worked on with reporter Judith Miller, a specialist in bioterrorism and chemical weapons, about Osama bin Laden and al-Qaeda that ran in January 2001. "It became clear he hadn't read it," Engelberg says. Frustrated, he then proposed examining the Bush and Clinton administrations' planning and response to warnings about attacks on American soil, but Raines dismissed the idea. ("Let's just say we had heard of Richard Clarke," Engelberg says dryly, referring to the Bush and Clinton antiterrorism adviser who, in the spring of 2004, ignited a firestorm when he criticized President Bush for dropping the ball on warnings about al-Qaeda. Clarke was quoted in Engelberg and

Miller's January 2001 series.) After a vague discussion in which Raines said he wanted to look forward, not back, he told Engelberg and Bronner, "I don't want my obituary to read that I was the editor who blew the biggest investigative story of my generation."

"I was just staggered," says Engelberg. "The sheer ego of it. It wasn't about doing great journalism. It wasn't about the thousands dead at ground zero. It wasn't about getting the story right. It was about his obituary."

Still, the newsroom needed a leader, and it's entirely possible that the *Times*'s staff might have embraced one in Raines if he'd been willing to show them he valued having them on his team. But Raines seemed uninterested in providing that sort of leadership. In his first month on the job, he had already begun to alienate a key constituency, a group of powerful newsroom brokers who could have helped interpret his vision: the desk editors. In taking authority and control away from the men and women who ran the paper's myriad departments, Raines immediately disenfranchised the layer of management that had the most interaction with reporters. "When you empower the desk editors, you in effect empower the reporters," says Gene Roberts, Joe Lelyveld's first managing editor. "Ten o'clock is the busiest time of the day for the assignment desk. Reporters are coming in, they're checking with sources, so between ten and eleven, reporters and editors are making deals about what their days are going to be like. And then meanwhile you have the AMEs [assistant managing editors] meeting with the executive editor and reflecting on yesterday's newspaper. So they come out of that meeting and give marching orders to the desk editors, but they've already talked to their reporters.

"At this point either the assignment editor basically ignores the assistant MEs or they have to go back to the reporters and say, 'Oops, I said you could do story X, but now you have to do story Y.' So you have a kind of institutional disconnect that gets built right into the system, and no matter what your personality is, having that kind of day-in-day-out problem starts unsettling people on a massive scale." By ignoring the desk editors, Howell Raines had all but forced them to make an unpleasant choice: either they could cheerily carry out Raines's marching orders and risk the wrath of their reporters or they could align themselves with their staffs and join in the griping. Most of them sided with their reporters—and against Raines.

There were also more personal reasons that the paper's midlevel editors felt frustrated. The *Times*, like any tribal institution, has its own set of social classes. One of the most important is made up of midlevel editors, the group of *Times* lifers between thirty and sixty years old who actually put out the paper on a day-to-day basis. They assign the stories, they edit the copy, they deal with complaints. They are, invariably, journalists who have made enormous sacrifices to work at the *Times*. "Where are these people going?" asks one *Times* editor. "They're not going to *Esquire*, they're not going to *Vanity Fair*. They carve out some small amount of space, they fight for some tiny bit of creativity, and they do it for the chance to be a part of something larger. Howell took that away."

As the year stretched on, the *Times* settled into a routine in which reporters and editors were working seven-day weeks. In the midst of this chaos, Raines began a campaign to more purposefully remake specific sections of the paper.

He began by focusing on both the national and business desks. Raines, working through Gerald Boyd and Andrew Rosenthal, would send marching orders to national editor Katy Roberts, who sometimes ended up in tears because she had to go to a reporter to whom she had already given a story and take back the assignment.

Raines had more success with the business section. "Early on," says Glenn Kramon, "there was this sense that Biz Day needed to be told what to do." Kramon responded by exhorting his staff to prove to Raines that they were worthy of his respect and praise. "As it went on, it became much more of a collaboration." In early 2002, no business story was more consuming than the collapse of Enron, and Raines's intense desire to dominate breaking news coupled with the hard-nosed work of Kramon's staff pushed the *Times*'s coverage of the story into the lead, ahead of *The Wall Street Journal*, which had dominated the story early on. On January 17, the *Times*'s David Cay Johnston broke a story on page one detailing how the company had avoided paying income taxes for four out of the previous five years. On January 25, Alex Berenson detailed how Enron had created illusory profits in a division run by Thomas White, who left Enron to become secretary of the army. And on February 10, Kurt Eichenwald authored a 6,460-word front-page story that to this day serves as an excellent primer on the downfall of a once mighty company.

"[Howell] recognized early on what a huge story Enron was," says Kramon. "And he pushed us hard to dominate the story, to stay ahead of competitors like the *Journal*. On days we did, he was extremely complimentary and enthusiastic. He had great instincts for stories that would excite readers."

Once Kramon showed he was able to lead his staff to dominate the coverage, Raines became less dictatorial as well. On days when Enron would be a major focus of the paper's news report, Raines, Boyd, and Rosenthal would meet with Kramon and other reporters and editors involved in the story to map out coverage. "It wasn't, 'You should do this or you should do that,' " says Kramon. "Which was in contrast to what happened early on.

"I always told my staff that they saved my job. We did so well on that story, it became clear to Howell that we were quite good already and that we could be trusted."

With the business and national staffs still trying to find their footing, Howell Raines set his sights on an even bigger project: reorganizing his old stomping grounds, the Washington bureau. It would become one of the most contentious managerial battles he would fight.

THE WASHINGTON BUREAU

Jill Abramson was hired by the *Times* from *The Wall Street Journal* in 1997. Abramson is a short, droll woman who draws out her words as she speaks. She's also a ferocious political reporter and was scooped up by the *Times* because she was regularly beating the paper on stories involving Clinton's fund-raising scandals. After only three years there, she was named the *Times*'s Washington bureau chief: On Election Day 2000, Abramson was in New York helping to coordinate the *Times*'s coverage when Joe Lelyveld called her into his office. "We don't know who's going to be the next president," Lelyveld said, "but we know who'll be the next Washington bureau chief." Abramson started her new post on January 1, 2001.

Only five months later, Raines was named as Lelyveld's successor, and that summer Raines asked Abramson to dinner. The two had met before—Abramson's best friend at the *Times* is Op-Ed page columnist Maureen Dowd, who was one of Raines's stars when he led the Washington bureau. Now, the agenda was the future. "He clearly wanted me to take a different job in New York," Abramson says. But Abramson had barely begun her new job, which was one she thought she "was born to do." Besides, her son was just starting high school in Washington.

Over dinner, Raines asked Abramson if she thought Patrick Tyler, the paper's London bureau chief and an old friend of Raines's, would make a good Washington bureau chief. Abramson was taken aback. "That struck me as odd," Abramson says. After all, Washington already had a bureau chief. But despite that awkwardness, Abramson liked Raines: "He had a really good sense of humor and a very sharp take on politics, which had always been my passion. I thought we would be kind of simpatico."

After Raines took over, things went downhill fast. The Washington bureau, Raines felt, had underperformed in its September 11 coverage, and he grew even more autocratic than usual when it came to deciding what stories the bureau should be pursuing. By October, Raines was dictating stories for the bureau to write over the daily squawk box meetings. "*He* became the Washington bureau chief," Abramson says. "*He* was deciding who he wanted to write most of the big stories. And *he* decided to have Pat Tyler come back from London. . . . I definitely had the feeling that he did not have the confidence in me and anyone else in the Washington bureau who hadn't been part of his own Washington bureau A-team."

Tyler's appointment reinforced Raines's reputation among the bureau's staffers as someone who was insensitive and arrogant. As far back as Scotty Reston's days in the 1940s and 1950s, the Washington bureau has resented what it sees as the meddling from New York; Raines himself had pushed back against the authority of the home office when he was bureau chief. In picking a fight with Abramson so early on, Raines virtually guaranteed that the bureau would unite against him. And in selecting Tyler as Abramson's designated successor, Raines also inflamed speculation that he was willing to dole out key positions based upon friendship rather than reportorial chops. Tyler was a fine correspondent, but he had also famously been a fishing buddy of Raines's for more than three decades. Before long, the fifty-person Washington bureau had begun referring to the paper's masthead as the Taliban and Raines as Mullah Omar. ("Jill Abramson never expressed any frustration to me . . . about my assignment to the Washington bureau," Tyler wrote to me in an e-mail. "On the contrary, she expressed gratitude to me that I would be bringing my extensive experience in international affairs . . . to the bureau management team.")*

In mid-October 2001, Gerald Boyd flew to Washington to meet with the staff there. He spoke about the importance of the Washington report but did so in a way that made the bureau feel inconsequential. "He kept saying, 'At nine o'clock, we [the masthead] decide, then at ten o'clock we decide, and at noon we decide.' That angered people," Abramson says. Boyd also explained how when something "major" happened in Washington, "we want Johnny Apple writing the story." R. W. "Johnny" Apple, who at one time had specialized in writing the *Times*'s trademark page-one comprehensive summaries of the issue of the day, hadn't been a daily presence in the bureau for years; by 2001, his input was increasingly felt in the Dining In/Dining Out section, for which he contributed articles about his gastronomical adventures. The bureau was surprised by this announcement, especially because Boyd seemed to overlook Adam Clymer, the *Times*'s Washington correspondent, who was the paper's presumptive go-to guy on major D.C. events. But as of late, he too had been forgotten—or neglected—in Raines's frenzied reorganization.

"The thing about Howell and Gerald to a degree is they'd been out of the newsroom for a while," Abramson says. "So they missed this whole generation of new reporters who'd broken incredible stories. It was like they didn't exist."

Boyd was shaken by the level of discontent he encountered in the D.C. bureau. "The issue of the heavy-handedness was a lot more personal than I certainly realized," Boyd told Ken Auletta for *The New Yorker*. "I didn't defuse it. I probably added to it, which wasn't good." After the bureau meeting, Abramson and Boyd sat outside on a bench facing the White House to talk one-on-one.

---

* Tyler did not speak with me for this book; however, he did send me several "clarifying comments" after I wrote to him explaining his presence in this book.

That meeting went much better than the one at the bureau. "What I appreciated about [Gerald] was that he was approachable," Abramson says. The two spoke in depth, and Abramson told Boyd that she felt Raines and Boyd were "especially disrespectful to the women managers in the newsroom." Abramson felt national editor Katy Roberts was being "run over" and Week in Review editor Susan Chira was "pretty desperate" because her weekly lineup was being dictated to her. Boyd told Abramson that things could get worse before they got better, but Abramson left the meeting feeling that she and Boyd had reached an understanding. "I felt like he was talking to me from the heart and honestly," says Abramson. "And I felt that he went back and at least conveyed my message to Howell."

But Raines and Abramson's relationship would continue to deteriorate throughout the new year, even though Raines did make attempts to reach out to his Washington bureau chief. In late January 2002, Raines's son's funk band, Galactic, was playing at New York's Irving Plaza, a standing-room-only concert hall just east of Union Square. Abramson's son Will is an aspiring musician, and Raines invited Abramson and Will up to New York for the show. He cooked a lamb dinner and then got a backstage pass for Will. By that time, Raines and the D.C. bureau were almost at open war, but both Howell Raines and Jill Abramson managed to put aside their professional animosity for an evening. "It was so nice," Abramson says wistfully, remembering that night more than two years later. "Actually lovely."

A Growing Mandate

The September 11 coverage put Howell Raines's plans to overhaul the paper temporarily on hold. "This story was so consuming that there wasn't a lot of time to think about organizational issues, staffing issues, and long-term strategy," Raines said in August 2002. "This was a matter of total immersion." By January 2002, he was ready to move again. One of his first decisions involved what to do about Kevin Sack, who had yet to hear a word from Raines since their contentious meeting in Atlanta the previous August. Raines dispatched Jill Abramson to Atlanta to meet with Sack and David Firestone, the paper's Atlanta correspondent. Abramson told Sack that he could have a national beat based out of D.C. Firestone was being asked to move to Washington as well. "I felt in the case of Kevin, it was clear they didn't really care whether he stayed or went," Abramson says. "But I cared a lot."

Sack asked Abramson if he'd be able to return to Atlanta on the weekends. Occasionally, she said. Abramson was sympathetic to Sack and told him she'd do her best to make sure he could return more often than not, at least every other weekend. Sack asked if any arrangement he made with Abramson would be binding to the next Washington bureau chief. Abramson said it wouldn't be. The next Monday, Sack declined the offer. He e-mailed Raines and Boyd to ask what he should do next.

Boyd shot back a terse e-mail declaring that Sack's next job for *The New York Times* would not be in Atlanta. Raines didn't even bother replying. "I just thought that was awful," says Mike Oreskes, who had worked extensively with Sack over the years. "I understand that Howell didn't want people staying in places forever, but Kevin is a rare talent, and I thought we should do whatever we could to keep him. And besides that, the way Howell dealt with the whole thing was so bullheaded and wrong."

Throughout the process, Raines never called Sack to discuss the situation. "He let Gerald carry all the water," says Sack, "to the point where I was getting e-mails and calls because other people were so outraged. Finally, after this had started leaking out he called and [we] had a very perfunctory conversation."

Sack began to look for another job. Meanwhile, word of the incident began to trickle through the *Times*'s newsroom. Raines's few public declarations—that national correspondents should expect to travel more, that he was looking to respond more quickly to the news—only heightened tension. At one meeting in Washington, Raines told the staff that he hadn't worked long and hard to get to his post just to sit back and passively watch the paper's staff do whatever they wanted. San Francisco–based Evelyn Nieves, Los Angeles–based James Sterngold, and Seattle-based Sam Howe Verhovek—longtime bureau chiefs or correspondents all—were told they'd be relocated or moved back to New York.

Particularly galling to the correspondents was the fact that while Raines was unwilling to compromise with Sack, he bent over backward to accommodate his personal friend Rick Bragg, who seemed to be permanently parked in New Orleans, a city where the *Times* didn't traditionally even have a bureau. Ever since Raines had been named executive editor, Bragg had frequently reminded other reporters how close he was to the paper's new boss. Bragg also appeared to get better play than virtually any other reporter on staff. In Raines's first six months on the job, ten out of Bragg's twenty-one stories ran on page one. From the time he was hired by Joe Lelyveld, Bragg had always been a difficult writer to handle, but Raines's coddling made things worse. Raines put out word to Bragg's editors that his copy shouldn't be edited unnecessarily; in fact, he said, he viewed *any* substantial editing of Bragg's work as unnecessary. When, immediately after September 11, Raines had insisted Bragg be sent overseas to Pakistan, he did so over objections from acting foreign editor Roger Cohen and members of the masthead. Bragg had little foreign experience and was known for being intractable. This was too important a story to assign to someone like Bragg, they felt.*

After joining the *Times* in 1994, Bragg, a native Alabamian, was quickly promoted to the paper's national desk. ("It was my dream to do this someday, but some things even I was afraid to dream," he wrote later.) He specialized in colorful stories about the American South, stories more lyrical and quirky than what the *Times* usually ran. He delighted in painting himself as the ultimate outsider: In an online autobiography, he described his appointment as one of Harvard's Nieman fellows as being made so the university could "fill . . . their white trash quota." From his early days at the paper, Bragg inspired wildly divergent opinions. Some readers—and some of the paper's other writers—loved his writing and felt it brought a dose of much-needed humanity and liveliness to the paper's pages. (The Pulitzer board agreed and in 1996 awarded Bragg the prize for feature writing.) Others decried what they saw as overwrought sentimentality. "I stopped reading him long ago," blogger and journalist Ana Marie Cox wrote in 2003, "about the time I realized that any article carrying his byline would, more likely than not, be the Platonic ideal of *Times*ian condescension. More specifically, they would be about people who lived in trailer parks (or some

---

* Bragg said he would be "unable" to speak with me for this book.

such lower-class milieu) but had the kind of stubborn dignity—or precocious skill—the middle class folks find so quaint."

In 1997, Bragg published his bestselling memoir, *All Over but the Shoutin'*, a highly acclaimed book that celebrated his mother's iron will. From then on, Bragg was a marquee writer, one of the few journalists at the *Times* who was better known for his accomplishments away from the paper. By the time Raines demanded Roger Cohen send Bragg overseas, Bragg's insistence on special treatment was more the rule than the exception.

Bragg's stories from Pakistan occasionally embarrassed the paper's more seasoned correspondents. An October 1 story headlined "Pakistan Is 2 Worlds: One Urbane, One Enraged" struck some staffers as simplistic and reductionist. Bragg's conclusion—that there was a divide between the country's upper classes and Islamic militants—was already obvious to anyone who had read anything about Pakistan. Three weeks later, a dispute over one of Bragg's stories all but led to the removal of Nicholas Kristof as the assistant managing editor in charge of the Sunday paper. The story, about a deformed Pakistani woman who was treated by her fellow villagers as if she had divine healing powers, was just the kind of soft-news tale Bragg specialized in. It began:

> Surrounded by caged birds and blessings, touched in reverence by throngs of people who believe that she is touched by God, the young woman with the startling deformity sat at the door of a place of miracles and pawed clumsily at the women and babies who bowed for her favor. The gatekeeper of a shrine to health and fertility, she has a shrunken head that is too small for her body, her words are nonsense and screams, and even her face, with its pointed forehead and wide, round jaws, is in the shape of a tear.

Raines wanted the piece on the front page of Sunday's paper. Kristof disagreed. Raines shot back, "What's wrong with putting on page one a story everyone will talk about?" In the end, of course, Raines got his way, and Bragg's story ran on the front page of the October 28 paper. By the end of November, Kristof was pushed out of his job and given a twice-weekly Op-Ed page column, a position that can be appointed only by the publisher. It was another signal of the close relationship between Arthur Sulzberger and Howell Raines.

By February 2002, other news outlets were beginning to report on the discord among the *Times*'s national staff. Correspondents told media reporters that they feared the paper was becoming antifamily and that Raines was rumored to be looking only for "unencumbered" writers for the national desk. "He's looking for 30-year-olds with no spouse and no children, people who can file from four datelines in five days," one correspondent told *New York* magazine. Another said, "There's suddenly this whole issue of what it means to be a reporter at the *Times*. It used to be if you were a star, you either went national or foreign. What do you do now when you're 40 or 50 years old?"

In response to these public reports, Raines sent out an e-mail on February 15, 2002, to the *Times* staff; it was addressed to "friends and colleagues." "I know that inaccurate reports have stirred anxieties among some of you about how people will be treated as we pursue this energetic vision," Raines wrote. "There will be no anti-family attitudes or actions at The Times. . . . Cooperation and personal respect in the service of quality journalism are the first principles at The Times. I do ask your consideration of the fact that in an international organization with over 1,100 staffers, orderly management and fairness of opportunity are necessary to achieve that journalism."

But Raines's actions seemed to belie his words. What's more, Raines hadn't bothered to try to gain the respect of his staff in his crucial first months on the job—and now, when he faced turmoil in the newsroom, his reporters and editors were more willing to give the benefit of the doubt to the colleagues they had been working with for years than to a man who'd spent the last decade secluded in the offices of the editorial page, seven floors up and a world away from the newsroom. Sack received over a hundred phone calls and e-mails from fellow *Times* reporters and editors, all bemoaning his treatment at the hands of Raines. "What seemed to happen," says Soma Golden Behr, "was as we got more kudos, [Raines] got more full of himself. And by this time he knew where the men's room was, he knew how to sub out a picture at the last minute, things he didn't really know when he walked in the door. . . . And as it went on, his resistance to criticism grew and grew, until finally it became this sense that to criticize [Raines] is to betray [him]. And then you're really in deep."

PUSHING BACK,
MOVING ON

By the spring of 2002, Raines seemed positively obsessed with the *Times*'s Washington bureau. For one thing, he was frustrated that Pat Tyler, the old fishing buddy he hoped to install as bureau chief, wasn't flourishing. For this, Raines blamed Jill Abramson. Soon after Tyler moved back to the bureau from London, there was a protracted dispute over the office space he would get. When Tyler arrived, only Abramson and Washington editor John Broder had offices. Raines wanted Tyler to have one as well, so Abramson suggested converting an empty office that was used for the daily page-one meetings.

Office space—indeed, any private space—is a rare commodity at the *Times*, as it is at most newspapers. The vast majority of reporters and midlevel editors work on open floors, sitting cheek by jowl with their co-workers. In New York, even masthead-level editors make do with windowless offices that open onto newsroom hallways. But Raines was determined that Tyler have a bigger office than Broder. Abramson considered just giving Tyler her office to keep the peace. "I didn't know what to do. I said to Howell, 'There is no other office,' " says Abramson. Raines replied that it was up to Abramson to solve the problem "creatively." Raines also asked former managing editor Arthur Gelb—who was one of Abramson's mentors on the paper—to talk to Abramson about Tyler's office. Eventually, Raines agreed that it would be acceptable for Tyler to remain in the former page-one office even though it was slightly smaller than John Broder's office. But the damage had been done: Raines had made it clear he was willing to undermine Abramson's authority over something as petty as office space for one of his favorites.

Word was starting to circulate in Washington's close-knit journalistic community about Abramson's difficulties with Howell Raines and Pat Tyler's apparent installation as the bureau chief–in-waiting. That was a perception Tyler disagreed with. "Far from being a shadow bureau chief, I was an adjunct to her management of the bureau on her initiative," Tyler wrote in an e-mail. "She said to me on a number of occasions that she was delighted to have someone with my experience on her team. Of course, I was aware of the tension between her and Howell Raines, but she and I had had two long dinners about how determined we both were to overcome it."

Abramson, on the other hand, remembers feeling frustrated and humiliated. "I went from [being] the first woman ever to be Washington bureau chief of the *Times* to going to book parties in Washington and having people ask me, 'How *are* you?' like I had cancer," she recalls. In the spring of 2002, Steve Coll, the managing editor of *The Washington Post*, asked Abramson to meet him for a drink. Coll told Abramson what she was quickly realizing: She was in an untenable position. He asked her to join his staff.

Abramson didn't dismiss the offer out of hand, and she told Coll she'd need to think seriously about her situation. Without making any decisions one way or the other, she kept on pushing forward. By then, even Raines had realized he had to address the tensions with his D.C. bureau. He decided the way to do this was to essentially promote Abramson out of Washington, much as he had orchestrated Kristof's promotion out of his way. Later that spring, Raines asked Abramson to come to New York and meet him for dinner at Aquavit, a Scandinavian restaurant on West Fifty-fourth Street.

The meal was over three hours long. Raines spent the first half of it discussing the symbolic importance of the meeting place. Aquavit, he told Abramson, was where he had made his pitch to Arthur Sulzberger about becoming executive editor of the *Times*. He explained his campaign: how he had argued that the *Times* was losing a step, how the culture report needed to be reinvigorated, how he wanted to fight against complacency. He described how he had mapped out a campaign that included individually wooing members of the *Times*'s board of directors and how, at each step along the way, he was amazed that Bill Keller wasn't doing the same thing. Then, finally, Raines told Abramson that he wanted her to join the paper's masthead. Abramson wasn't sure how to react.

"It's very hard for me to evaluate your offer," she remembers telling him. "Part of the reason is that I feel I have to disclose to you I'm in very, very serious talks with *The Washington Post* to go work there." Raines was thunderstruck. The meal concluded soon after. Before they departed, Raines said, "If you're not coming to the prom with me, I need to know."

Abramson might have actually left the paper were it not for the intervention of the two men who were widely seen as Raines's biggest supporters. Shortly after she told Raines she was considering the *Post*'s offer, she met Gerald Boyd for lunch at the Mayflower Hotel in Washington. The two briefly discussed the situation and Abramson's offer from the *Post*. After listening to Abramson, Boyd looked across the table and said, "Don't you be afraid to fight Pat Tyler for your job."

"It never occurred to me I could do that," says Abramson. "I just assumed Gerald was totally with [Raines] and with the plan of putting me in the icebox and making Pat bureau chief." Abramson, it seems, did not realize the extent to which many in New York also viewed Raines's preoccupation with Tyler as something attributable more to Raines's personal relationship with him than to Tyler's journalistic merit. "A lot of people did not see in Pat Tyler's work a vindication of Howell's position on him," says Al Siegal, a *Times* assistant managing editor.

Then, soon after her lunch with Boyd, Abramson got a call from Arthur Sulzberger.

"What would it take for you to be able to be happy at the *Times* and remain here?" Sulzberger asked.

"It would take removing the sole of Howell Raines's shoe off my ass," Abramson replied.

Sulzberger didn't miss a beat: "Do I tell him or do you?"

Abramson said she would do it. "That was amazingly empowering," she says. That afternoon, she called Raines to tell him she would remain at the *Times*—but as the paper's Washington bureau chief.

Raines was angry. Immediately, he began to focus on Tyler. "He was saying that meant I had to make sure Pat flourished and that Pat was a star," Abramson says.

———

BY THE SPRING OF 2002, it wasn't just journalists in the Washington bureau who were frustrated. The situation in the newsroom had grown outright hostile. Now even the assistant managing editors were being cut out of the loop. Raines had by then stopped attending the 10:30 a.m. meeting he had instituted during his first week on the job, because, he told people, he was sick of listening to their ridiculous ideas. Things got so bad that current and former *Times* staffers began complaining directly to Arthur Sulzberger, who is said to have laughed them off. "I'm hearing Abe's back!" Sulzberger was quoted as saying in Ken Auletta's June 2002 *New Yorker* profile of Raines. Sulzberger was referring to former executive editor A. M. Rosenthal, who had ended his seventeen-year tenure at the head of the paper in a state of bitter isolation.

Auletta's piece was a landmark moment for Raines. It was his first major profile as executive editor, and one with which he had enthusiastically cooperated, to the point of once suggesting that Auletta be permitted to sit in on company retreats and strategy sessions. Auletta quoted a thirty-year veteran of the paper as saying, "There is enormous resentment, the likes of which I've never seen." But overall, the piece was largely positive and dwelled at considerable length on the *Times*'s triumphs after September 11. Raines, however, thought the piece was an "unsophisticated" analysis of the situation. It was foolish, Raines complained, not to expect there to be friction when a new leader tries to implement his vision.

It became increasingly clear that that vision would mean both the loss of some valued *Times* staffers and complaints about favoritism. By March, Kevin Sack had left *The New York Times* after more than a decade at the paper. Dean Baquet, the managing editor of the *Los Angeles Times*, hired Sack and told him he could stay in Atlanta for as long as he liked. (Soon after, Sack set to work with the *Los Angeles Times*'s Alan C. Miller on a large, in-depth investigative project examining a military aircraft nicknamed "the Widow Maker" for its high number of fatalities. Sack—and the *Los Angeles Times*—would win a 2003 national reporting Pulitzer for that work, beating out *The New York Times*'s entry on the country's business scandals.) By the end of the year, a number of other national correspondents had also either retired or left to work for other papers, including Gustav Niebuhr, who became a visiting fellow at Princeton's Woodrow Wilson School; Evelyn Nieves and Blaine Harden, who both joined *The Washington Post*; James Sterngold, who was hired by the *San Francisco Chronicle*; and Sam Howe Verhovek, who left for the *Los Angeles Times*.

Rick Bragg, on the other hand, wasn't going anywhere. Copy editors were again explicitly instructed to lay off his work, and Raines gave the general impression that his stories, no matter their topic, were invariably destined for page one. In fact, of the twenty-three stories Bragg filed in the first six months of 2002—for an average of less than one story a week—fourteen ran on the front page. "Florida Town Finds Satan an Offense Unto It," was the headline for one Bragg front-page dispatch; "Key West Is Tiring of Chickens in Road," read another. In Salt Lake City, where Raines dispatched Bragg to write about the 2002

Winter Olympics, Bragg had boasted to other *Times* writers about his relationship with the paper's executive editor; at one lavish dinner, he insisted on picking up the check, explaining, "Howell won't mind."

It's easy to see why the unabashedly literary, confident Bragg appealed so strongly to Raines, a man who still hoped one day to be known as a great novelist. The author's bio in Raines's 1977 novel, *Whiskey Man*, reads, "Howell Raines grew up among great storytellers from the hill countries of northern Alabama," just the kind of self-conscious detail Bragg favored in his writings. In many ways *Whiskey Man*, which centered on a young man living in Prohibition-era Alabama, struggling to break free from his Scripture-quoting father while falling under the influence of a bootlegger named Bluenose, was filled with the kind of down-home flourishes that Bragg used to strong effect in his newspaper work.

As Howell Raines continued to indulge his favorites, he also maintained his dismissive attitude toward those whose opinions and perspectives differed from his own. Investigative editor Stephen Engelberg, who had clashed with Raines over the September 11 coverage, was beginning to find the *Times*'s new order unbearable. By the spring of 2002, he had become quite vocal in his dissatisfaction with Howell Raines. Raines, Engelberg wrote later in a March 2004 article for Portland's *The Oregonian*, was a "boss from hell" and had made the atmosphere at the paper "ugly." He disagreed, too, with the quick turnaround Raines was demanding for full-page stories on the hot topic of the week, whether it was the Olympic ice-skating scandals or the controversies in the Catholic Church. On November 1, 2001, after polishing off two successive, Raines-assigned 3,500- and 4,000-word stories, Engelberg turned to Matthew Purdy, a colleague who was helping to edit the stories. "This can't work," Engelberg said. "It will end in tears." The first piece, an examination of anthrax, actually *had* worked: It was insightful and contained new information. But the second story, about the risks of biological and chemical attacks, was hardly impressive. "It was embarrassingly bad," says Engelberg. "I went to Gerald and said, 'Give us one more day and we can do something

worthwhile.' But for Howell, the story was just a means to an end to
the buzz it created. What the stories said weren't important; it was just
important that there *were* stories."

In April 2002, Engelberg quit, leaving his post as head of investigations to take a job managing enterprise reporting at *The Oregonian*, a
350,000-circulation daily. Life at *The Oregonian* has been an adjustment
after the *Times*. "I often want a story on international affairs and I can't
get it because we don't have a foreign staff," Engelberg says. But *The
Oregonian* is one of the strongest regional papers in the country and has
long had a reputation for devoting ample resources to big stories. Just
as important, Engelberg says, he is happy. "After 9/11, I began thinking, had I been in the World Trade Center, would I have spent my life
and time devoted to the people I wanted to be devoted to?" says Engelberg, who has three young daughters. "Thinking about it like that
made leaving a pretty easy decision."

To replace Engelberg, Raines eventually settled on Douglas Frantz,
a *Times* reporter who at the time was based in Istanbul. "It was a potentially great job," Frantz says. "In some ways, it was the job I had
spent my entire career getting ready for." Frantz asked Raines if he'd
support larger investigative projects and was answered with an enthusiastic yes. "He made a very persuasive case," Frantz remembers.
"Howell certainly convinced me that he wanted to have an investigative unit that did both the run-and-gun stuff for which the unit had become best known and longer-term, more serious investigations. That
was certainly something I was concerned about, like a lot of other people. It's hard to devote serious resources to other projects when the
world is coming down on your shoulders, but Howell convinced me he
really wanted it. He convinced me he fully intended to become known
as the greatest editor in the history of *The New York Times*." On October 1, Frantz became the paper's new investigative editor.

Upon arriving in New York, Frantz, who had been away from New
York for years, was surprised by what he found. "The whole paper was
so Howell-driven in every way," Frantz says. "Nobody wanted to argue
with him, nobody wanted to give him any news. Even Gerald. And that
was a real problem."

Frantz also witnessed what he viewed as incredibly dysfunctional management. "I had been on the job for two or three weeks," Frantz says. "Gerald was one of the people I knew who pushed for me to get the job. He'd asked me in a meeting what I needed in terms of staff. And I said what I really needed was a couple of young guns who would go out and work really hard and do whatever it is I ask of them. We were talking about outside candidates. Gerald said, 'That sounds good. Get me a list of two to four people and we'll talk.'

"So a few days later he and I were sitting in Howell's office and the notion of my hiring outsiders came up again. I told Howell I was putting together a list of possible outside hires. Howell looked at me and said, 'Who told you you could have outside hires?' I pointed to Gerald, and he just shook his head. Howell went on to give this long explanation about the economic situation and how tight things were. And the whole time, I was just floored. When we left the meeting, Gerald put his arm across my shoulder and just said, 'Sorry about that.' I figured he just didn't want to have talked out of school."

Boyd's refusal to acknowledge what he had said in a private conversation with Frantz was emblematic of everything that was going wrong with the *Times*. Even the second most powerful editor in the newsroom was afraid to contradict Howell Raines. Nor did Boyd seem concerned with the effect of his humiliating reversal on the editor who worked below him.

Another episode that occurred in February 2003 further alienated Frantz. At an editors' meeting, Frantz and national editor Jim Roberts pitched a story about the space-shuttle disaster. According to a story that later ran in *The Wall Street Journal*, Boyd dismissed the idea, saying he had read a similar story that morning in *USA Today*. But when Frantz handed Boyd a copy of *USA Today* to show the story hadn't been in the paper, Boyd became furious.

"You shouldn't humiliate the managing editor," Boyd snapped at Frantz. He then handed Frantz a quarter and told him to go call Dean Baquet. The next month, Frantz did just that, quitting the *Times* to work for Baquet at the *Los Angeles Times*. His term as investigative editor lasted less than six months.

"Gerald is a very likable if unpredictable fellow," says Frantz. "You never know what's going to come out of his mouth and how he intends some of his digs. But he has a real good heart. But by that point, I'd come to the conclusion that Howell Raines was not somebody I wanted to work for. I found he took a point of view on a story and pushed that point of view as hard as he could. And too many reporters and editors were willing to fold in the face of his pressure."

After Frantz left, Raines and Boyd pushed for investigative reporter Tim Golden to accept a reassignment to a daily news beat. Instead, Golden quit as well, but not before, according to several people at the *Times*, having a one-on-one conversation with Arthur Sulzberger about the discord that was spreading in the *Times*'s newsroom.

Raines had alienated another important desk, and more and more staffers were considering leaving the paper. "Everybody started to get calls," says Jon Landman, the metro editor at the time. "And some of the people who stayed, it had nothing to do with professional satisfaction. It had to do with things like 'I've got to pay for college education. I've got to pay the rent.' "

The Daily Report

Throughout the first half of 2002, it was easy for Raines's supporters—and Raines himself—to dismiss the newsroom's unhappiness as mere whining. After all, Raines's methods seemed to result in the sorts of accolades dreamed of by publishers and editors alike: April 2002 brought the paper's unprecedented Pulitzer haul. But even when the breakneck pace of the news slowed, Raines kept riding his staff. Indeed, in his 2004 *Atlantic* piece, Raines wrote how he hoped to practice newsroom management by systematically exhausting some of his correspondents—as if they were racehorses or mules. "One person quits—sometimes in response to stepped-up metabolism—and another can be hired," he wrote. "Inevitably, removing underperformers created newsroom grumbling. But I felt that if we could all stand being rode hard and put up wet until the end of 2003, an entire new cast of editors would be in charge at the lagging departments, and we could all begin to get some rest."

Some members of the masthead tried to warn

Raines off this tactic. Many of the correspondents and editors being lost were a far cry from being "underperformers." But Raines kept isolating himself, and even top managers began to conclude that he perceived any advice, regardless of its origins, to be the result of jealousy and ill will.

Had the problem been only Raines's increasingly bitter fights with some of the paper's editors and reporters, he might have been able to march onward with at least the passive support of most of the staff. The *Times*, after all, is a great, lumbering institution, one that trudges forward on its own momentum, regardless of management intrigue. But as the year wore on, the newsroom began to feel that Raines was forcing bad journalism into the paper. The staff began to view him as an editor concerned at least as much with burnishing his own image as with putting out a great newspaper. The feeling intensified after Raines began forcing his beloved "all-known-thought" pieces into the paper whether they were worthwhile or not; after all, he was the editor who had pioneered the genre.

"These [all-known thoughts] were often a repetitive thing," says Soma Golden Behr. "We may have already done fifty stories on this subject. So we'd summarize those fifty, plus add in one other fact. If you're a regular reader, you wonder why you should bother with the story. And if you do bother, you get pissed off. It's three thousand words, it takes you half of Sunday to read, and for what?"

One example of Raines's obsession with making a big splash regardless of whether or not the news warranted it was an April 21, 2002, front-page story warning of the dire economic impact of a recent drought in the Northeast. "If the drought drags on," read the 1,700-word story, "possible delays in linking new housing or businesses to overburdened water systems could cause economic setbacks. . . . The potential for damage to the economy is considerable. . . . Restrictions on water use could hurt small businesses, forcing car washes, for example, to cut back their hours. . . . Some tourists might alter their vacations, avoiding the Northeast and its hotels." Rarely had conditional clauses gotten such a robust workout on the front page of the *Times*.

Worst of all, the report contained this caveat: "So far, the economic damage has only been spotty and minor."

"He decided we were undercovering [the drought]," says Jon Landman. "We were not undercovering it. We were covering it appropriately. We were not saying the world was going to end. And he wanted it to be faster, more, bigger. And he commissioned that piece that was an embarrassment.

"He gave the impression it wasn't about journalism, it was about making a statement. When the making of a statement doesn't coincide with good journalism, you have a real problem."

By this point, Landman was another one of the paper's desk editors feeling increasingly alienated and frustrated by Howell Raines. "I worked for him in Washington," says Landman. "I learned a lot. I was excited that he was going to be editor. But this was not the same guy that I had known. . . . In Washington I found him to be an excellent listener, a guy with a genuinely deep interest in the things we were covering. He really enjoyed the back-and-forth of it." Once Raines took over as executive editor, Landman says, something changed. Raines, who maintained that he thought the metro section was one of the strongest in the paper, kept killing stories for no apparent reason; at other times, he'd give orders with little regard to reality.

"I objected to the general thrust of things, and I told him so," says Landman. "He didn't want to hear it. Nor did Gerald. They were losing people, they were killing stories by first-class people. I don't know why. It wasn't because all of a sudden all these [writers] lost their journalistic standards. But he didn't want to hear it. He said I should stop making a big deal out of it, that I was emotionally labile."

As spring turned into summer, Raines continued to recast the *Times*'s news report to reflect his preoccupations. American journalism has a long, weighty tradition of aiming for objectivity in its news pages. That, of course, is a canard: Every news judgment, every article placement, every lead, reflects snap judgments about what is and isn't important, what should and shouldn't be emphasized. Investigative stories are a publication's way of announcing that there's an issue that is not receiving the attention or scrutiny an editor or reporter thinks it deserves. In hundreds of small ways, every editor is "guilty" of pushing an agenda; after all, editors are hired at least in part for their news judgments and convictions.

Raines, however, seemed not to be content with using the *Times*'s resources to spotlight specific stories he felt weren't being covered. Much as he had with campaign finance reform while running the editorial page, Raines wanted to set the national agenda. It was this sense of journalistic activism that critics had worried about even before Raines took over as executive editor. "Every editor and reporter holds private views," wrote Robert Samuelson in a *Washington Post* column a week before Raines took over the newsroom. "The difference is that Raines's opinions are now highly public. His [editorial] page . . . was pro-choice, pro–gun control and pro–campaign finance 'reform.' . . . Does anyone believe that, in his new job, Raines will instantly purge himself of these and other views? And because they are so public, Raines's positions compromise the Times' ability to act and appear fair-minded."

By August 2002, media critics and conservative gadflies alike were accusing the *Times* of trying to shape, rather than chronicle, the national debate. In two successive front-page stories, the *Times* wrote about growing Republican dissent over the seemingly inevitable war with Iraq. "Leading Republicans from Congress, the State Department and past administrations have begun to break ranks with President Bush over his administration's high-profile planning for war with Iraq," began an August 16 story co-authored by Todd Purdum and Patrick Tyler. "These senior Republicans include former Secretary of State Henry A. Kissinger and Brent Scowcroft." The next day, another front-page piece, by Elisabeth Bumiller, noted that President Bush was "listening carefully to a group of Republicans who were warning him against going to war with Iraq. . . . It was the first time Mr. Bush had so directly addressed the growing chorus of concern from Republicans, which now includes former Secretary of State Henry A. Kissinger."

But Kissinger had never argued against invading Iraq; all he had done was express some realpolitik reservations in an August 11 *Wash-*

ington Post op-ed piece. In fact, he'd written, "The imminence of pro-liferation of weapons of mass destruction, the huge dangers it involves, the rejection of a viable inspection system and the demonstrated hos-tility of Hussein combine to produce an imperative for preemptive action."

But the damage had been done. On August 18, Charles Krautham-mer wrote in *The Washington Post*, "Not since William Randolph Hearst famously cabled his correspondent in Cuba, 'You furnish the pictures and I'll furnish the war,' has a newspaper so blatantly devoted its front pages to editorializing about a coming American war as has Howell Raines's New York Times." The *Times* had always been con-sidered liberal, but now it was Raines himself who was being singled out as the source of the *Times*'s bias.

After several days of brutal criticism, the masthead asked David Carr, a *Times* media reporter, to write a story on how the American press was increasingly seen as driving the debate on Iraq. Carr re-searched the project, reading the clips and making calls, before return-ing to the paper's editors. "I had to tell them the media wasn't driving anything," Carr says. "It was only us. It was only the *Times*." In lieu of a story, the *Times* ran an editors' note on September 4, explaining its mistakes.

"This is certainly a shift from *The New York Times* as 'the paper of record,' " Alex Jones said at the time. "It's a more activist agenda in terms of policy, especially compared to an administration that's much more conservative." It was as if Raines were determined to question the Bush's administration's push toward war, even if no one else was doing so. Tradition dictated that the *Times* needed someone in the nation's elite to voice the sentiments it actually wanted to come out and say on its own. Now, it seemed, when they couldn't find the right person, they simply wrote the story anyway.

It was Tyler, already seen as Raines's favorite, whose reputation suf-fered most. "By this time, there were other reporters in the Washing-ton bureau who were refusing to work with [Tyler] because they didn't trust his reporting," says Jill Abramson. Around that time, she ran into Paul Steiger, the managing editor of *The Wall Street Journal* and her old

boss. "He said he thought the credibility of the *Times* was suffering because of [the Kissinger story]," Abramson says.

And it wasn't just biased political stories that the staff felt Raines was
hurrying onto the front page. That fall, Raines became convinced that
Britney Spears was trying, and failing, to reinvent herself as an adult
pop star. The ensuing 1,600-word, Sunday front-page story was yet another embarrassing example of Raines's certainty that he had his finger
on the pulse of American culture. "Ms. Spears," the piece read, "who
made her debut as a wholesome bubblegum star with a penchant for
sweetly flashing her belly button, is caught in a vicious conundrum of
fame acquired young: the qualities that made her accessible and popular as a teenage star may be precisely the ones choking her career as an
adult, leaving her looking like an unseemly parody as she tries to become a grown-up recording artist." In November 2003, Spears's fourth
album, *In the Zone*, hit number one its first week on the charts, making
Spears the first woman ever to have four consecutive number-one
records.

"There's nothing wrong with putting stuff like Britney on the front
page," says Jon Landman. "If she's on the front page because it's an interesting story, great. But if she's there because we're so eager to show
our youthfulness, then that's a problem. People sense that. They understand what's going on."

AUGUSTA

As 2002 stretched on, Raines's *New York Times* was about to show readers and critics alike that it would continue to tell the rest of the country what was and wasn't newsworthy, regardless of what anyone else felt. On November 25, 2002, the *Times* ran a front-page story headlined "CBS Staying Silent in Debate on Women Joining Augusta." It was the thirty-second piece the *Times* had run in less than three months about whether the Augusta National Golf Club, which hosts the Masters Tournament, would admit women as members.

The story spanked CBS, which airs the Masters, for "resisting the argument that it can do something to alter the club's policy," although it was unclear who—other than the *Times*—was making the argument; as the piece eventually noted, "Public pressure on CBS to take a stand has been glancing." "[The Augusta coverage] was just shocking. It makes it hard for us to have credibility on other issues," said a *Times* staffer at the time. "We don't run articles that just say so-and-so is staying silent. We run articles when something important actually *happens*." Media coverage of Raines's Augusta obsession was scathing. Slate's Mickey Kaus and Jack Shafer rode the story for days, and *The New York Observer*'s Sridhar Pappu added damning dispatches. "Raines is on the verge of a breakthrough reconceptualization of 'news' here," Kaus wrote, "in which 'news' comes to mean the failure of any powerful individual or institution to do what Howell Raines wants them to do." After praising the *Times* for its aggressive coverage of the Bush administration, Shafer wrote, "At some point, saturation coverage of a story begins to raise more questions about the newspaper's motives than about the story being covered."

In some ways, the criticism was familiar. "We're *The New York Times*," Arthur Sulzberger told me in a 2004 interview. "People are going to hold us to a standard that's higher than others'. That's okay. We like to think we hold ourselves to higher standards, too." Historically, staffers had rallied against any attack on the paper, defending it to their peers and colleagues. This was different—this time reporters within the *Times*'s newsroom were embarrassed as well.

"I remember being surprised by the relentlessness of [the *Times*'s Augusta coverage]," says Daniel Okrent, who was named the *Times*'s first-ever public editor (an ombudsmanlike position) in the fall of 2003. "There are a lot of things to worry about in the world besides whether some millionaire CEO who happens to be a woman gets into the Augusta Golf Club. There was this clear campaign at the *Times* . . . the whole coverage was out of proportion."

"The Masters story," says then business editor Glenn Kramon, "was like a crusade. The perception in the newsroom was that it was an agenda that went beyond the bounds." The outcry over the paper's Augusta coverage grew much more intense. On Wednesday, December 4, the New York *Daily News*'s media columnist, Paul Colford, reported that the *Times* had spiked two sports columns because they disagreed with the *Times*'s activist position on Augusta. Harvey Araton's column asked whether there weren't more important battles to be fighting in regards to discrimination in sports, and Pulitzer Prize winner Dave

Anderson's column disagreed with a *Times* editorial that had called on Tiger Woods to sit out the Masters.

The reaction to Colford's story was immediate and furious. Online media forums, such as Jim Romenesko's media blog, overflowed with letters ridiculing the *Times*. In the newsroom, reporters and editors were shell-shocked—usually, rumors of columns being spiked on ideological grounds were just that: rumors. Later on December 4, Gerald Boyd, who had personally spiked one of the columns and was running the newsroom while Raines was away in Paris dealing with the *Times*'s takeover of the *International Herald Tribune*, wrote a staffwide memo that only made the situation worse. It was at once long-winded and unsatisfying, defensive and arrogant. Boyd's memo read:

Howell and I believe you should know The Times's response to questions that have been raised by some published reports in recent days about our coverage of the Augusta Golf Club story and our handling of sports columns on the subject.

First, we are proud of our leadership in covering this story. Our sports staff, with help from many desks, is doing exactly what some "accuse" us of doing: asking questions that no other organization is raising, and pressing energetically for the answers our readers want.

Augusta's restricted membership policies have been legitimate news for decades. With the ascendance of Tiger Woods and the campaign by the National Council of Women's Organizations, the club has become an inescapable story.

The decisions faced by CBS, a leading network that is a 46-year Masters partner of the club, are a significant part of the story. There is only one word for our vigor in pursuing a story—whether in Afghanistan or Augusta.

Call it journalism.

Columnists in the news pages hold a special place at The Times. Each has wide latitude to speak with an individual point of view, always informed by diligent reporting and intelligent reasoning. In the sports pages, columnists have unique license to go beyond analytical writing and—still informed by their reporting—engage in robust argument, even express personal opinions on any side of an issue, within the bounds of sport, broadly defined.

Still, these columns are not on the Op-Ed page, and all newsroom writers are subject to our standards of tone, taste and relevance to the subject at hand. We are an edited newspaper: that is one of our strengths, and we believe our staff takes pride in it.

Recently we spiked two sports columns that touched on the Augusta issue. We were not concerned with which "side" the writers were on. A well-reported, well-reasoned column can come down on any side, with our welcome.

One of the columns focused centrally on disputing The Times's editorials about Augusta. Part of our strict separation between the news and editorial pages entails not attacking each other. Intramural quarreling of that kind is unseemly and self-absorbed. Discussion of editorials may arise when we report on an issue; fair enough. But we do not think they should be the issue.

In the case of this column, the writer had previously dealt with the Augusta controversy at least twice, arguing on October 6 against pressuring the golf club to admit women. His freedom to argue that way was not—is not—in question.

The other spiked column tried to draw a connection between the Augusta issue and the elimination of women's softball from the Olympics. The logic did not meet our standards: that would have been true regardless of which "side" the writer had taken on Augusta. The writer was invited to try again, but we did not think the logic improved materially.

None of what appears here should be taken as criticism of our columnists, whose work we value tremendously. And we would be happy to discuss our thinking over lunch or in any appropriate setting. Perhaps we need better-understood definitions or a more pronounced sense of column boundaries.

At any rate, we hope no member of our staff really needs this assurance that our news columns enforce no "party line." But all of you are welcome to come and talk with us whenever you have concerns or want to hear ours.

Media critics were not impressed. "If Boyd's memo is an example of his idea of 'logic,' I *really* don't want to read the columns he killed because 'the logic did not meet our standards,' " Mickey Kaus wrote in Kausfiles, his Slate blog, within minutes of the memo's inevitable leakage.

Reaction in the newsroom was just as severe. "Gerald's memo was totally disingenuous," says Clyde Haberman, a *Times* metro columnist. "And I told Gerald, 'I don't understand how this mistake could be made.' How could they not have foreseen the reaction? How did they not know people would see this as a crusade? It was totally blind of them."

Raines, meanwhile, had returned from Paris. When he heard that news of the spiked columns had leaked, he wanted to post the columns immediately on the *Times*'s website. Boyd disagreed. Raines didn't give any extensive interviews about the flap at the time, but he did speak to *Sports Illustrated* writer Alan Shipnuck for his 2004 book, *The Battle for Augusta National*. Raines acknowledged to Shipnuck that it was unusual for the executive and managing editors to become involved in a debate on a column's tone: "I guess it was because of the whole buzz about the Masters," Raines said by way of explanation.

In recounting the story to Shipnuck, Raines belittled the very people he had entrusted with the power to lead the paper. "There was a very strong feeling on Gerald's part, and others', that [running the spiked columns] was the wrong thing to do on principle, that in both cases we had acted on reasonable journalistic principles," he told Shipnuck. "And we shouldn't simply reverse ourselves. At that point, I had to face a decision. Do I overrule my masthead—whose authority and confidence I'm trying to increase—from [Paris] three thousand miles away, or do I wait and get back to meet with them? I chose the latter. I wish I had gone on my initial impulse, but managerially, you can't overrule your six top executives without them having a chance to meet with you." He also told Shipnuck that Boyd's decision to hold Araton's column hadn't even been the right one. "I think Gerald made the wrong decision," he said.

On Saturday, December 7, the *Times* ran a one-thousand-word story on the debacle. The piece noted that Colford's *Daily News* dispatch "prompted critical commentary in the news media and resentment in the *Times* newsroom." The next day, both Araton's and Anderson's columns finally ran in the paper.

The Augusta chapter was a sorry episode for the *Times*, a moment in which Raines seemed to have shamelessly co-opted the paper for his own crusades. Slate's Jack Shafer noted that it was as if the *Times* had set itself up as a de facto opposition party on any issue that Raines felt wasn't getting enough attention otherwise. *Times* staffers looking for a silver lining hoped that Raines's public dressing-down would serve to temper his activist zeal.

It didn't. In early 2003, when the *Times*'s submissions for the Pulitzer Prizes were due, Raines insisted the paper's Augusta coverage be included as an entry. A longtime veteran of the *Times* who was for years a close personal friend of Raines's says, "I was appalled. It was at that moment when I realized the newsroom was out of control. It was anarchy. . . . [Raines's] arrogance had actually become blinding."

By the beginning of 2003, as Howell Raines began his second full year as executive editor, it seemed as if the paper, much like the country, were settling into its new normal. Despite frequent frustrations, Raines had made his mark on some of the paper's key sections. Katy Roberts was no longer the editor of the national section; she had been moved over to the Week in Review and was replaced by Jim Roberts (no relation). Many of the national correspondents had either moved or moved on, and Raines had replaced them with younger staffers. The Sunday Arts & Leisure section, one of the areas of the paper Raines thought had suffered most under Lelyveld, had been shored up under the direction of Jodi Kantor, an energetic young editor Raines had hired from Slate. Visually, the *Times* looked better than it ever had. Raines even joked about the staff dissension. "If there's ever a revolt," he'd crack, "at least photo and graphics will defend me." After more than a year of chaos, it appeared that Raines was finally getting his chance to put an enduring mark on *The New York Times*.

It seemed that 2003 was to be a banner year personally as well. On March 8, Raines wed his longtime girlfriend. Raines had met Krystyna Anna Stachowiak, a Polish-born thirty-nine-year-old public relations executive, in 1996 when she brought in a client, Poland's president Aleksander Kwaśniewski, to meet with the *Times*'s editorial board.* The day after the wedding, Raines hosted a reception at Ilo, a restaurant in Manhattan's Bryant Park Hotel. The event had the air of a coronation. New York's senior senator, Charles Schumer, was there, as were Governor George Pataki and Mayor Michael Bloomberg. NBC's Tom Brokaw, CBS's Dan Rather, and PBS's Charlie Rose attended as well, as did a number of *Times* heavies, including Arthur Sulzberger, Max Frankel, and A. M. Rosenthal. In another effort at détente, Raines had invited Jill Abramson up from Washington. Rick Bragg was in from New Orleans, and Grady Hutchinson, Raines's former maid and the subject of his Pulitzer Prize–winning magazine article, came in from Alabama. It was one of the most buzzed-about weddings of the year.

The New York Observer described Raines's new wife as a "blue-eyed brunette" who wore "strappy white sandals and a shiny, backless white silk gown that revealed the small curve of her abdomen and porcelain-perfect shoulder blades." (Alex Kuczynski, the *Times* Style-section writer, helpfully told the *Observer* the dress was designed by Monique Lhuillier.) All of Raines's best qualities—his forceful charm, his natural sense of authority, his theatrical flair—were on display that night, and for a moment the turmoil of the last year seemed to be forgotten.

Toward the end of the reception, Stachowiak was asked if she thought wedded life would lead to a "kinder, gentler" era at the *Times*. "I don't know about a new era," she said, laughing. "But I know this is going to be a happy marriage."

---

* Raines had proposed in Paris the previous December, just as the furor over the spiked Augusta National columns was breaking.

Part Two

SPRING 2003

THE FIRST SIGNS
OF SCANDAL

On Saturday, April 26, 2003, Robert Rivard, the editor of the *San Antonio Express-News*, woke up and drove two hours out to his weekend cabin in the Texas hill country along the Llano River. He was planning on spending a weekend off the grid, catching up on his reading and relaxing. Rivard brought a pile of newspapers with him, including Friday's *Wall Street Journal* and Saturday's *New York Times*. Rivard started with the *Times*. "I got out there and I put my feet up, and immediately, this front-page story caught my eye," Rivard says. The story was about Juanita Anguiano, a Texas woman whose enlisted son was the only American soldier still missing in action in Iraq almost a week after retired U.S. general Jay Garner had set up office in Baghdad as the country's new civil administrator. It was written by a reporter named Jayson Blair, and it got huge play—three columns spread across the most valuable real estate in journalism. The headline read, "Family Waits, Now Alone, for a Missing Soldier."

Rivard chuckled to himself when he saw the

dateline. Los Fresnos is a tiny farming community—it has a population of fewer than five thousand people—nestled in the southernmost tip of Texas along the Mexican border. "I was pretty sure that was the last time I'd see Los Fresnos on the front page of the *Times*," Rivard says. The *Express-News* had recently written a similar story about the Anguianos—the monthlong conflict had officially ended the week before, and newspapers around the country were searching for ways to keep readers interested in the situation in Iraq. Even before he started reading, Rivard assumed the *Times* had seen his paper's story and decided to follow up with a dispatch of its own. That kind of regional poaching is a common (and more or less accepted) practice among national correspondents at the country's largest dailies; indeed, one of the implicit responsibilities of the *Times*'s regional reporters is to read the local papers and see if any of them had uncovered any good stories that deserved a broader audience.

For the editors of many of the country's midsize dailies, reaction to this kind of story appropriation ranges from pride to frustration to outright anger. It's nice to see your work validated in the most powerful paper in the world, but not quite as nice when there's no attendant acknowledgment. Rivard had worked as a senior editor at *Newsweek* in the 1980s and understood how New York City journalism worked. What's more, he was, perhaps, oversensitive to suggestions of pilfering by the *Times*. Four years earlier, in the spring of 1999, Rivard had accused a *Times* reporter of lifting material from one of his reporters' stories about a suspect in the disappearance of atheist leader Madalyn Murray O'Hair. Rivard had complained to then managing editor Bill Keller, who wrote back a snippy and belittling note. Rivard let the matter drop but never forgot about it.

The *Express-News* story on the Anguianos, written by a young *Express-News* reporter—and former *New York Times* intern—named Macarena Hernandez, had run on April 18, eight days earlier. As Rivard began reading the Blair story, he felt suddenly uncomfortable; it seemed to him there were frequent echoes between the *Times* piece and the piece his paper had run. Since Rivard's cabin has no Internet hookup and no phone, he couldn't look through his paper's electronic archives online or call an editor at his paper's offices to compare the two stories. On Monday, he thought, when he was back in the office, he'd check this out.

Back in her office, Macarena Hernandez had also seen Blair's story and had recognized entire passages of her piece—lifted nearly verbatim—immediately. She was furious. Hernandez knew Blair: The two were part of the same minority internship program at the *Times* in 1999. "Jayson was always just a big kiss-ass," Hernandez says. "He wasn't even very smooth about it. I thought he was always more interested in being at *The New York Times* than he was in being a journalist. But he seemed harmless. A little misguided and immature, but harmless."

Both Blair and Hernandez were offered the chance to stay on at the *Times* after their internships ended, an offer Hernandez said she planned to accept until a few days later, when her father died in a car accident. "Instead of going to the Times, I moved in with my mother, who doesn't speak English or drive," she wrote in *The Washington Post* in June 2003. "I took a job teaching English to high school sophomores and tried not to cry when my students asked me why I had left journalism." In 2001, she got a job writing for the *Express-News*.

Now, four years after she had left the *Times*, it appeared as if Blair had brazenly ripped her off. "It was just completely obvious that he had taken major chunks of [my story]," Hernandez says. The second paragraph of her story read:

So the single mother, a teacher's aide, points to the ceiling fan [Edward Anguiano] installed in her small living room. She points to the pinstriped couches, the tennis bracelet still in its red velvet case and the Martha Stewart patio furniture, all gifts from her first born and only son.

Blair's story began:

Juanita Anguiano points proudly to the pinstriped couches, the tennis bracelet in its red case and the Martha Stewart furniture out on the patio. She proudly points up to the ceiling fan, the lamp for

Mother's Day, the entertainment center that arrived last Christmas and all the other gifts from her only son, Edward, a 24-year-old Army mechanic.

The rest of Blair's piece was filled with identical quotes and turns of phrase. In both stories, Juanita Anguiano says, "I wish I could talk to a mother who is in the same shoes as I am." In both stories, the author writes how Anguiano's sleep comes only with "a pill." "I was blown away," Hernandez says flatly. What's more, the Anguianos' Martha Stewart patio furniture wasn't on a patio, as Blair had written—when Hernandez had seen it, it was still in its boxes in the middle of the living room.

First thing Monday morning, Hernandez talked to Rivard and then placed a call to Sheila Rule, the *Times* recruiter who had hired both Hernandez and Blair, to let her know about the situation. Rivard decided to wait and see what the *Times*'s reaction to Hernandez's call would be before doing anything else. "Since someone at the *Times* already knew about this, I didn't want for us all to gang up on it. I decided to give them a news cycle to acknowledge and correct this," Rivard says.

In New York, Sheila Rule told Gerald Boyd about Macarena Hernandez's complaint. Boyd immediately summoned national editor Jim Roberts. Blair's Los Fresnos story had run in Roberts's section, and Blair—a seemingly indefatigable twenty-seven-year-old reporter—had been working for Roberts for the previous six months, ever since he had been drafted as an extra set of legs in the Washington, D.C., sniper story, in October 2002. Boyd, Roberts, Rule, and Bill Schmidt, an associate managing editor in charge of newsroom administration, met in the managing editor's office. It was a dispiriting meeting. "By the time I got there, they had already concluded this looked really bad," says Roberts.

———

IN THE SPRING OF 2003, Jim Roberts was perhaps one of the happier desk editors at *The New York Times*. He'd been with the paper since

1987 and had worked his way up the editing ranks, moving from copy editor to deputy national editor to national political editor. While some of the paper's desk editors disagreed with Howell Raines's "flood the zone" mentality, Roberts enjoyed—and excelled at—dispatching his correspondents around the country. He agreed with Raines's philosophy of riding breaking news stories hard.

That afternoon after the meeting, Roberts called Jayson Blair on his cellphone. Blair answered. He was supposed to be in Washington, covering the trial of the suspects in the previous fall's sniper shootings. In fact, unbeknownst to Roberts, Blair was in Brooklyn, shuttling between his apartment and a local diner for infusions of caffeine. Roberts explained that questions had been raised about the Anguiano story and asked Blair if he had read Hernandez's story in the *Express-News*. Blair said he hadn't, and he mumbled out an explanation. Roberts's heart sank. "His initial response was fairly implausible," says Roberts. "What he tried to say was that he had just mixed up his notes. But during that period I wanted things to turn out a lot better than they did. I had a real hope that the implausible was still possible."

After he hung up with Roberts, Blair called Macarena Hernandez at her desk at the *Express-News*. "He calls, and he says, 'I just want you to know I didn't see your story,' and I was like, 'Jayson, come on. Of course you did,'" Hernandez says. "Then he says that maybe the quotes were so similar because he got the daughter to translate and she probably just said the same thing. At that moment, I knew. Juanita Anguiano speaks English."

Meanwhile, Howard Kurtz, *The Washington Post*'s hard-charging and high-profile media reporter, had received a tip about the possible scandal from a colleague who had been assigned to follow up Blair's Saturday story in the *Times*. The *Post*'s Manuel Roig-Franzia had been dispatched to Los Fresnos to write about the Anguianos and, while reading the clips, had noticed how similar Blair's and Hernandez's stories were. Kurtz, after reading the pieces side by side, agreed. He called Howell Raines's office and left a message for the editor to call him back. He then called Catherine Mathis, the *Times*'s spokeswoman, who said only that the paper was looking into the issue. Finally, Kurtz called

Robert Rivard, who still hadn't heard back from anyone at the *Times*. "At that time, he hadn't decided whether he wanted to make an issue of it," Kurtz says. "I could have jammed the story in, but it was already late in the day, so I decided to follow up the next day."

A couple of hours later, Jim Roberts called Jayson Blair back. Blair, Roberts told him, was being pulled off the sniper case—he'd need to come back to New York to answer some questions. Adam Liptak, the paper's national legal correspondent, was already on his way down to Washington to cover Tuesday's sniper hearing. "Even then, I had no idea what we were getting into," says Roberts.

JAYSON BLAIR

Ever since he first took a journalism class in high school, all Jayson Blair had ever wanted to be was a reporter. Blair, who would later present himself as a perennial outsider—"just another black man without a college degree," he'd joke—grew up in integrated neighborhoods in suburban enclaves. He attended high school in the heart of middle-class Fairfax County, in northern Virginia, where his parents bought a two-story, four-bedroom house in an upscale subdivision for $255,000 in 1990. The Blair home is on a private cul-de-sac in a neighborhood of plush, manicured lawns and tree-lined parks.

Blair's father, Thomas, is an inspector general at the Smithsonian, and his mother, Frances, is a Fairfax County schoolteacher. Both were extremely active in their local church while Jayson was growing up. They tutored children and donated money for local scholarships. In a community of involved parents, the Blairs stood out. "They are the finest people I have ever known,"

Pamela Latt, Blair's high school principal, said later in an interview.

In high school, Blair founded a chapter of the Fellowship of Christian Athletes despite the fact that he never played any sports—at just over five feet tall, he didn't have the build or natural ability to excel on the playing fields. At times, he appeared deeply religious, quoting Scripture extemporaneously. He also joined the yearbook staff. But it was journalism that excited him most. Blair spent his days hanging out at the third-floor offices of the school's biweekly student newspaper, the *Centreville Sentinel*. He loved knowing the secrets and the gossip; he loved trafficking in information, loved seeing his name in print. "He charmed me from the get-go," Latt said. "He had a very clear focus of what he wanted to do." In high school, Blair began what would become a lifelong pattern: cozying up to adults while alienating his peers. "I always felt that if he had been our age, we would have been friends," Latt said. "We would have hung out. A lot of teachers felt that way."

While still in high school, Blair interned for the *Centreville Times*, a local weekly paper. "He just bounced in one day," remembered Steve Cahill, executive editor of the chain that runs the paper. "He struck me as a kid who wanted to go places." Cahill describes Blair in language similar to that used by virtually everyone who worked with him over the next decade—he was charismatic and had boundless energy. He had an "electric smile." But he was also unreliable. Blair disappeared at critical times. He missed deadlines. That was understandable, Cahill figured. After all, Blair was just a high school student. In time, he'd learn to be more responsible.

Blair was also the index editor of his yearbook. The yearbook index lists only two entries for Blair, even though he is pictured on more than a dozen pages—including the page that features a photo of the yearbook's staff, for which there was no entry. The two entries that do appear feature two different spellings—he's identified once as "Jason Blair," the name he was given at birth, and once as "Jayson Blair," the spelling he decided to adopt in the eighth grade.

Toward the end of the book, there was an advertisement that Blair's parents had purchased. It read:

Congratulations, Jayson. What a gift you have been to us! We have memories of you as a 4-year old praying for the healing of your great-grandmother, Susie. We have watched you grow as you continued to extend your caring hands out to others. We saw you with a vision to make the Fellowship of Christian Athletes an effective force at Centreville High School. Keep pursuing your dreams of speaking and writing. You are a very special person for whom God has special plans. Love Mom, Dad and Todd.

Blair seems to have faked his first newspaper story in high school. The September 22, 1993, issue of the *Centreville Sentinel*, the student paper, ran an article titled "God Attracts 62 Students and 4 Teachers." At the time, Blair was the news editor of the *Sentinel*. The article is by-lined to Chris Mergerson, who was a columnist for the paper. "Jayson attached [my name] without my knowledge or consent," Mergerson says today. "I absolutely did not write the article." If that is indeed true, perhaps the reason Blair—who even then loved seeing his name in print—inserted Mergerson's name on the story was that Blair is by far the most extensively quoted person in the piece. "It was unbelievably uplifting to see so many students gathered in His name," Blair is quoted as saying in the piece. The story ends with a paragraph-long, off-the-cuff speech attributed to Blair:

We are ready for anyone who needs us, just like Jesus says in Revelations 3:20: "Behold! I stand at the door and knock, if anyone opens the door I will come in and eat with Him and him with me." If you want a translation of that, what we mean is this: God is waiting for each and every one of us. He has already paid the price; He is only waiting for us to take the gift.

"I confronted him," Mergerson says. "He just kind of smirked and went off. It was like, 'Yeah, I did this. What are you going to do about it?' " Later, Blair would alternately say that he didn't remember high school, that he spent high school manipulating other students to win their approval, and that he never faked a story in high school. In 2004,

Blair wrote in an e-mail that it did "not make sense . . . that Chris Mergerson refused an assignment and then his byline was put on a story where he did no reporting." When asked directly whether or not he had written the piece himself, Blair did not respond.

————

AFTER GRADUATING IN 1994, Blair enrolled at Liberty University, a Baptist school founded by Jerry Falwell. After college, Blair would identify religion as his first "drug of choice," the first time he tried to hold on to something greater than himself to find his moorings. After a few months at Liberty, however, his attitude toward God changed dramatically, predicated on Blair's disillusionment with Falwell and his own evolving views on religion and homosexuality. While in high school, Blair had written at least one vitriolic letter to the editor of a local paper condemning gay personal ads. But while at Liberty, he became upset with his church after what he termed the persecution of a minister who was outed as being gay. Furthermore, he found Falwell to be duplicitous and racist. After one semester, he left Liberty, and in the winter of 1995, he transferred to the University of Maryland. "He was easy to pick out in a crowd," said Chris Callahan, the associate dean of the university's journalism school, in a 2003 interview. While many students cultivated an air of aloof insouciance, Blair was tiny, puppyish, and eager to please. Callahan was so impressed that he hired Blair to work for him in the Annapolis bureau of the Capital News Service. "He was completely defined by being a newshound. He didn't know when to turn it off," Callahan said.

But while Blair was busy charming the powerful adults on campus— the ones who could arrange for prestigious internships and write glowing recommendations—he was alienating almost everyone he worked with on *The Diamondback*, the student newspaper he would eventually run from 1996 to 1997. His tenure as editor was marked by strife, allegations of racism, problematic stories, and fantastical tales. "When Jayson was initially hired, people were really upset," Danielle Newman, who worked as an editor under Blair and succeeded him after he resigned, said in a 2003 interview. "We said we just didn't think he was qualified." (Newman now works as a layout editor on the sports desk of *The Washington Post*.) Blair, according to several people on *The Diamondback*, responded to his peers' doubts by intimating to the paper's board of directors that the staff was filled with backstabbing racists.

While in college, Blair began exhibiting behavior that he would repeat over the course of his career. When his fellow students complained—about his failure to pay reporters* or to complete assignments or about his cribbing copy—he would remind them how well connected he was with the paper's faculty leadership. When he was accused of incompetence, he charged his colleagues with racism.

Despite Blair's later claims that the first time he ever fabricated or plagiarized a story was at *The New York Times*, there were several stories in *The Diamondback* that his colleagues identified as problematic. There were concerns about a football game Blair covered—his story was filled with quotes from people another reporter at the game didn't think existed. Then there was a story in which Blair tried to insert quotes from an Associated Press wire story. "We definitely had our suspicions about his reporting," said Newman. "But what could we do?" While he was the editor—a post he was appointed to by faculty members—Blair's spelling and grammar were so poor that at least one reader sent in a complaint. As his tenure progressed, Blair's behavior became more erratic. Once, when the paper was putting out a spring-break guide, Blair disappeared without handing in a story he was working on. "We kept paging him and paging him," Newman said. When he finally did come into the office later that week, Blair claimed he had almost died from gas poisoning when his roommate left the burner on. "At the end of the meeting . . . he told me his doctor said he needed to rest," Newman said. "I told him to go home. After he left, someone leaned over and asked, 'Do you believe him?' I said no. She said, 'Good, neither do I.' "

That night, Newman and others realized the Maryland campus

---

* *The Diamondback*, like some college papers, pays its reporters.

didn't even have gas stoves. Later, when Newman confronted Blair, he offered to take her to his apartment. "But when I said, 'Let's go now,' he said we had more important things to talk about," she said. During the argument that followed, Blair suddenly fired one of *The Diamond-back*'s managing editors. Several hours later, Blair resigned from the paper for "personal reasons," effective a month later.

Before he left, however, Blair initiated a final scandal. That year, a Maryland student died in his sleep. It turned out the student had died of an undiagnosed heart ailment. Blair, however, was convinced he had been a drug abuser and forced through articles that contained unverified, anonymous rumors about the student's cocaine habit. "He just kept saying, 'I'm in charge. I'm writing the story,' " Newman said. *The Diamondback* story became a hugely divisive issue in the university community and was the subject of protests and letter-writing campaigns. "It was terrible. I ended up writing an apology that ran in the paper a month later," said Newman.

———

THERE'S A GALLOWS-HUMOR SAYING in journalism: When a reporter brings a guaranteed home run of a story in to an editor, the joke is it's "too good to check." In 1996, when Jayson Blair began applying for internships on newspapers, he was simply too good to check—a young, ambitious, talented black reporter eager to succeed in an industry that was desperate to diversify its ranks. Blair came with the enthusiastic recommendations of Maryland's faculty, but even a cursory examination of his work at *The Diamondback* would have revealed serious problems with his journalism. That probing never took place, and despite Blair's problems—with reliability, with accuracy, with his colleagues—he landed a series of prestigious internships. While still at Maryland, Blair worked for both *The Boston Globe* and the *Times* and freelanced for *The Washington Post*.

Blair's first internship was at the *Globe*. In the summer of 1996, he worked for the paper's Washington bureau, and he spent the next summer in Boston on the paper's metro desk. At the *Globe*, the twenty-year-old Blair had a reputation for trafficking in nasty gossip, stealing story ideas, and cozying up to superiors so he could get credit for work he didn't do. "All of us were ambitious," said one of Blair's fellow interns. "He was to a dangerous extent." "He tried to undermine our efforts," said Jennifer McMenamin, who worked with Blair as a *Globe* intern and is now a reporter at Baltimore's *Sun*. Another intern says Blair frequently tried to eavesdrop while reporters were discussing story ideas and then pass them off as his own. Before the summer was out, Blair's gossiping became such a problem that Chris Callahan, the school's dean, felt compelled to talk to him about it. Blair, Callahan says, was spreading information about a colleague's marital strife; he also seemed preoccupied with staffers' sexual orientation. "It was like, 'I have a piece of information and I want people to know,' " Callahan said. "It was a wonderful journalistic instinct turned on its head."

In his interactions with colleagues, Blair was obsessed with the salacious and trivial. But with superiors, he talked often about his preoccupation with social justice. "I've seen some who like to abuse the power they have been entrusted with," Blair wrote in his 1997 application for an internship at the *Times*. (At the time, the internship was open only to minority applicants; it has since been opened to everyone.) He wrote that his "kindred spirits are the ones who became journalists because they wanted to help people." In the summer of 1998, Jayson Blair arrived at the *Times*. By this point in his young career, he already had a loaded reputation: *Globe* reporters had warned their friends at the *Times* to be careful around Blair.

The *Times's* reaction to Blair was mixed from the beginning. Joyce Purnick, then the metro editor, was never impressed with Blair's reportorial abilities. She told him the *Times* was not a place that was able to nurture young reporters. Blair should, she said, go and learn the trade at a smaller, regional paper. Blair paid Purnick lip service in face-to-face conversations, but behind her back, he accused her of racism and noted derisively that she had had to start *her* career at the *New York Post*. He also made much of the fact that Purnick was married to Max Frankel, a former executive editor at the *Times*.

Nevertheless, when Blair's internship was over, in August 1998, he was offered an extended stay, as were all three of the other reporting interns in the program, including Macarena Hernandez. (The other two—Edward Wong and Winnie Hu—are still at the *Times*.) Instead, he returned to Maryland, where, he told *Times* officials, he would graduate in December 1998. Then, as now, the *Times* had a woeful record on newsroom diversity, and there was enormous pressure to find and promote African American reporters. The top two editors were both white men, as they had been throughout the *Times*'s history. Gerald Boyd, then a deputy managing editor, and Dean Baquet, then the paper's national editor, were the only two African Americans on the paper who seemed to have even a chance at moving up the newsroom's food chain anytime soon. (According to Arthur Sulzberger, less than 10 percent of the journalists working at the *Times* are African American.)

Jayson Blair was a beneficiary of this pressure. He did have some talent to go with his energy and exuberance, although neither his writing skills nor his reporting abilities were exceptional, and there are dozens of genuinely talented, eager reporters trying to fight their way into the *Times* every day. In June 1999, Blair was invited back to the *Times*, this time for a probational reporting position. Newsroom administrators later said they had assumed he had graduated from Maryland on schedule, in December 1998. In fact, Blair still had extensive course work outstanding when he returned to the paper.

Blair began his career at the *Times* working in the "cop shop," the pressroom at New York City's police headquarters. From very early on, Blair bragged of his relationship with senior editors at the *Times*, particularly Gerald Boyd. There were reasons to believe him: Many reporters were under the impression that Boyd took African American reporters under his wing. What's more, Blair seemed to have an inside track to people's personnel files, and he made frequent references to employee evaluations or private notes sent between editors, which he hinted he had gotten through his supposed connections.

From the get-go, Blair's performance was spotty. There was the time Blair was at a party when he was supposed to be covering a crime scene. He told friends he once passed out at *Times* headquarters and woke up there the next morning. He consumed copious amounts of Scotch, and he seemed to blow through money. He showed up to work in dirty, stained clothes. Charles Strum, his editor at the time, said later, "I told him that he needed to find a different way to nourish himself than drinking Scotch, smoking cigarettes, and buying Cheez Doodles from the vending machine."

"He always struck me as having really bad boundaries and being really immature," says a *Times* reporter who first met Blair during those years and remained friendly with him throughout his time at the paper. "His biggest skill seemed to be office politics. You'd see his stories, and they never stood out. There was nothing really memorable in his writing." But he was always eager for more assignments.

That November, Blair was promoted to the position of intermediate reporter. Over the next four years, Blair furthered his reputation for being one of the paper's most tireless gossips. He knew, or claimed to know, virtually everyone who worked in journalism. He was the type of voracious self-promoter who constantly bragged about his connections to editors at the *Times* and to reporters at other papers, and he made a particular point of discussing his supposed connections to Boyd. He made no secret about the fact that he was often an anonymous source for several of the city's media columnists. He gravitated to places he knew he'd be seen, such as Robert Emmett's, a bar near the *Times*'s headquarters, and Siberia, a downscale media hangout that had recently moved from the entranceway of a subway stop to an equally divey location near the Port Authority Bus Terminal. And although Blair rubbed many people at the *Times* the wrong way, many others liked him: He was gregarious and seemed to have an endless appetite for socializing.

In January 2001, Jayson Blair was promoted to full-time staff reporter. At the *Times*, landing a staff position is similar to getting tenure at a university; because the *Times* is a union shop, it's very difficult to fire full-time reporters.* Gerald Boyd headed the committee that recommended Blair's promotion, despite the fact that Jon Landman, by

---

* The *Times* also has an institutional tendency to exile undesirable staffers to unpopular beats or bureaus rather than fire them outright.

then the editor of the metro section, didn't think it was a wise idea. "It was clear that Gerald felt pressure to promote Jayson and that he thought it was the right thing to do," Landman said later. "The racial dimension of this issue and Gerald's obvious strong feelings made it especially sensitive. . . . I think race was the decisive factor in his promotion." Boyd disagreed. Later, he told a newsroom committee investigating Blair's career at the *Times*, "To say now that his promotion was about diversity in my view doesn't begin to capture what was going on. He was a young, promising reporter who had done a job that warranted promotion." But Blair's performance, which had already been uneven, was about to get markedly worse.

———

OVER THE NEXT YEAR, Jayson Blair disappeared with a company car, was sexually suggestive with *Times* news clerks and interns, and began lying to get out of assignments. After September 11, he pretended he had a cousin who had died in the Pentagon to avoid writing any "Portraits of Grief," the *Times*'s short, unbylined biographical sketches of the victims that collectively won a Pulitzer Prize. Blair seemed to bridle at the notion of doing work for which he might not get explicit credit.

In October 2001, he wrote a story so riddled with errors that it attracted the attention of the newly installed Howell Raines. Blair had been assigned to cover a September 11 memorial concert at Madison Square Garden. His story ran in the paper on Sunday, October 21. Two days later, the *Times* ran the following correction:

An article in some copies on Sunday about a benefit at Madison Square Garden for victims of the Sept. 11 terror attack misstated the price of the most expensive tickets. They were $10,000, not $1,000. The article also quoted incorrectly from a remark by former President Bill Clinton to the audience, many of them police officers and firefighters. Mr. Clinton said he had been given the bracelet of Raymond Downey, the deputy fire chief who died in the attack—not Chief Downey's hat.

Referring to the terrorists, he said, "I hope they saw this tonight, because they thought America was about money and power. They thought that if they took down the World Trade Center, we would collapse. But we're not about mountains of money or towers of steel. You're about mountains of courage and hearts of gold, and I hope they saw you here tonight." He did not say "hearts of steel."

The next day, there was yet another correction to the story:

An article in some late editions on Sunday about the benefit concert at Madison Square Garden for victims of the Sept. 11 attack referred incorrectly to scenes in a short film made for the event by Woody Allen, "Scenes From a Town I Love," which showed New Yorkers talking on cellphones. An actor in one scene complained that his anthrax drugs had been stolen by muggers; he did not say the police took them. Another man talked about opening Starbucks coffee shops in Afghanistan after the war; he did not say one had already opened there.

The article also included two performers erroneously among the participants. Bono and the Edge, of the band U2, were scheduled to appear but canceled before the concert.

Blair, it turned out, had not even gone to the concert. He had written his review after getting drunk and watching a broadcast of the event at a local bar. Blair was given a formal reprimand, and he lashed out at his superiors, telling them that the people who hired him were more powerful and important than they. Still, Landman continued to bear down on the young reporter. In January 2002, he sent Blair a negative review. He also sent copies of the review to Boyd and Bill Schmidt, along with a note. "There's big trouble I want you both to be aware of," Landman wrote. In response, Boyd called Blair into his office for a one-on-one meeting. "You have enormous promise and potential," Boyd said. "But your career is in your hands. I don't know what you're doing, drugs or what, and I don't care. The issue is your performance, and unless you change, you are blowing a big opportunity." A formal warning was placed in Blair's personnel file.

Instead of working to earn the trust of his editors, Blair reverted to behavior he'd been exhibiting at least as far back as college—he accused Landman of racism.* It was a shrewd move: By this point, Landman's and Howell Raines's private resentments had spilled out into the newsroom. Gerald Boyd had also said privately that he was not fond of Landman. That spring, Bill Keller had confirmed to *The New Yorker* that had he been named executive editor, he would likely have appointed Landman as his managing editor, a pronouncement that did nothing to help soothe Landman and Boyd's testy relationship. (In the same article, Boyd described Keller as not "inclusive"—"a word," *The New Yorker* noted, "with deep meaning for a fifty-one-year-old black man.") Over the next several months, as his performance worsened, Blair took two personal leaves from work. He said later he was being treated for drug and alcohol dependencies. After he returned from his second leave, two of Blair's supervisors, Nancy Sharkey and Jeannie Pinder, devised a written plan to oversee Blair and his performance. Gerald Boyd refused to let them present Blair with the plan. It was, Boyd said, "something we had never done" and therefore could be seen as discriminatory.

By the summer of 2002, after months of shoddy work and erratic behavior, Blair orchestrated a transfer to the *Times*'s sports department. Landman warned Blair's new supervisors about Blair's track record. Before he moved up to his sports-department desk on the fourth floor of the Times building, Blair told national editor Jim Roberts that he was available for assignments if anything came up.

From May through October 2002, Blair wrote fifty-six stories— about two a week—along with three short squibs for the paper's gossip column. (In the first six months of 2001, Blair wrote fifty-eight full stories in addition to fifty shorter items.) Despite his putative placement in the sports department, most of his stories continued to be filed to the metro desk, and they focused on mundane subjects like a new Con

---

* During this time, Blair also joked publicly about how Landman and another editor on the metro staff "hijacked a plane and flew it into my career."

Edison substation in midtown Manhattan or a new waterfront TV tower. The vast majority of Blair's stories appeared deep inside the *Times*'s metro section, and many of them ran only in the editions of the paper printed and distributed in the New York metropolitan area.

Blair's correction rate also went down during this time. Later, in several conversations, Blair would say that Jon Landman was the only editor at the *Times* who realized he just needed to slow down. "In a weird way, I think he's a real honest and honorable man," Blair told me in the spring of 2003. "I actually have more appreciation for him, in particular for the way he helped my recovery in the beginning."* At the time, though, he told colleagues how much he despised the metro editor. Meanwhile, Blair's personal life seemed to be spinning out of control. He was besotted with a young intern in the *Times*'s photo department, a Polish émigré named Zuza Glowacka, with whom he was spending most of his free time. His apartment in Park Slope, Brooklyn, was littered with broken furniture and rotting food, according to his landlord at the time. There was fungus growing in the bathroom and mold in the kitchen. When Blair moved out that fall, the landlord, who had considered herself a friend of Blair's, contemplated taking the young reporter to court. "It was real filth," she said. "Imagine using a bathroom for two and a half years and never cleaning it."

According to his own accounts and those of his friends, Blair was sleepless for days on end. For the first time in his life, he started talking about leaving journalism for good. "He was just spinning out," says a friend of Blair's. "Talking about how he had to kill Jayson Blair the journalist so Jayson the person could live."

---

* Blair would later disavow these comments and refer to his time with Landman as one that induced something akin to post-traumatic stress disorder.

Sniper Time

In October 2002, an unknown sniper began a murderous rampage in the Washington, D.C., metropolitan area, the final denouement in what had been an exhausting and bewildering year. Since September 11, the *Times* had been on overdrive, pouring money and manpower into the terrorist attacks, the war in Afghanistan, the anthrax letters, the corporate scandals roiling the country, and the threat of an invasion in Iraq. It felt as if the paper were on a war footing all the time. That pace suited Howell Raines just fine—he had no problem driving his troops hard.

What he *did* mind was getting beaten, and he was worried the *Times* was getting beaten but good on the sniper story. Howell Raines, Gerald Boyd, and national editor Jim Roberts scrambled to find reporters to parachute in and flood the zone. At the time, Raines said he and Boyd had decided to appoint Jayson Blair to the paper's sniper coverage. After all, Blair had grown up and studied in the D.C. area and had some experience covering local law enforcement for *The Washing-*

ton Post. "This guy's hungry," Raines said. Neither Raines nor Boyd informed Roberts about Blair's extensive disciplinary record or numerous corrections; Raines would later claim he hadn't even been aware of Blair's problems.

On October 30, six days after arriving in Maryland, Jayson Blair broke out of the pack with a front-page story that featured exclusive details about the arrest of John Muhammad. The piece was sourced to five anonymous law enforcement officials—two reportedly from Maryland and the other three from federal agencies—and said that investigators had stopped an interrogation of Muhammad under orders from the White House. Blair also wrote that Muhammad had been on the verge of explaining "the roots of his anger" when the interrogation was halted.

The piece caused an immediate uproar. Reporters and editors in the *Times*'s Washington bureau raised questions about Blair's story even before it ran—how was it, they asked, that a green metro reporter was able to land multiple anonymous law enforcement sources on one of the most hotly contested stories of the year? What's more, the D.C. bureau's own reporting indicated Muhammad hadn't been talking about anything like "the roots of his anger" but was instead discussing mundane details of his confinement, such as when he'd be allowed a shower.

"We had sources waving us away from that," says Jill Abramson. She called Jim Roberts in New York, and the story was changed to reflect dissent in the reporting. The Washington bureau's reporters were still not thrilled with the story, which now contained as many caveats as it did assertions.

"When I read that first story, I remember thinking, Holy cow, could this really be him?" says David Barstow, a forty-year-old investigative reporter who sat next to Blair in metro when the two first joined the paper in 1999. "I assumed he got the byline because he got the first tip or something. But everyone knew there's no way some reporter could just wander into that situation and get three federal law enforcement sources and two state sources right away. It would be an extraordinary thing even for the most extraordinary reporter. It wasn't just his age, but the arc of his career. There was no history of that type of report-ing."

After Blair's story ran, the U.S. Attorney from Maryland and an FBI official issued public statements refuting parts of the story. Within days, *The Washington Post* was running multiple articles picking apart central components of Blair's piece. In the media dustup that followed, Blair told Erik Wemple at the *Washington City Paper*, "The *Post* got beat in their own back yard, and I can understand why they would have sore feelings." *Times* reporters cringed at Blair's statements; his showboat-ing went against protocol at the *Times*, where reporters let their work speak for itself.

Howell Raines, however, told colleagues he had no problem with Blair's comments. And indeed, at no time during the furor over Blair's reporting did Raines or Boyd ask Blair to tell them who his anonymous law enforcement sources were. Furthermore, even after complaints were made about his work, no one told Jim Roberts or other editors on the *Times*'s national desk about Blair's disturbing track record. Instead, incredibly, Raines sent Blair an e-mail, which he also forwarded to a broad group of editors, including Jim Roberts, Jon Landman, and Jill Abramson, praising Blair for his work. "Jayson," Raines wrote, "I should have already emailed to congratulate you on that great scoop in Wednesday's paper. The Post's follow up merely served to confirm the strength of your sources. This is great shoe-leather reporting and es-pecially impressive because you were dropped in the middle of a very big running story being covered by scores of other reporters. I am very impressed and most grateful. All best, Howell."

Raines's memo was viewed as much as a thinly veiled message to Landman and Abramson as it was an "attaboy" to Blair. "I interpreted it as, 'Fuck you, Washington bureau, with your scaredy-cat jealous re-porters who shoot down someone else's story because they can't get their own,' " says Abramson.

Later, Blair's editor on the sniper stories, Nick Fox, said he would have felt much more wary of Blair's work if he had been warned in ad-vance. "I can't imagine accepting unnamed sources from him as the basis of a story had we known what was going on," he said. "If somebody had said, 'Watch out for this guy,' I would have questioned every-thing that he did. I can't imagine being comfortable with going with the story at all, if I had known that the metro editors flat out didn't trust him." But instead of warnings, the editors were being given every indication that Blair was a favorite of the paper's top editors and, more-over, trustworthy. At one point, according to several people in the newsroom, Boyd walked by the *Times*'s metro desk holding one of Blair's front-page exclusives. "See?" Boyd said. "At least national knows how to get good work out of this guy."

Less than two months later, another Blair exclusive would receive public rebuke. In a December 22 front-page story, Blair wrote that all the evidence in the sniper case indicated that teenage suspect Lee Malvo was the triggerman in the shootings. Again, all of Blair's sources were anonymous. Again, a prosecutor publicly denounced the report. This time, Raines checked Blair's reporting by comparing what he had written against what had appeared in *The Washington Post* and, not find-ing any major discrepancies, decided his reporting was solid. (This hadn't always been Raines's modus operandi. The previous February, business reporter Gretchen Morgenson had written a story about Enron that detailed how the company was a house of cards built on the momentum of a constantly rising stock price. The piece contained one crucial anonymous source. Upon reading the piece, Raines demanded Morgenson tell him the source's identity. Morgenson, who had prom-ised she wouldn't reveal the source's identity under any circumstances, refused, and Raines spiked the story. Two months later, Morgenson won a Pulitzer Prize for her subsequent Enron coverage, and for the next two years, Glenn Kramon, Morgenson's editor, carried her spiked story around with him in his briefcase. "I couldn't throw it away," he says. "It was so good. And—this is totally irrational—I kept thinking, I'll get it in the paper someday.")

Blair was not just *covering* the snipers' trial. He was increasingly identifying with Lee Malvo, the teenage suspect. Within months, Blair was circulating drafts of a book proposal on the sniper story in which he discussed his own anger and frustration as an African American. "Zuza [Glowacka] encouraged me to look for answers about the history of violence in my own family and that of Lee Malvo, suggesting the search would not be in vain, if it at least ended my restless angst," Blair wrote. "The observations about the present day criminal justice system and the historical context are what sets this work apart, giving it a broad appeal to all those interested in uncovering this rare blend of shattered dreams and violence that is endemic in our society."

Over the next several months, Blair continued to get high-profile assignments from the *Times*, writing about the families of missing American soldiers and the unfolding sniper story. He also was becoming more entwined with Glowacka, the daughter of a Polish friend of Raines's Polish wife. Several of the people closest to Blair during this time remarked later that Blair was something of a chimera; seemingly unable to develop a core personality of his own, he instead tried to become like the people around him. In college, while writing about sexual abuse, he suddenly and publicly claimed he himself was a victim. When the space shuttle blew up, he said his father worked at NASA. When Illinois governor George Ryan pardoned all the prisoners on death row in his state, Blair said his uncle was on death row. After September 11, of course, he said he had had a cousin in the Pentagon. And when Howell Raines married a Polish woman, Jayson Blair found a Polish girlfriend.

That spring, Blair pushed his deceptions to the breaking point. In his 2004 memoir, *Burning Down My Masters' House*, Blair would describe himself during this period as being "fully psychotic." Staggering under the pressure of his national assignments, he stopped traveling for work and instead used his cellphone and laptop to make it seem as if he were jetting around the country. At times, he was writing from inside the paper's newsroom when he was supposed to be hundreds of miles away.

Instead of his usual manic self, Blair was outwardly calm, even listless. Roberts says he went out to lunch with Blair in March, two years after Blair had been hired on the *Times* full-time, to discuss the young reporter's goals. "He did not seem to have any strong desires," Roberts says. The national editor met with Blair again in early April 2003. "He seemed even more distracted, and I remember telling other people I thought that was a bit odd, because he had been so ambitious before."

To some members of the *Times*'s newsroom, Blair's April 26, 2003, front-page story on the family of missing army sergeant Edward Anguiano was seen as further proof of the maturation of a once troubled reporter—it was elegantly written, with fluid transitions and nuanced turns of phrase.* Several of Blair's fellow reporters sent him e-mails praising his work. To more than one, Blair responded with a description of how emotionally draining it was to interview a woman whose son was, in all likelihood, dead.

---

* The story had initially been suggested by a *Times* researcher who had dug up the names of the two soldiers still missing in action. Before Blair began the assignment, one of the soldiers was confirmed as having been killed in action.

RESIGNATION

After being summoned by Jim Roberts on April 29, Blair went to the *Times*'s headquarters on Forty-third Street. He brought reporter's notebooks containing what he said were his notes from Los Fresnos. "I was still wondering, Is it sloppiness? Is it plagiarism?" says Roberts. "But in those first twenty-four hours, even in my wildest imagination I wouldn't have conceived that he didn't go to San Antonio."

Already, Blair was changing his story. On Monday, he insisted he had never seen Macarena Hernandez's piece. By Tuesday, he said he had seen a version of it. Actually, Blair said, he'd downloaded it onto his computer and had simply gotten his notes mixed up. Blair told Roberts he was exhausted, and perhaps he had been trying to do too much. As Blair was talking with Jim Roberts, Robert Rivard of the *Express-News* checked with Hernandez to see if anyone from the *Times* had gotten in touch with her about her complaint. No one besides Blair himself had. No one had contacted Rivard, either, or anyone else at the *Express-News*, even just to say they were looking into the situation. After his experience in 1999 with the *Times* and his paper's Madalyn Murray O'Hair story, Rivard knew he had to do something.

"Many people in my newsroom were already on edge because of that situation," Rivard says. In 1999, the first time Rivard had been on the receiving end of an apparent non-attribution, he had written a letter to Bill Keller, then the *Times*'s managing editor. "We believe your Houston reporter . . . has made improper use of material without attribution from an article written by a *San Antonio Express-News* reporter," Rivard wrote. Looking back at the two pieces, it's hard to understand why there was so much frustration over this one story. The *Times* account went out of its way to credit the *Express-News*'s reporting for serving as the impetus for reopening the investigation into O'Hair's disappearance. But Rivard, and *Express-News* reporters, were undoubtedly responding to the accumulated frustration of feeling as if they were nothing more than a bottomless well of story ideas for the country's national papers. What's more, the *Times* story did unquestionably use one quote, without attribution, that had been printed only in the *Express-News*.

A week later, Keller wrote back. "Having reported for a couple of regional papers," he wrote, "I understand the feeling of reporters there that when they have a good story, the bigshot press pays them no respect. Perhaps some such feeling has made you a little thin-skinned in this case. . . . Whatever's going on, I don't see that we owe you an editor's note."

Rivard was offended, but he let the issue drop. "Hearst [the corporate owner of the *Express-News*] doesn't have me here to pick industry fights with *The New York Times*," he says. But this time, Rivard vowed, the outcome would be different: "I wasn't going to let this end the way the last one ended." That afternoon, Rivard began composing a formal complaint to Gerald Boyd and Howell Raines. He also decided to go on the record with *The Washington Post*'s Howard Kurtz. "It's not quite plagiarism," Rivard told Kurtz, "nor is it as simple as an error of non-attribution. It's definitely a problem of presenting previously published material without an appropriate acknowledgment." Around the same time, Rivard got a call from Erik Wemple, the editor of the *Washington City Paper*, an alternative weekly. Wemple, who had written about the minicontroversies surrounding Blair's coverage of the D.C.-area sniper case the previous fall, had also been tipped off to the similarities between Blair's and Hernandez's stories. When Rivard got off the phone with Wemple, he finished his e-mail to the *Times* editors and sent it out at 5:00 p.m., eastern standard time.

Kurtz, meanwhile, had reached Jayson Blair on his cellphone. "The first words out of his mouth were, 'I really fucked up, man,' " says Kurtz. "He was very smooth. He immediately pled guilty to a limited offense—mixing up his notes. He says he can't be quoted, but explains the situation to me, one reporter to another, saying, 'Look, I'm not going to defend myself.' I wasn't completely buying his explanation." Kurtz was aware of Blair's sniper stories because of the small ruckus they caused in the *Post*'s newsroom, but he hadn't ever dealt with the reporter before. "The notes excuse, that's the first refuge of every plagiarist. And besides that, there was more that was similar than just the quotes. It wasn't adding up."

The press queries from other reporters meant there was no longer any way for the *Times* to deal with the situation quietly. Kurtz and Wemple knew they had a juicy scoop on their hands. Kurtz had already held off for a day, and both reporters rushed to post their pieces online. The *Times*, Kurtz wrote, was aware of the situation and was "looking into it." Wemple's story indicated Blair might have cribbed from at least one other source—it identified a quote Blair attributed to Edward Anguiano's sister Jennifer ("I'm just not feeling a lot of hope right now") that had also appeared in an Associated Press dispatch on April 14.

At 7:03 p.m. on Tuesday, after Kurtz's and Wemple's stories were already posted online, Gerald Boyd wrote back to Rivard. "Dear Bob," Boyd wrote. "Thanks for your letter and the considerate tone it strikes." Boyd wrote that he remembered Hernandez well from her days at the *Times* and thought of her with "considerable respect and affection." He requested some time to resolve the problem and promised he'd be back in touch soon.

That night, Blair asked for the sympathy and support of his colleagues. He e-mailed reporters on the national desk to complain about how unfair Jim Roberts was being. He talked to one reporter who was under pressure to file a story of his own about ways to protect against confusing previously published clips with your own work. He broke down crying at least once. "I know this doesn't erase all the good work I've done," Blair said, sobbing. "It doesn't change who I am as a person."

Meanwhile, the paper's top brass were still scrambling to determine what exactly had happened. The *Times*, like all newspapers, hates embarrassing corrections, and it hates to correct its corrections even more. When the editors finally printed something about Blair's Anguiano story, they wanted to make sure it was the final word on the matter. Roberts was growing more suspicious, and that night he called the paper's photo desk and asked for the unpublished shots from the Anguiano story.

On Wednesday, April 30, Gerald Boyd met with Jayson Blair for the first time since he had been alerted about the similarities between Blair's and Hernandez's stories. Boyd told Blair that he had always been a vocal advocate for the young reporter's career, and Blair asked for forgiveness. Despite Blair's efforts over the past few years to paint Boyd as one of his mentors, this was one of only a handful of face-to-face meetings the two men had ever had. Blair also met twice more with Jim Roberts that day. At the first meeting, Roberts made Blair describe the Anguiano household. Using pictures from the *Times*'s unpublished photo archive as a point of comparison, Roberts was temporarily persuaded the reporter had at least been in Texas. But a couple of hours later, Nick Fox, Blair's editor on the sniper story, found the AP story that Blair seemed to have plagiarized as well. Roberts exploded. "This is bullshit," he screamed at him. "I need you to tell me what's really going on."

Finally, at 4:00 p.m., Blair met with Bill Schmidt and members of the paper's legal staff. Blair brought Lena Williams, a representative of the paper's Newspaper Guild and a three-decade veteran of the *Times*, with him to the meeting. "He just seemed nervous," Williams says. "I've learned in thirty years in this culture, no matter how bad the truth is, just give it to them. He knew me. He knew Bill. I said it would be okay." Blair, Williams thought, would likely face a suspension for plagiarism.* "I said, 'They might not want you traveling all over the country, but that's not that bad. I wouldn't doubt if by the 2004 election they didn't ask you to go back out and do some work.' "

Throughout the meeting, which lasted almost five hours, Jayson Blair continued to work the angles. He apologized—for not working hard enough or not spending enough time with sources. He explained how he had confused his notes and promised nothing like that had ever happened before. But as the meeting progressed, Schmidt—a former national correspondent—realized Blair's story wasn't adding up. His supposed flight route didn't make any sense. Blair said he'd been unable to rent a car from Avis or Hertz, because they were closed when he got to the airport. He said he'd slept in the backseat of the car he did finally rent, and that was why he didn't have receipts from his hotel. After the meeting, back in his office on the corner of the fourth floor, Schmidt quickly confirmed that Blair was lying. The Avis and Hertz counters at San Antonio International Airport were open twenty-four hours a day; the rental agency Blair said he got a car from was not. Schmidt realized then that the paper would need to fire Jayson Blair.

But the *Times* never had the chance. The next morning, Thursday, Blair came in and went straight to Lena Williams. He announced he was going to resign. "He's so tiny and endearing," Williams says. "And since I've never had children, here was someone I looked on as a son I never had, and he was breaking down." The previous day, Blair had described a gas station in Los Fresnos that he had visited. Williams still believed that Blair had been in Texas, and she told him she'd call the station. "I said, 'Sometimes it's good to be a five-foot-tall black man,' " Williams says. "They'd remember him. And that's when he told me: 'I

---

* The *Times*'s journalistic integrity statement, issued in 1999, says that falsification of any part of a news report "will result automatically in disciplinary action up to and including termination." A typical punishment for the first instance of plagiarism—assuming there was not a previous disciplinary record against the employee—would be an unpaid suspension. At this point in his *Times* career, Blair already had a disciplinary letter in his personnel file that warned him that his continuing problems with accuracy were putting his job in peril.

don't want to do this. I'm not going to get through this. Don't make me do this.' " Blair started to sob. "I had a belt around my neck last night and I should have jumped," he said.

"I just held him," Williams says. "I was crying, too. I just held him and said, 'It's gonna be all right.' "

Williams went and told Bill Schmidt that Jayson Blair was resigning from the *Times*. That night, metro columnist Clyde Haberman sent Blair a supportive e-mail. "I said I was an expert on life after death at *The New York Times*," says Haberman, who had been banned for life from the paper by A. M. Rosenthal when, as the City College of New York stringer, he had inserted a fake graduation award in a write-up of the 1966 commencement exercises.* "I said I could be a shoulder he could lean on. That was before I learned the full extent of his behavior, of course. Then I probably would have thrown him out a window."

Elsewhere at the paper, Blair's editors were realizing they were dealing with something much larger than simple plagiarism. Gerald Boyd got hold of Jim Roberts, who had flown down to Washington to meet with Rick Berke, an editor there, and summoned him back to the office. That afternoon, Roberts and Nick Fox began to check out the stories Blair had written for the paper's national desk.

"I got back to the office around four-thirty," says Roberts. "Nick had already put together stacks of Jayson's war stuff. I took a few, he took a few, and we started making phone calls." Roberts reached Reverend Tandy Sloan, the father of a dead soldier whom Blair had supposedly written about from Cleveland. "He remembered the story, remembered disliking it," says Roberts. "He didn't remember ever talking to Jayson. It was becoming clear by the minute that all these stories were screwed up." As Fox and Roberts were going over Blair's stories, Bill Schmidt and his staff also began to look into Blair's career. They pulled all the records they could find—expense reports, cellphone records, personnel files. By the end of the day, Boyd told Roberts to return to his regular work. Raines, who had been at his fish-

---

* The fictitious award was the "Brett Award," given "to the student who has worked hardest under a great handicap" and was given to "Jake Barnes." The reference was to Hemingway's *The Sun Also Rises*, in which the impotent Jake Barnes falls in love with Lady Brett Ashley.

ing cabin in Pennsylvania, decided he'd come back into the office the next day, and he and Boyd agreed they needed to assign a team of reporters the task of examining Jayson Blair's career at the *Times*. The solution to bad reporting, Howell Raines said, was good reporting.

Later that day, Jayson Blair sent a letter to both Raines and Boyd in which he apologized for his "lapse in journalistic integrity."

> This is a time in my life that I have been struggling with recurring personal issues, which have caused me great pain. I am now seeking appropriate counseling. Journalism and The New York Times have been very good to me and I regret what I have done. I am deeply sorry.

Raines would later say that he accepted Blair's apology and that there was no need to demonize the young reporter. But as much as Raines and Boyd may have wanted to close an embarrassing chapter in their stewardship of the paper, they couldn't. The story was far from over.

————

ON FRIDAY, MAY 2, *The New York Times* ran its first story on the Jayson Blair situation. The piece, which was written by Jacques Steinberg, the *Times*'s newspaper beat reporter, said that Blair had resigned from the paper. Blair, who refused to speak to Steinberg, gave a brief statement to the Associated Press in which he once again said, "I have been struggling with recurring personal issues." Immediately, New York's overactive media watchers became preoccupied by news and gossip about Blair's misdeeds. That same day, Howell Raines told New York's *Daily News* that Blair had "trouble with basics of the craft," leading many people to wonder why, if that was so, Blair had been sent to cover some of the past year's highest-profile national news stories. Raines also acknowledged that he had assigned a team of staffers to check the rest of Blair's stories for mistakes. "We have good reason to believe we've published flawed journalism," Raines said. That weekend, Howard Kurtz devoted a segment of *Reliable Sources*, his weekly CNN media roundtable, to Blair. On that show, Kurtz raised the race angle, one that would come to dominate the next phase of the story's coverage. "Look," Kurtz said, "this was a promising young black reporter. I wonder if a middle-aged hack would have gotten away with fifty mistakes and still be at that job." Middle-aged *white* hack was more what he had in mind.

Kurtz's comments were notable because they articulated what others were saying privately. Even in better economic times, it was extremely rare for any reporter, white or black, to begin his career at *The New York Times*. Usually, reporters had to spend time proving their mettle on scrappy dailies in smaller markets. Blair had broken in at the top—his first full-time job was at the *Times*. In those first days after his resignation, Blair's suspiciously accelerated career path became a focus of many white reporters who didn't advance as quickly as they would have liked.

Still, even with all the attention the story got that weekend, the Blair scandal looked as if it would remain more or less contained within the industry's hyperoxygenated and self-referential media columns. That week, the *New York Post* ran some small items on Blair peppered with snarky anonymous quotes. Mickey Kaus, the blogger, posted an item connecting Blair's flameout to affirmative-action programs. The *Washington City Paper* put together a cover story on the many errors in Blair's coverage. Slate's Jack Shafer, who himself had been snookered by a writer who convinced him to run a largely made-up account of something called "monkeyfishing," wrote about how any editor can be fooled by a reporter determined to perpetrate a fraud. And the *Daily News*'s Paul Colford filled in his readers on what the *Times* said it was doing next.

Over the coming week, *The New York Times* would demonstrate once again its power to shape the national news agenda. A team of five reporters, three editors, and a handful of researchers were digging into Jayson Blair's career with an intensity and scrutiny usually reserved for corrupt public officials. Their report would transform the Jayson Blair story into a full-blown national scandal, one that would affect the culture of the paper, as well as that of other newspapers around the country, for years to come.

————

ON THURSDAY, MAY 1, Jacques Steinberg had arrived at the *Times*'s offices only dimly aware of Blair's situation. Like everyone in the building, he'd read the Kurtz and Wemple pieces but hadn't heard much else. Steinberg began his tenure at the *Times* as a Washington-based assistant to James "Scotty" Reston, the man closest to a personification of an institutional voice that *The New York Times* had ever had. Reston's career at the *Times*—which stretched from the eve of World War II through the elder Bush's administration—included a brief stint as executive editor, but he was best known as a D.C. correspondent and political columnist. Within the *Times*, Reston, who died in 1995, was seen almost as an adopted member of the Sulzberger family. "He adored this newspaper," Steinberg says. "And he adored the family that ran it." Steinberg grew up in southern Massachusetts, but his father was born and raised in Brooklyn. Every day, when Steinberg's dad got home from the hospital where he worked, he'd pick up his son and drive into town to buy a copy of the *Times* from the drugstore. "Here's my father, going out of his way to pick up this newspaper with this incredibly small print," Steinberg says. "I learned by example that it was important."

After his time working with Reston, Steinberg moved from Washington to New York, where he covered education for the paper for eight years. Then, in April 2003, after briefly filling in at the paper's Los Angeles bureau, he moved over to the newspaper beat. It was a high-profile assignment: Media coverage was one of the areas Howell Raines was most interested in beefing up. Steinberg's introduction to the industry's major players occurred on April 27 through 29, at the Newspaper Association of America's annual conference, which was held that year in Seattle. Once Steinberg got back to New York, he continued cultivating industry sources. On April 30, he had a get-to-know-you dinner with Lachlan Murdoch, one of Rupert Murdoch's sons. (Lachlan Murdoch is in charge of all of the News Corp.'s stateside publishing interests, including the *New York Post*.)

As the day wore on, word of Jayson Blair's resignation began to make its way around the newsroom, although there hadn't been an official announcement. Early that afternoon, Steinberg and Lorne Manly, the *Times*'s acting media editor, were called into Gerald Boyd's office. Manly, a bespectacled, curly-haired journalism junkie, had been covering the media industry for over a decade—as a reporter for *Ad-Week* and *MediaWeek*; as a reporter and editor for *Folio:*, an industry trade magazine; as the "Off the Record" columnist at *The New York Observer*; as one of the first hires at *Brill's Content*, a now-defunct general interest magazine covering the press; as a media editor for Inside.com, a short-lived online publication covering the information industries*; and then in a return engagement as the editor of *Folio:*. He was brought to the *Times* as the deputy media editor in early 2002 as one of Howell Raines's first hires. In April 2003, media editor Dave Smith became an editor at the Sunday paper's Week in Review section, and Manly settled into his new role.

By this point, Bill Schmidt and employees from the paper's news administration staff had worked through Blair's expense reports and other records. "It was suggested to me that there was a suspicion that he might not have been [in Texas]," says Steinberg. But no one had actually reached Juanita Anguiano, the mother of the soldier Blair wrote about.

That afternoon, Steinberg tracked down Anguiano at her home in Los Fresnos, Texas—he was the first reporter to reach her since the story had broken earlier that week—and began to ask her about conversations she'd had with reporters, including one from *The New York Times*. As Steinberg continued his interview, some of the reporters seated at the desks surrounding his realized what was going on. They gathered around his cubicle. It was at that point that Anguiano said she

---

* For about six months in 2001, Manly served as my editor at Inside.com.

had to get off the phone. She was, she said, on her way to her son's funeral—in the five days since Blair's story had run, Edward Anguiano's remains had been identified.

"I very gently told her I just needed to confirm this one fact," Steinberg says, "that Jayson had actually been there to see her." Anguiano said he hadn't. "I kept apologizing profusely," Steinberg says. "But I asked her—several times, as I recall—if she was sure he hadn't been there. Was there any chance she had forgotten? Remember, it was just a completely alien thought, at that point, to me or any other reporter, that Jayson would have datelined a story and not gone there. This was thought to be just a dustup over plagiarism."

Steinberg hung up the phone, stunned. He assumed there had to be an explanation. Maybe Blair had been in Texas but reached the woman only by phone? Maybe Anguiano just completely forgot about Blair's visit? After all, she had had a traumatic several weeks: Her son, first thought to be merely missing, was then presumed dead, and now she was off to bury him in a military funeral. Steinberg conferred with Manly and then punched in Jayson Blair's cellphone number. His call was returned by Lena Williams, who was across the street at a hotel bar, trying to comfort Blair. Blair, Williams said, wouldn't comment. Steinberg explained that Juanita Anguiano had just told him that Blair had never been to her house and that he needed to know if Blair had, in fact, even been in Texas.

"I said, 'Lena, you know how this works. I need to show the reader that I've tried to convey this information to Jayson to get a comment. I spoke with the people in Texas, with Juanita Anguiano.' Even at that point, as a colleague, I'm thinking there's got to be some explanation for this," Steinberg recalls. Williams put down the phone for a minute and then returned to the line. Blair, she said, was covering his ears. "And so I went back and said, 'Lena, you have to tell him, it's not just that I spoke with her, it's that she says he wasn't there. She says he was never in Los Fresnos.' And she said she'd try, but then whenever she went to him he'd cover up his ears."

"I couldn't ask the question. He didn't want to hear the question you had," Williams said. Steinberg hung up the phone and turned to Manly. It now seemed entirely possible, they agreed, that Jayson Blair had never been in Texas.

"I keep trying to come up with a better word than 'surreal,' " says Manly. "But that's what it was. It was like *The Twilight Zone*. . . . I mean, people would kill to get these assignments, to get a chance to go and talk to and write about people around the country. And here was this guy that might not even have bothered to get on a plane? What for?"

Steinberg wrote up his story, a 644-word piece that ran on page A30 the following day, a Friday. Blair, Steinberg wrote, had resigned; he attributed that revelation not to any editor or spokesperson but to "The Times." Steinberg quoted Juanita Anguiano saying, "No, no, no, he didn't come." He also reported that before his phone call, Juanita Anguiano was unaware of the *Times*'s article by Jayson Blair.

As the reporters and editors were finishing up for the day, Gerald Boyd wandered over to the media cluster, on the far west side of the newsroom. Steinberg had known Boyd for years, from back when Steinberg was a clerk in Washington and Boyd was covering the White House. Steinberg, like all reporters, wanted more space for a good story. He asked Boyd if he could give the Blair saga the "David Shaw treatment," referring to the *Los Angeles Times* media reporter who wrote a thirty-one-thousand-word report on a scandal that erupted in 1999 after the publisher of the *Los Angeles Times* had arranged to produce a 168-page Sunday magazine supplement devoted to the Staples Center, a downtown arena, splitting the $2 million in advertising revenue with the center. "I was thinking about Reston and what he'd want me to do in a situation like this," says Steinberg. "And he'd say to just report the hell out of it. And much of who I am as a reporter was taught to me by Gerald himself. I just wanted to use all the techniques the paper has invested in me to just turn loose on this."

Without making any decisions, everyone went home for the night. "We both knew there was more to be done," Manly says. "We were going to go back in the next morning and tell Gerald we should really go back at this."

"Whatever happened, I knew when I went home that night that my life was going to be very different on Friday," Steinberg says. That night, Steinberg—who has two children under five years old—told his wife, "You can expect not to see me for a while." He was right.

A TEAM ASSEMBLED

On the morning of Friday, May 2, 2003, Gerald Boyd's secretary summoned Adam Liptak to the managing editor's office. Liptak, the *Times*'s thin, balding legal correspondent, had traveled an atypical path to the *Times*'s newsroom. For years, he had served as one of the paper's in-house lawyers, working closely with the editorial side of the paper on libel and First Amendment issues. He'd always maintained an interest in writing— he'd written a fair amount for the *Times* and had once written a "Talk of the Town" piece for *The New Yorker*—but was still surprised when, in 2002, Howell Raines asked him if he was interested in serving as the paper's national legal correspondent. Liptak, whose five-year-old daughter, Katie, was in kindergarten at the Bank Street School on 112th Street, had a parent-teacher conference scheduled for lunchtime, and when he was summoned into Boyd's office, he called his wife to tell her he might not be able to make it. "I had no idea what this was about," Liptak says, "but whatever it was, I assumed it was some issue that had to do with me." Liptak arrived first and sat alone, waiting.

Boyd's secretary also called Jonathan Glater. Glater, an African American reporter with wavy hair and braces, is exceedingly polite. He was coming up on his three-year anniversary at the *Times;* he'd arrived during the paper's (and the industry's) last big round of hiring, back in the fall of 2000. Before that, Glater had been removed from the world of daily journalism for half a decade, since he left *The Washington Post* in the mid-1990s. After the *Post*, Glater went to Yale Law School and then spent two years working as a lawyer, first in private practice in Buenos Aires and then as a litigator in the New York office of Cleary, Gottlieb, Steen & Hamilton. The whole time he was practicing law, Glater says, he missed writing. In the summer of 2000, he decided to send out his clips. "The great thing about law is, sometimes you can make a difference—usually for one client at a time," Glater says. "As a journalist, you can make a difference for a whole lot of people at once." To his surprise, he was offered a job on the *Times*'s business staff covering law firms, accounting firms, and consulting firms. He knows his timing was fortuitous. "Six months later in 2001 [after the stock market bubble burst], no one was hiring at all, least of all one more wannabe law firm refugee with various journalism internships but no clips in years," he says.

Glater thought he'd been summoned for a debriefing about his recent monthlong reporting stint in Los Angeles, where he had replaced Jacques Steinberg, who had also been there on a temporary posting. It was Glater's first real assignment for the paper's national staff, but he knew it might not be his last. Ever since September 11, the *Times* had been in triage mode, as many of the paper's most enterprising reporters were recruited to cover the first terror strikes, then the war in Afghanistan, then the war in Iraq. Adding to the staffing problems was the fact that Howell Raines had forced out a handful of the paper's national correspondents in 2002. Glater, whose wife works in a Manhattan law firm, didn't have the flexibility to ask for a posting overseas, but earlier in the year he had gone to Boyd and said he would welcome the chance to spend a month or so filling in at one of the paper's domestic bureaus.

When Glater saw Liptak in Boyd's office, he concluded that Liptak had been tapped as the next person to fill in at the L.A. bureau. To pass the time until Boyd showed up, Glater spoke to Liptak, recounting details from one of his more amusing and memorable stories. "Adultery May Be a Sin, but It's a Crime No More," published on April 17, 2003, was a lighthearted piece about a gated community more than an hour's drive from Los Angeles that had recently removed from its books a statute outlawing adultery. (The piece quoted a retired banker who dated another woman during his divorce: "Arguably that would've run afoul of this," the banker said. "I try not to violate these provisions.") Glater told Liptak about how he drove all the way out to the community, called Rolling Hills, only to be turned back at the gate. As he was finishing his story, Boyd walked into the room.

"Well, at least you went," said Boyd. That was the first hint Glater got that the meeting wasn't going to be about Los Angeles. Jacques Steinberg and Lorne Manly arrived soon after. (Earlier that morning, Manly had been told he'd have the "acting" removed from his title and would be made the paper's permanent media editor.) Boyd told the three reporters and one editor that he wanted them to work on a team that would examine the career of Jayson Blair at *The New York Times.* "The notion that Jayson wasn't in Los Fresnos changes things substantially," Boyd said. "We need to go back and look at everything, starting with the work he did for the national desk." The team, Boyd said, should get started immediately. "The initial marching orders were not incredibly precise," says Glater. "Our sense was we'd need to come up with twenty-five hundred words by Monday or Tuesday."

"Gerald started to lay out a working hypothesis of what he expected us to find out about Jayson," Liptak says. "And that's that Jayson had no credit, that he had reached his limit on the company credit card, and this was why he got boxed in to this position where he'd either need to turn down assignments or make stuff up." The *Times,* like many media companies, requires its reporters to front their travel expenses and file receipts to be reimbursed. For a national reporter making last-minute reservations and flying around the country, this can result in outlays of thousands of dollars. Glater mentioned how he had been fronting significant sums of money while he was in Los Angeles.

Boyd also made it clear that the team would need to report on their superiors, including himself and Howell Raines. "He told us that he was going to be deciding what sort of cooperation to extend us," Liptak says. "He was saying, 'There are some things I might tell you, some things I might not. There are some records we might share, and some we might not.' He was plainly setting up an independent unit in the paper to report on the paper."

"We were going to report this as *Times* reporters," Steinberg says. "It wasn't even clear yet who was going to lead us, so we were told to just kind of sit tight, and they were in the process of getting in touch with people who might head up the team. But it was clear we were heading into uncharted territory." Later, Steinberg called his wife and told her, "It's happening exactly the way I'd thought it would happen."

After Glater, Liptak, and Steinberg left Gerald Boyd's office, Boyd spoke to Manly about how the project would evolve. "I wasn't going to be the main editor," Manly says. "But Gerald had no idea who would be. He talked vaguely about wanting someone who wasn't involved in the newsroom but knew the culture. But at this point he was mainly just stressing that they wanted the record corrected." Manly had been in charge of the paper's media coverage for only two weeks, and he was still trying to feel his way around the *Times*'s power structure. "Gerald can talk in riddles sometimes," Manly says. "So it was a little hard to tell exactly what was happening."

Several hours later, in Portland, Oregon, David Barstow was returning to his hotel room. Barstow was a four-year veteran of the *Times*. After graduating from Northwestern, he spent three years as a reporter on the *Rochester Times-Union*. Then he moved to Florida to work on the *St. Petersburg Times*, one of the best regional papers in the country. It was in Florida that Barstow learned how to handle the pressure of producing the day's big story. "When I got [to *The New York Times*] I got down on my knees and thanked God that I didn't get hired here when I was in my twenties. I was not ready," Barstow says. "Everyone has this experience at some point: It's three o'clock and the spotlight swivels and you're the man and you need to deliver by six. [At the *St. Petersburg Times*], I was the go-to guy on a lot of big stories in a lot of weird circumstances. I'm glad I learned how to do that there." While in Florida, Barstow was a finalist for Pulitzer Prizes in three separate categories—breaking news, investigative reporting, and explanatory reporting. At the *Times*, Barstow worked in metro before becoming one of the linchpins of the paper's investigative unit.

Barstow can be an intimidating presence in the newsroom. He's tenacious and fearless and gets so immersed in projects that he essentially disappears down a wormhole for weeks at a time. In Portland, he was working on a follow-up to a three-part series he had co-authored with Lowell Bergman on McWane, Inc., a Birmingham, Alabama–based pipe company the *Times* called one of "the most dangerous employers in America." (The series, coupled with a later project by Barstow and Bergman titled "When Workers Die," won the 2003 George Polk Award, the 2003 James Aronson Award, the 2004 Sidney Hillman Award, the 2004 duPont Award, the 2004 Goldsmith Prize, and the 2004 Pulitzer Prize.) When Barstow arrived at his hotel the morning of May 2, he had several urgent messages telling him to call Gerald Boyd. Barstow called Paul Fishleder, his editor back in New York, who told him that he didn't know what the calls were about, either. Even though that day's *Times* had run Steinberg's story about Blair's resignation, and the newsroom had been rife with speculation about the former reporter for days, Barstow didn't know anything about the situation. "I was deep into my other story," he says. "I hadn't heard anything about it."

Barstow's first desk at the *Times*, back in the spring of 1999, was across from Blair's. Barstow isn't involved in the *Times*'s social scene; he never got to know the young reporter well. But he saw enough to know he wasn't impressed. "On his best day," Barstow says, "he was mediocre." Barstow finally called in to the office and was told he was needed immediately for a project examining Blair's career at the paper. He was to fly back to New York City as soon as possible.

In the meantime, Steinberg, Liptak, and Glater worked on dividing up what was in front of them. They quickly realized the difficulties of investigating one of their colleagues. "You're suddenly looking at the newsroom as sources of information," Steinberg says. Colleagues began to e-mail the three reporters with tidbits about Jayson's career at the cop shop or pointing out stories they remembered as being not quite right. "Almost as soon as we put word out, my phone started ringing," Liptak says. "Lots of people had lots to say. So right off the bat, we're working these two tracks—trying to get a fix on who Jayson is and was and trying to rereport the damn stories."

Rather than meet out in the open, the three reporters gathered in a small, windowless room that sits right outside the greeter's desk on the third floor. The first thing the team did was draw up a list of documents they wanted access to. The list they came up with included all the obvious things—all of Blair's articles from the *Times*, examples of Blair's work at *The Boston Globe* and *The Washington Post*, and stories from other news organizations that covered the same topics. They also requested internal communications about Blair or his work at the paper, his application and résumé, all his employee evaluations, his personnel file, his reimbursement requests, and any internal memos tracking corrections or error rates. Adam Liptak and Jonathan Glater—the team's two attorneys—signed the request and sent it on to Gerald Boyd. There still wasn't an editor besides Manly assigned to oversee the project. "It was similar to a litigation document discovery request," says Liptak. The request included language like "including but not limited to," because, Liptak says, "we meant to be comprehensive."

According to people in the newsroom who spoke with him at the time, Boyd was stunned by the request. "He couldn't believe we didn't wait to get an editor," Steinberg says. "The normal *Times* protocol would be, editors talk to editors." Boyd redoubled his efforts to figure out who was going to lead the reporting team. "Fairly early on," Liptak says, "it became clear this was not going to be good for anybody's career."

Everyone on the team had been chosen at that morning's masthead meeting for a specific reason. Liptak was chosen because he was a recent transplant from the legal department. "He had a kind of mental rigor that we thought would be hugely valuable," says Al Siegal, the *Times* assistant managing editor who was eventually put in charge of the project. Steinberg, as one of the paper's media writers, was an obvious choice: "This was the biggest story conceivably he'd need to deal with ever," says Siegal. Barstow is one of the paper's top investigators. And Glater, in addition to his legal background, is black. "We had decided on the other guys, and I said, 'Wait a minute, this group is awfully white,'" Siegal says. "The fact that we had a reporter who was young and black and a lawyer was a no-brainer."

GLENN KRAMON, the *Times*'s business editor, had a lunch meeting on May 2. He didn't get back to the *Times* until around 3:00 p.m., and by the time he made his way up to the third-floor newsroom, several people had already told him that Gerald Boyd wanted to talk to him.

Boyd told Kramon about the team that was being assembled to examine Blair's fabrications at the *Times* and asked Kramon to work on the project. "I had never worked with Jayson, which I think is one of the reasons they put me on this," says Kramon. "I knew him to say hello to, but not much more than that. I did remember people warning me, 'Boy, this guy is trouble.'"

Steinberg, Liptak, and Glater, meanwhile, were realizing that a significant part of their job would include reporting on their colleagues—the reporters who shared bylines with Blair, the editors who assigned him stories, the managers who promoted him. No one on the team knew about Blair's sloppiness or the widespread concern about his work on the metro desk, but reporters and editors in the newsroom were soon seeking the team out to share their stories. "It became clear that we could not do this and work in the newsroom," Steinberg says. "Already at that point, we're digging up memos, we're getting a paper trail going. We could already see that there had been issues with Jayson that were brought to people's attention from way back. So I went to Gerald and said, 'You gotta get us a place to work.' Within an hour, there were tech people coming through the newsroom with carts and taking our computers off our desks." The team was moved to the eleventh floor, to a temporary office space.

Outside of the third-floor newsroom, the eleventh floor is one of the busiest at the *Times*'s headquarters. The paper's cafeteria is on the east side of the floor, through a pair of defunct turnstiles. The building's ATM is there as well, and beyond that, on the west side of the floor, is a catchall office space. On one side are several rows of desks, where reporters sometimes come when they're working in teams or on special projects. The other side houses the work space for the *Times Magazine*'s special supplement sections. In May 2003, James Glanz and Eric Lipton were in a room off the back, working on their book about the World Trade Center, *City in the Sky*. It was here that the Blair investigative team was first moved. "There was no way to get any privacy here," says Steinberg. So he and his colleagues asked news administration to try to find a more secluded location.

That afternoon, Glater, Liptak, and Steinberg, along with Manly and Kramon, assembled around a squawk box in one of the business department's conference rooms and called Barstow in Portland. It was the first official meeting of the team that, in a bit of dark humor, some in the newsroom would call the Blair Witch Project. The meeting—and the assignment the team was asked to complete—was unprecedented in the history of *The New York Times*. The closest parallel to the team's endgame—producing a published report on the paper's doings—was an April 1, 1963, report filed by A. H. Raskin documenting the causes and repercussions of the 114-day newspaper strike that crippled the paper. (Raskin filed what amounted to a follow-up in 1974, detailing another bout of labor trouble for the *Times* and the city's papers.) But the 1962–1963 newspaper strike had affected not only the *Times*; it had shut down all nine of the city's daily papers, crippling the entire industry. The mayor's office and then the White House got involved with the negotiations. Thousands of jobs and millions of readers were affected—Raskin estimated in his story that "600,000,000 daily and Sunday papers went unprinted." The *Times* had to cover the newspaper strike if it had any hope of reestablishing itself in readers' daily routines.

Other times, the paper avoided reporting on its own mistakes. On May 6, 1964, at the height of race tensions in New York, the *Times* published a front-page story about the Blood Brothers, a black youth gang in Harlem that was said to be recruiting and training forces to kill whites. The article, by staff writer Junius Griffin, claimed the gang already had four hundred members who were being trained by dissident Black Muslims and were suspected in four recent murders of whites in Harlem.

Almost immediately, the story came under fire. On May 11, the *Times* reported on page 27 that the NAACP had challenged law enforcement to prove the gang existed. "No doubt hoodlum groups do exist throughout the city and the crime rate is alarming, but it is inequitable, immoral and dangerously inflammable to scandalize an entire community on the basis of the flimsy evidence offered to date," the NAACP said in a statement. The story was blamed by many in the black community for fanning the flames that led to the July riots that engulfed Harlem for five days. Griffin, the reporter, eventually resigned, and the story is now generally acknowledged to be wildly exaggerated, if not completely made up. The *Times* never published a retraction or correction of any kind relating to the Blood Brothers.

More recently, when the *Times* has been faced with potential scandals concerning its journalistic standards, it has usually tried to address the matter quietly and privately—if at all. In 1991, when executive editor Max Frankel published a profile that identified Patricia Bowman, the woman who had accused William Kennedy Smith of rape, there was outrage in the newsroom that the *Times* had named an alleged rape victim. Anna Quindlen, then a *Times* Op-Ed page columnist, wrote a critical essay, calling the Bowman piece a "mistake." Media watchers at other news outlets wrung their hands about the collapsing standards at the Good Gray Lady. But apart from a defensive editors' note* that was published nine days after the initial story ran, the *Times* remained mostly silent on the controversy.

Seven years later, under Joe Lelyveld, the *Times* once again faced criticism from within. This time, the subject was the initial paroxysm of the Monica Lewinsky coverage. The paper, some staffers felt, had ignored its own rules about sourcing and attribution in an effort to bite off a chunk of the story that was overwhelming the country. Lelyveld, who had been named executive editor in 1994, didn't commission a reported review or order up an editors' note. Instead, he asked Marty Baron, then an associate managing editor (and now the editor of *The Boston Globe*), who had been on vacation in Mexico when the story broke, to review the paper's coverage. It was not an easy task for Baron, who was uncomfortable criticizing his colleagues' decisions and understood both their intentions and the difficulty of the decisions they had had to make. "I feel a bit uneasy evaluating our performance in the matter of sourcing during the first wave of Lewinsky stories," Baron wrote. "At the height of the frenzy, the biggest decision I had to make was whether dinner would be sea bass à la Veracruzana or chicken with mole sauce."

Baron's report, which was circulated only internally, was harshly critical of the sourcing in two lead stories. He accused his colleagues of "repeating sensational reports . . . without confirming them," "questionable exercises in mind-reading," "passive voice . . . as a substitute

---

* On the day the Bowman profile ran, the *Times* also published an unbylined story explaining that the paper "normally shields the identity of complainants in sex crimes, while awaiting the courts' judgment about the truth of their accusations" but that the naming of Bowman in other news outlets, including a British tabloid, an American supermarket tabloid, and an NBC News report, "took the matter of her privacy out of [editors'] hands." Nine days later, the editors' note read: "An article on April 17 portrayed the life and background of the woman who has accused William Kennedy Smith of rape at the Kennedy estate in Palm Beach, Fla., on March 30. The article drew no conclusions about the truth of her complaint to the police. But many readers inferred that its very publication, including her name and detailed biographical material about her and her family, suggested that The Times was challenging her account. No such challenge was intended, and The Times regrets that some parts of the article reinforced such inferences. . . . The Times regrets its failure to include such a clear statement of the article's limits and intent. It remains The Times's practice to guard the identities of sex crime complainants so long as that is possible and conforms to fair journalistic standards. In cases of major political or civic interest, that practice needs to be continually reviewed. . . . Whenever possible, The Times intends to continue its longstanding practice of withholding the names of sex crime victims while informing its readers in the fullest and fairest ways about major cases."

for sourcing," "speculation," and "overstatement based on evidence seen or heard." But readers of the *Times* never learned of Baron's criticisms; indeed, for the most part the paper publicly defended its Lewinsky coverage.

Almost three years later, Lelyveld again had to ask one of the paper's insiders to conduct a review of reporting that had come under fire. This time the stories were about Wen Ho Lee, a Chinese American scientist who was fired from Los Alamos for security violations in March 1999. Over the next year and a half, the *Times* was often out in front of the story and just as often drew fire from media critics and Lee's defenders, who argued the *Times*'s coverage had resulted in a witch hunt.

When the din got too loud to ignore, Lelyveld asked Dave Jones, the former national editor who had competed with Lelyveld for the managing editor's position under Max Frankel, to review the paper's work. "Joe wanted me to just examine the coverage and tell him what I thought," says Jones. "It wasn't an assignment I was looking forward to. When Joe first came to me, I said, 'Let this cup pass from my lips.' But I felt an obligation to Joe and the paper, particularly since I was under contract."

Jones was allowed to interview anyone on staff, with the exception of the reporters who wrote the articles. At the end of his investigation, he told Lelyveld and Bill Keller, then the paper's managing editor, that too much credulity had been given to the prosecutors, that there was a lack of adequate balance in the coverage, and that the paper hadn't asked its science reporters to help with the coverage early in the story, which could have helped prevent problems that arose later. The lesson, Jones said, was to bring the full resources of the paper to bear on a story at the outset.

Lelyveld and Keller, Jones says, seemed to agree. They commissioned an editors' note, and on Tuesday, September 26, 2000, the paper ran a 1,600-word, unbylined, page two "From the Editors" column. It didn't satisfy anyone. The *Times* reporters and editors who had been involved in the project felt attacked, and the paper's critics were unappeased. The piece read, in part:

As a rule, we prefer to let our reporting speak for itself. In this extraordinary case, the outcome of the prosecution and the accusations leveled at this newspaper may have left many readers with questions about our coverage. That confusion—and the stakes involved, a man's liberty and reputation—convince us that a public accounting is warranted. . . . In those instances where we fell short of our standards in our coverage of this story, the blame lies principally with those who directed the coverage, for not raising questions that occurred to us only later. Nothing in this experience undermines our faith in any of our reporters, who remained persistent and fair-minded in their newsgathering in the face of some fierce attacks.

It was these types of stories that would, at other papers, be addressed by an ombudsman, a quasi-independent person on a newspaper's staff who investigated and reported on lapses in quality or judgment or addressed readers' complaints. Since the first ombudsman was appointed in the United States, at Kentucky's *Courier-Journal* and *Louisville Times* in 1967, many big-city papers, including *The Washington Post* and *The Boston Globe*, had installed some type of public representative. The *Times*, however, had always resisted, both out of a fear that an insider critiquing the paper's judgment would give ammunition to the paper's ideological critics and out of a philosophical belief that *all* editors and reporters are meant to serve the public.

When Raines decided to turn his reporters loose on Jayson Blair, he called Dave Jones at home and asked him to oversee the assignment. Jones was no longer under contract to the *Times* and, to his relief, was able to refuse. "This time," Jones says, "I did let the cup pass from my lips."

————

BACK IN THE business-department conference room, members of Bill Schmidt's office in news administration were guiding the reporters toward stories that deserved further examination. Using Blair's expense reports and phone records, Schmidt's staff had been able to determine several other instances when it seemed as if Blair had said he was on assignment but had remained in New York. Schmidt suggested the team pay particular attention to a dispatch from Hunt Valley, Maryland, where Blair had supposedly gone on March 24 to write about the parents of a marine who was missing in Iraq, and one from April 7 in Cleveland, Ohio, where Blair said he had interviewed Reverend Tandy Sloan, the father of a dead soldier. Liptak, meanwhile, was still talking with news administration over whether the team would have access to Blair's personnel files. As a former *Times* in-house attorney, he'd been on the other side of transactions like these many times. Now, the paper's lawyers were arguing that if they gave the reporting team access to Blair's personnel records, they'd be obligated to share those records with other news outlets as well, an argument Liptak thought was specious.

In the middle of the meeting, there was a knock on the door: Jayson Blair was on the phone and wanted to speak with Steinberg. Blair, ever mindful of the machinations of the media, told Steinberg he had a statement, and he was going to give it only to the *Times* and the Associated Press, thereby assuring it would be available to every paper in the country. "It was just a simple thing, expressing regret. We didn't even write about it," Steinberg says. "I just went back to the meeting and told them what he'd said."

From Portland, Barstow asked how many stories Blair had written, and the response that came back stunned everyone: over six hundred. "I said, 'This is nuts,' " Barstow says. " 'We need to be real about the magnitude here.' "

By Friday evening, the paper's top editors agreed to assign at least one more reporter to the project. Kramon called Abby Goodnough, a reporter on the paper's metro staff. "We needed someone else to help, at least just with the writing and wrapping it all together," says Kramon. "I was aware, too, that this was an all-male team." But Goodnough was out for the evening and didn't get the call until the next day. Kramon also asked Joan Nassivera, the weekend editor for the metro desk, if she would call Dan Barry, then a general assignment reporter. Barry cut his teeth at *The Providence Journal*, where he shared a George

Polk Award and a Pulitzer Prize for investigative projects. He grew up on Long Island, and the past several years had been overwhelming: He'd been diagnosed with cancer, had gone through chemotherapy and radiation treatments, and had written a memoir titled *Pull Me Up*. Barry can be intimidating to some people. Even Blair, who made a point of befriending as many people in the *Times*'s newsroom as possible was rattled by Barry; after Barry was warned about Blair's supposed after-hours snooping in the *Times*'s offices, the two reporters didn't speak for more than a year. But after Blair's story on Reverend Sloan, Barry had sent Blair a congratulatory note. "It was a good story," Barry says. "I told him so." Blair so disbelieved that he would ever get a congratulatory note from Barry, he thought someone had hacked into the reporter's computer and sent him the e-mail as a joke.

By the time Barry's name was put forward, he was already at home in New Jersey. Before Barry made up his mind, he called Jon Landman, the paper's metro editor, on his cellphone. Landman was at Yankee Stadium for the first game of a three-game series with the Oakland A's. "I hadn't had the assignment explained to me by Glenn or anyone else," Barry says. "I basically just wanted to know what the deal was. It sounded like kind of an internal affairs thing—like the assignment would involve going around and pulling people aside, including our superiors. And I wanted to be assured that this was going to be an endeavor of integrity."

"Anytime you're doing a project that might end up casting a really bad light on the people who run the joint . . . these issues come up," says Landman. "By that time, things were pretty poisonous. But I told him to do it. I thought it would be good for the paper. And I didn't think anyone would let the process be corrupted." At 11:30 that night, Dan Barry called back to the *Times* newsroom with the following message: "I'm in." The final team was in place.

ONE WEEK IN MAY

On Saturday, May 3, Dan Barry, David Barstow, Jonathan Glater, Glenn Kramon, Adam Liptak, Lorne Manly, and Jacques Steinberg met in their quarters on the eleventh floor of *The New York Times* to discuss their assignment. The marching orders were vague. The team was told to root out Blair's errors and correct the record. At that point, they still weren't sure if that meant they would be writing a story and supplying a list of corrections or just focusing on the errors. Jayson Blair had worked at the *Times* for four years. Were they expected to look at all his stories? Only the ones from the previous year? "We had no idea how deep this went," says Barstow, who had flown back the night before from Portland. "It was literally a reporting problem: How do you begin? How do you attack the story? So we decided to focus first on the work he did on the national staff. That's a more manageable series of time"—about six months—"and it was logical to us that if he was going to pull any funny business, it would be easier to do on a longer leash."

By that time, the research staff had printed out stacks of Blair's clips, and the five reporters started to divide them up. David Barstow and Adam Liptak dove into the sniper pile, Jonathan Glater took the stories Blair had written about the family of Jessica Lynch, and Jacques Steinberg grabbed the missing-soldiers pile. Dan Barry, meanwhile, was examining the arc of Blair's career and trying to piece together details about his rise in journalism. By now, the working assumption was that the final analysis would be in the paper the following Tuesday or Wednesday, May 6 or 7, and would run around 2,500 words.

Even that seemed like a tall order. "It was starting to sink in that this was going to be an extraordinarily draining experience," says Liptak. The subject of the project obviously made it unique, but it was atypical in other ways as well. Many investigative teams have experience working together. The reporters understand one another's strengths and weaknesses. The editors know when to push harder, when to ask more questions, and when to pull back. This team had no experience working together on what would prove to be an immensely tiring and harrowing project. Glenn Kramon and Lorne Manly had worked together on the business desk, and Glater and Steinberg were both business reporters (although Steinberg had just been transferred several weeks earlier). Neither Barry nor Barstow had worked with the men who would edit and shape their copy, and on an assignment like this everyone was going to need lots of support and protection. "That day, I remember my shoulders just slumping," Glater says as he recalls the piles of clips and the implications of the project. "And just thinking, This is going to be a really miserable task. And besides that, I worried it could be a crappy career move—if the article was something Gerald or Howell was unhappy with, that would or could be a really bad thing. It was going to be a very sensitive exercise."

The team decided its first task would be to try to reverse engineer Blair's national desk stories to determine if Blair had routinely collected details and quotations from secondary sources instead of firsthand reporting. The reporters were working with librarians, and as they went through Blair's articles, they'd mark anything that stood out—specific physical descriptions of a house or a living room, for example, or a particularly poignant quote. The librarians would then pull other clips written about the same subject and search for similar phrases or descriptions that might prove plagiarism. The examples kept piling up: On April 3, Blair had quoted Donald Nelson, a friend of Private Jessica Lynch's, reacting to a letter he had received from Lynch: "We just bawled like babies when we got the letter," Blair wrote. With a couple of clicks of the mouse, the librarians realized an Associated Press dispatch from April 2 had included the exact same quote. On April 7, Blair described a funeral service for Private First Class Brandon Sloan, the son of a Cleveland minister. Blair wrote: "The senior pastor, the Rev. Larry Howard, opened the prayer service by reminding the several hundred people who gathered that God was 'bigger than Hussein.' Mr. Sloan bowed his head and closed his eyes." Soon, the librarians found a March 29 article in *The Washington Post* in which Tamara Jones wrote: "Now, as the Rev. Larry Howard opened the prayer service for Brandy Sloan, reminding several hundred congregants that 'God is bigger than Hussein,' Tandy Sloan closed his eyes and bowed his head."

The reporters were also reaching out to *Times* reporters and photographers who had shared bylines with Blair or worked with him on assignment. Time and time again, photographers and other *Times* reporters told the team that, yes, they had been on location with Blair. But time and time again, it turned out that Blair had never actually met with them—he'd said he was on his cellphone down the block, or around the corner at a deli, or just driving away from a church. Haraz Ghanbari was a freelance photographer assigned to shoot an April 6 church service in Cleveland attended by the Reverend Sloan the day after his son had been pronounced dead in Iraq. Ghanbari called Blair fifteen times that day and reached him three of those times. Blair told Ghanbari he had momentarily left the church to get his cellphone fixed. Ghanbari took the pictures, and Blair filed the story, but they never met up. Only Ghanbari had actually been there.

———

JOURNALISM, its practitioners like to joke, is the perfect profession for people suffering from extreme attention deficit disorders. Reporters and editors can bore in on a subject for a week or a month or even a couple of years and then move on to something totally different. On a large daily paper like the *Times*, it's not unusual for a single career to include stints as a foreign correspondent, a science reporter, a metro editor, and an arts writer. One of the delights of working at an institution with ample resources is the chance to get out and actually explore, to see the country (or the world), to meet new people, to not be tethered to a desk all day. Reporters fight—sometimes viciously—for the chance to travel on assignment. Even after Steinberg's reporting had uncovered the likelihood that Jayson Blair had not gone to Texas, there was still an inability to fully accept that he might not have been traveling on assignment at all. Plagiarism was one thing. It might be the result of crumbling under deadline pressures, raging insecurity, or just bad writing chops—and in his brief career, Blair had repeatedly demonstrated just these tendencies. But not showing up at all? Then what was the point of being at the *Times*, of being a journalist?

Late on Sunday, May 4, the team began to discuss how their piece would progress. Barstow and Barry were especially vocal in their desire to have the piece be edited by someone other than Howell Raines or Gerald Boyd. They also said they thought a Tuesday deadline was unreasonable, as was a proposed length of 2,500 words. "Even by Sunday, the big drama for us was, Were they going to give us the space we need? Were they going to recuse themselves? And if they don't, what do we do?" Barstow says. "I don't think there was any doubt that if they tried to fuck with it, we would have walked." Kramon did all he could to reassure his colleagues. "I gave them my word that [Raines and Boyd] wouldn't influence the piece in any way," Kramon says. "That weekend, Barry was saying, 'They're gonna cook this.' And I just said, 'No, they won't. I'll lie in front of it.' "

On Monday, May 5, as the newsroom returned to its weekday rhythms, the team was moved from the eleventh floor to an empty room on the fourth floor where new hires were trained on the paper's computer system. Technically, the fourth floor is also part of the newsroom—it houses many of the paper's "soft news" sections, including the sports and culture departments. But it was removed from the din of the main third-floor newsroom and, more significantly, from the metro and national desks, where Blair did most of his work.

That morning, the team asked Howell Raines to send a formal staffwide e-mail asking reporters and editors to cooperate fully with any questions that arose. Raines refused. He told the reporters if anyone on staff had reservations about cooperating, they could come to him and he'd reassure them. For a team that was growing ever more certain that Raines would be a likely subject of their piece, it wasn't the answer they had hoped to hear.

By this point, the reporting team was realizing the degree to which the increasingly dysfunctional culture of *The New York Times* had affected Blair's career, especially in its latter stages. The *Times*—like every newspaper in the country—has always had its share of editors and reporters who feel disenfranchised or resentful. But under Howell Raines, the frustration that normally simmered just below the surface seemed to explode. Desk editors weren't speaking to one another. Reporters were almost at the point of open revolt. There was such fear of Raines's temper and dismissive attitude that some editors said they kept to themselves concerns about shoddy stories or reporters.

A newsroom where editors are scared to voice their concerns is a disaster waiting to happen. Newspapers are built on trust, and for that trust to survive there needs to be a robust and open exchange of information. Even worse is the newsroom where concerns are raised but ignored by the top editors. As the reporters were discovering, that seemed to be the case under Howell Raines. The more warning signs and public admonishments the reporters found scattered throughout Jayson Blair's files, the more they became aware of a culture that seemed to discourage an open exchange of information, an exchange that likely would have prevented Jayson Blair from ever getting assigned to the sniper story in the first place. That weekend, the reporters discovered an April 2002 e-mail from Jon Landman that seemed particularly damning. The e-mail, sent to newsroom administrators, including Bill Schmidt, said, "We have to stop Jayson from writing for the Times. Right now."

By the afternoon of Monday, May 5, "we were already seeing that there were going to be some pretty awkward questions that we were going to have to ask our bosses," Barstow says. "It was clear we had to address management issues," says Manly. "We all worked there. We knew the problems. The obvious question for the reader was, How the hell did this happen? Part of the answer was that Jayson was well liked in spite of his problems. But part of it was how things changed under Howell, how senior management felt frozen out, how a malaise set in and people just stopped fighting back." The team grew more nervous as the day went on and sought ways to protect itself and whatever it might uncover. That day, Glenn Kramon and Lorne Manly asked Howell Raines and Gerald Boyd to recuse themselves from the editing process. Boyd, without making any commitments one way or the other, said it was his fiduciary duty to read every story that went into the paper. Still, by Monday afternoon, Al Siegal was brought in to oversee the entire project.

To call the sixty-four-year-old Siegal a *Times* institution is an understatement. He was first hired at the *Times* in 1960 and, aside from a brief stint as a reporter, has worked mainly as a copy editor and then masthead editor. Since 1977, he has overseen usage and style throughout the paper. More than any other person—more than Arthur Sulzberger, more than Howell Raines, more than famed Washington correspondent R. W. "Johnny" Apple—Al Siegal is the institutional memory and conscience of *The New York Times*. He's in charge of the paper's corrections. He co-authored The New York Times *Manual of Style and Usage* and wrote the introduction to *Kill Duck Before Serving: Red Faces at* The New York Times, a compendium of the paper's most humorous errors. Siegal is the person editors go to when they want to know what the precedent is—if the *Times* ever let its columnists disavow a news story, for instance. And it was Al Siegal who named the special section created to cover the aftershocks of the September 11 attacks "A Nation Challenged." For Siegal, Howell Raines's tenure had been a happy change. He felt more vital than he had under Joe Lelyveld and appreciated the extent to which Raines made him realize he was needed in the day-to-day operations of the paper.

Siegal's seriousness, dry manner, and physical presence make him an intimidating force in the *Times*. He's a heavyset man, and he moves with purposeful intent. Not a small number of reporters and editors find him cutting and occasionally cruel, and his public dressings-down can make reporters and copy editors feel both superfluous and stupid. But no one doubts his love of *The New York Times*. After he was put in charge of the project, members of the reporting team began to petition Siegal, asking for a guarantee that neither Howell Raines nor Gerald Boyd would see the final product before it was printed. "They half begged and half demanded," Siegal says. Some reporters said they'd heard Blair had protectors among members of the masthead. The reporters tried to argue on precedent, drawing a comparison to the report filed by the ombudsman of *The Washington Post* in the wake of the 1981 Janet Cooke scandal, in which a young reporter was found to have invented an eight-year-old heroin addict about whom she wrote a Pulitzer Prize–winning feature story. Siegal told the reporters that Blair didn't have any protectors and that *The New York Times* didn't have an ombudsman. The story would be edited in whatever way the executive editor saw fit. "I don't seek that kind of autonomy," Siegal says. "The editor is the editor. But I told them I would do what I can do to see there is no tampering. I will throw my body in front of it."

By Monday night, the reporting team had begun to get a handle on the extent of the deception they were facing. That evening, in an almost five-hour meeting, Jacques Steinberg and David Barstow had met with members of the paper's news administration office. The team would not be given access to Blair's employment records; however,

Steinberg and Barstow were shown physical copies of Blair's expense reports, cellphone records, and filed receipts. They took copious notes.

For the rest of the night, the two reporters tried to triangulate Blair's whereabouts, comparing cellphone records, receipts, datelines, and stories. They realized he had handed in receipts from restaurants and coffee shops in Brooklyn during times when he said he was out of town—Blair submitted a receipt for Tutta Pasta, a Brooklyn restaurant, when he said he was eating with a law enforcement official in Washington. Blair's cellphone records occasionally indicated that a call was made from somewhere outside New York City—from Washington, for instance. Steinberg and Barstow realized that on the *Times*'s plan, a call from within the home calling zone would show up as blank, so they could determine when he had been making calls from New York City and when he had been elsewhere.

As they continued working through the night, the reporters realized that Blair had, in all likelihood, remained in New York City for most of the last six months, a period during which he was supposedly jetting across the country on assignment. Every time the reporters thought maybe Blair actually had been reporting from the field, they would soon realize they were wrong. "[Later that week], I interviewed [national editor] Jim Roberts about his confrontation with Jayson" about the Anguiano story, Barstow says. "Jim's telling me how Jayson described this red stucco house, how he described the two Jeeps out front and the rose garden. And how Jim asked for the photo of the house from the photo department, and that Jayson was right on every detail. I began to think maybe he was there." But it turned out that Blair had simply gained access to Merlin, the *Times*'s internal photo-archiving system. "It was like a horror movie where the killer is actually on the phone inside the house," Barstow says. "We realized he had actually been in the building when he said he was out in the field." Increasingly, the reporters were toggling between excitement over the incredible story they were uncovering and dismay at what Blair had done to their newspaper. "None of the reporters took glee in what we were finding," says Barry. "Having said that, though, there's no question that our journalistic juices were flowing. We had a big story, and we couldn't wait to tell it. The only questions were time and space."

At 9:00 p.m. on Monday, May 5, the team gathered in the page-one conference room for dinner. It was a ritual that would last all week. The conference room sits at the top of the staircase that connects the third and fourth floors. Several times every day, the masthead and desk editors meet here to discuss the next day's paper, with Al Siegal and the executive and managing editors presiding over the meetings. "We would talk a little bit about what was going on," Barry says of the team's dinners, which often featured large amounts of barbecue. "But we'd also just sit there with this sense of exhaustion."

After dinner, Steinberg and Barstow continued checking records. "It was excruciating," Steinberg says. "We're sitting there trying to fig- ure out—okay, if he had breakfast at this restaurant in Brooklyn, maybe he still had time to get to D.C. by the afternoon?" Adam Liptak and Jonathan Glater were making calls to the subjects of Blair's stories, and Dan Barry was prowling the newsroom, looking for people to in- terview. "I'd walk around, and it would be like, 'Uh-oh, here comes IAB,' " Barry says, referring to the police department's Internal Affairs Bureau. "Boy, did we laugh." Glater had to call several people who had lost family members in Iraq.

"That night, I couldn't sleep because I was so mad," he says. "I was calling this person up who suffered an incredible loss. And of all the inane and irrelevant things to talk about, I'm asking, 'Do you remem- ber talking to such-and-such a reporter?' It just felt gross."

"We were seeing indications that he was literally e-mailing the na- tional editor about his progress on a story from another floor in the building," Steinberg says. "That night, we're sitting there as a group, saying for the first time, 'Okay, this could be a gigantic fraud.' The ini- tial mandate—to correct the record—wouldn't be enough. To say he got this story wrong was not explaining who is this guy and how did he carry it out and how did he rise?" These were questions the reporters themselves desperately wanted answered.

It was hard not to be shocked. There had been numerous cases of journalistic malfeasance in the past—the *Times*'s Blood Brothers dispatch, say, or the *Post*'s Janet Cooke story. But with the exception of Stephen Glass, a *New Republic* reporter who had completely fabricated a number of feature stories in the late 1990s, there weren't any comparable cases of widespread, almost sociopathic fraud. And *The New Republic* is a rarefied political weekly that reached a tenth of the *Times*'s daily audience; Glass was writing feature stories about fringe groups he made up out of whole cloth. Blair was stitching his fraudulent accounts into some of the most heavily covered stories of the day. His "reporting" had been featured on the front page time and time again. It was moved on the *Times*'s newswires and reprinted by other papers around the country. The *Times* is the paper of record. What it writes is history. Blair had fabricated history.

Once again, the reporters struggled to find a way to describe the situation. Again, the only word they could think of was "surreal." "It was an amazing story," says Barstow. Blair's use of technology was also startling. "As we went on, we realized the level of journalistic crime here is much worse than some cribbed notes," Barry says. "He was literally not showing up. It was dawning on us that with cellphones and laptops, this was a whole new age in terms of journalism and integrity. [Blair] showed how someone could get away with this. And to explain this, we wanted to do a classic *New York Times* takeout."

At the start of Monday night, the five reporters had identified half a dozen stories they had questions about. After an all-night session, Steinberg and Barstow had identified thirty more stories that seemed to be problematic. On Tuesday, Manly reported to Al Siegal that the number of suspect stories was now up to thirty-six—almost exactly half of the seventy-three stories Blair had written since he had been temporarily reassigned to the national desk in October. "Siegal just said, 'Well, it looks like it's more than a half-page story, now, doesn't it?' " Manly says.

———

THE REST OF THE WEEK was marked by the growing tension between the reporting team and the paper's two top editors, as both sides realized the extent to which Raines and Boyd would necessarily figure in any accurate explanation of the Jayson Blair saga. "[Monday, May 5] was the one time Howell got really mad at me," says Kramon. In a meeting with Kramon and Manly, Raines barked out that he wanted to know why none of the reporters had asked to speak with him yet—if he was running the show, Raines said, he'd damn well have talked to the people in charge. "He was saying that I didn't know how to do an investigation, that I was doing it all wrong," Kramon recalls. "He was as angry as I've ever seen him.

"He was realizing it was getting out of control. This was a far worse problem than anyone had realized. But I just said, 'I've been through enough of these, and I'm gonna do it the way I always do it,' " Kramon says. "I knew the guys were already working eighteen-hour days. There was no way I was going back in that room and telling them I caved, because they just would have killed me." Unbeknownst to him, Raines's intractability was helping to strengthen the bond between the reporters and their editors. He was also painting his own portrait as the classically combative, defensive subject of an investigative report. Kramon stood firm. "I was used to having chief executives in my face [because of reporters' articles]," he says. "You have to ask yourself, Do you think you have a case? And if you do, you stick with it. And in this case it was pretty clear we had a case, so I just said to Howell, 'I'm working with a bunch of professionals. You've got to let us do our job.' "

Gerald Boyd, meanwhile, took the opposite tack and went out of his way to appear congenial. On Monday afternoon, he walked up the staircase to the fourth floor and walked into the room where the team was working. Everyone froze, and several of the reporters moved to cover their screens. Lorne Manly stood up and walked over to the door. "I just wanted to see if anyone needed anything," Boyd said. Manly walked him outside. Boyd later complained about what he interpreted as "adversarial body language." Manly explained to him that the reporters were just trying to do their job and were taken by surprise when he charged into the room.

"We knew they wanted us to talk to them," says Liptak. "In the ordinary course of things, you'd jump. But we wanted to move as methodically as we could from start to finish." Liptak agreed he would talk to Boyd. Jacques Steinberg, who'd already dealt with Arthur Sulzberger as part of his beat, would talk to the publisher. And Barry and Barstow would interview Raines.

Liptak met with Boyd, more to appease the managing editor than to ask specific questions. "I found him to be very defensive, in a very unseemly way," Liptak says. "It made me think that he viewed Jayson's story and his own as quite intertwined. He seemed to feel there was a whole lot riding on this. He kept ticking off all the things he and Jayson didn't do together. 'We didn't have lunch, he never came to see me in my office, we never talked about his career.' For him to be running for cover like that struck me as very unbecoming. The reality is, he *did* play a very significant role in Jayson's advancement."

Dan Barry scheduled an appointment with Raines. "I just went and said, 'I hear you have something you wanted to say,'" Barry says. Raines was welcoming and friendly. He focused on Blair's record of corrections—how corrections weren't necessarily a good indication of a reporter's progress, how some of the corrections were due to caption errors or simple misspellings. "We had already gone so far beyond that," says Barry. "But I just heard him out."

As the week went on, the reporters continued interviewing their bosses. Jonathan Glater had now teamed up with Adam Liptak to talk to Boyd. It wasn't a job he was eager to do. "When we were talking about who was going to talk to whom in the newspaper, I was not particularly eager to interview either Howell or Gerald," he says. "As a young reporter who had not been at the *Times* that long, I would be interviewing them, and at the same time they would be evaluating me." But Glater agreed it made more sense for both reporters to be present. They interviewed Boyd on Wednesday and again on Friday.

By this point, the reporters had zeroed in on the decision to send Blair to help cover the sniper shootings around Washington, D.C., as a crucial moment in their story. Liptak and Glater pressed Boyd repeatedly: Had he been the one to recommend Blair to Jim Roberts? "Several times, in a very bureaucratic and disingenuous way, he said something along the lines of how this had been a consensus decision and he had been the most senior person in the room," Liptak says. Blair's name had first come up during a meeting that included Boyd, associate managing editor Andrew Rosenthal, and Roberts. "Everyone seems to remember it being Gerald's call," Liptak says. "I don't think even Gerald disputes that. But he's holding on to this notion that there's a consensus. The *Times* is not a consensus-decision type of place. Certainly not at that juncture in its history." Boyd seemed to be formulating a defense that would enable him to hold on to his job rather than helping the reporters come up with the most accurate picture possible.

Steinberg, meanwhile, began talking to Arthur Sulzberger on Thursday. That day, Steinberg told the paper's publisher that there were at least three dozen stories by Jayson Blair that contained plagiarized or fabricated material. "I was calling him as a source, and I asked him to keep this to himself. I felt strongly and the team felt strongly that we as a newspaper needed to be the first to report this number," Steinberg says. Sulzberger, Steinberg says, was unequivocally accepting of that arrangement.

———————

ON MARCH 1, 2003, C. J. Chivers, a reporter and former marine, sent metro editor Jon Landman an e-mail from Iraq, where he was stationed. Chivers had spent weeks at ground zero after September 11 and had distinguished himself as one of the paper's shining talents. "I have a story," Chivers wrote to Landman. He continued:

> [Photographer] Ruth Fremson and [reporter] David Rohde showed up here a few days ago . . . and, no shit, David had two partial copies of the paper. It was quite a smuggle, because the papers provided a chance to show our translators and drivers the thing we make very [*sic*] day. I handed the larger edition to my translator, who is a young MD, and after a minute or two of deliberate study he snatched the

Metro section and started to flip through it at this quick speed, amazed. *"All this news is from New York,"* he said. *"Just from New York?"*

Then he used a Kurdish word, twice: *"Zora! Zora!"*

Roughly translated, it means "So much! So much!"

He's been with us for a while, and he more or less knew that The Times was special, but the page-by-page, tactile experience of reading the broadsheet rounded him out, and for a while after his face was really full of something that looked like pride. It was a good moment for me, because I've been a bit lost in my notes and isolation here, and it brought me back, throughout the day, to remembering what a whole bunch of our readers think. . . .

Jon, I haven't seen the English language paper in months, and suddenly I was reading this one. It was a jolt. I know that people who put this thing out everyday [*sic*] probably take it for granted, but it was a moment of discovery for my translator and rediscovery for me, and it's incredible how just this one day of production made a lot of us over here feel pretty fucking good.

Chivers sent the e-mail during a particularly bleak period for *Times* staffers. Landman forwarded the e-mail to Howell Raines, and the two men decided to print up T-shirts for the metro staff, with ZORA! ZORA! on the front and SO MUCH! SO MUCH! on the back.

By Thursday, May 8, the Blair team had been working around the clock for four days. The fourth-floor room they were working in was unventilated. "My shirt was getting rancid. My teammates were complaining," says Barstow. After printing up the ZORA! ZORA! shirts, Landman had given one to Barstow, which he stowed away in his desk. On Thursday, desperate for some clean clothes, Barstow walked down to his regular desk, got the shirt out of his drawer, and put it on. But the newsroom had by that time become so divided and suspicious that even Barstow's change of clothes was seen as a significant, cloaked message. "I'm walking through the newsroom, and I'm starting to get this weird vibe," Barstow says. "At that point so much of the staff was convinced of this Landman-versus-Howell thing that some people interpreted my wearing the shirt as my giving a shout-out to the Landman faction." That day, he and Dan Barry went to a Gap store in Times Square to buy fresh clothes for their Friday interview with Raines.

The reporting team wasn't getting much sleep, and the pressure to produce a story was mounting. On Thursday night, May 8, the reporters met in the page-one conference room to map out their assignment. It was still somehow supposed to come in somewhere between 2,500 and 4,000 words. Instead of quibbling over word counts, Glenn Kramon told the reporters to just write as much as they felt was needed. If the story deserved the space, Kramon said, it would get it. Time, too, was becoming an issue. The reporters knew that Raines was hoping to get the story into Sunday's paper, which meant they'd need to produce a draft by Friday night. Because the *Times* produces a bull-dog edition of its Sunday edition that's available on New York City newsstands on Saturday evening, they'd lose almost a full day of reporting time.

Dan Barry and David Barstow both live in suburban New Jersey, but for most of that week they remained in Times Square. One night, they caught a catnap for a couple of hours in a small windowless reception area to one side of the elevator bank on the third floor. Even when they tried to grab some sleep in a hotel, they were stymied. On Friday morning, Dan Barry wrote until almost 4:00 a.m. and then was going to trudge over to a recently opened Westin hotel on Forty-third Street. When he got to the *Times*'s lobby, he couldn't leave because the floor was being waxed. Finally, he was allowed to tiptoe out and walked the half block west to the hotel. "I get to the front desk, and the guy says he can't check me in right away because the computers were down," Barry says. "So I just sat there, just so tired, until after five in the morning. And then finally they let me in, and I slept for an hour and a half and came back to the office." The Westin had recently introduced a new feature, the Heavenly Bed. It included a custom-designed pillow-top mattress, three sheets, and a down blanket. Even though—or maybe because—Barry slept in his for only ninety minutes, he said it more than lived up to its billing.

Dan Barry and David Barstow delivered a preliminary draft of the story on Friday morning, May 9. At 9:00 a.m., they were due for their final interview with Howell Raines. It would be the last time they would talk to him before they filed their story the next day. "We did not look like two professionals in the mother ship," says Barry. "I'm completely unshaven," says Barstow. "We looked like two hungover, mangy dogs."

By then, Raines's demeanor had changed. Earlier in the week, he had been comfortable with the explanation that Jayson Blair was a sociopathic reporter who would have been impossible to catch under any circumstances. By Friday, as the team's understanding of the situation grew, Raines's own self-confidence had waned. Yes, Blair was a sociopath. But there had been ample warnings, and at times Raines and Boyd seemed pointedly to ignore those warnings because of their disdain for the editors who were doing the warning. Raines was taking dozens of media calls a day, and on some level he must have realized that he was fighting for his job. At 9:00 a.m., when Barry and Barstow showed up at his door, he had still not said whether or not he'd edit the final piece.

"At that point in time, given how tired we were, I felt like I just found my foundation in the core principles of journalism," Barstow says. "We were blocking and tackling, reverting to the basic essence of who you are when you go in to talk to a powerful person." Barry agrees. "There was little sense of us talking to our superior," he says. "All three of us had our game faces on."

The two reporters each had his own legal pad on which he'd listed topics to address. How well did Raines know Jayson Blair? What was Raines's connection to Blair's girlfriend, Zuza Glowacka? How had Raines responded to complaints from the federal prosecutor about Blair's sniper coverage? Had Raines ever seen Blair's personnel files? Had he been aware of his problems on the metro staff? Had he seen the infamous Landman e-mail? Had he signed off on Blair's promotion to the national staff?

"He did all the things you typically see in those kinds of interviews," says Barstow. "Sometimes he used Rumsfeldian intimidation. Sometimes it was Clintonian hairsplitting." Raines had his own written notes, and he referred to them frequently. "This," Barry says, "could not have been fun for him."

The interview lasted nearly three hours. At the end, Barry and Barstow told the executive editor of *The New York Times* the extent of Blair's deception—that of the seventy-three stories Blair had written between October 2002 and May 2003, at least thirty-six had substantial problems. "He was floored," Barry says. "He didn't know that."

As dismaying as the investigation was for the team, they appreciated a good story and were proud of their work. "In the piece, we were already heading in the direction of this being a low point in the 152-year history of the paper, and this was our scoop," Barry says. "We didn't want [Raines] to deliver it to our competitors." The reporters knew when the news broke that Blair had falsified dozens of stories, it would become one of the biggest journalistic scandals ever. They also felt sure that the fiercely competitive Raines would protect the scoop for the paper he ran, even if it was a personally painful exclusive. "We're walking out the door," Barry says, "and we tell him we'd hope he'd keep it to himself. He assured us that he would keep this as a *Times* exclusive. Then we shook hands and walked back up to the fourth floor."

Raines had also finally agreed not to read the report unless there was a last-minute need. Sulzberger, too, had called Siegal to ask if there was any reason he needed to see the piece before publication.

"Clearly, if you're putting a story in the paper that bears upon the organization being dysfunctional and is going to reflect badly on its top leadership, a case can be made that the publisher should see it ahead of time, or the executive editor, or both," Siegal says. "But given the climate of opinion and morale in this newsroom, I think they saw value in being able to say, 'Let the chips fall where they may.' At that time, I was conscious of the nervousness of the reporting team, which had asked me several times and at many stages, 'Are you sure that what we write is going to go in the paper?' And I told them, 'What you write is going to go into the paper if I think it is accurate, responsible, and proportional.' "

Siegal asked assistant managing editor Craig Whitney and deputy

managing editor John Geddes to read the finished piece with him.
They decided that if all three men did not agree unanimously that
the report was responsible and complete, they would either get it
fixed or go to Raines with their concerns. On Friday night, the three
assistant managing editors read a draft of the piece. There were several small holes that needed filling, a handful of explanations still
needed. But these were minor issues. "The team immediately agreed
[to the fixes]," Siegal says. "There weren't many problems with the
piece." There was no need, the men decided, for Howell Raines to
see it before publication.

———————

THAT FRIDAY, MAY 9, at 6:00 p.m., Raines appeared on PBS's *News-
Hour*, where he spoke with former *Times* correspondent Terence Smith.
Raines wore glasses and a striped tie, and he looked puffy and ex-
hausted. He described the formation of the reporting team:

> We also told this team that we wanted them to have full access to all
> executives of the *Times*, including me, and to the information that
> we possessed. And we also assured them that their findings would go
> in the paper in an independent way. My plan is to read this story for
> the first time on Sunday—if they're able to get it ready in time for
> Sunday—along with the rest of our readers.

Smith then asked Raines to explain how Blair's deceptions had been
discovered and what else was being done to examine his work. Raines
answered:

> One of the things that we have asked this reporting group to do is to
> work through the record. They tell me, in the course of interview-
> ing me today, two of our reporters told me that they had already
> found 36 instances of fabrication. As I say, we're committed to fully
> disclosing every circumstance of this.

On the fourth floor, Jacques Steinberg's phone rang. It was a colleague from the Washington bureau who said he had no idea there had been so many stories. When Steinberg asked him what he meant, he repeated what Raines had just said on TV. "I said to the other guys, 'You're not going to believe this, but Howell just went on PBS and gave them the thirty-six number,' " Steinberg says.

Barstow and Barry were furious. They flew out the door and bounded down the stairs connecting the third and fourth floors, looking for Raines. They never found him and eventually calmed down. "It was probably good we didn't find him right then," says Barstow. "He was exhausted. We were exhausted. For all we know, he just forgot about his promise."

All that night and into the next morning, the team banged out the final version of their story. They knew many on the paper's staff were hoping for a takedown of the paper's leadership. "It was pretty palpable that week that there were a sizable number of people on *The New York Times* that wanted this to be the story of Howell Raines," Barstow says. "This one incident at long last revealed all the pent-up grievances about Howell's tenure as executive editor. And it wasn't that we didn't feel this was a valid subject of inquiry down the road, but on this story, our assignment was to explain Jayson Blair. And even just writing about how he carried all this out was going to mean we were pushing our six-thousand-word limit [for two of the *Times's* inside pages]. It was ludicrous to try to attempt to do a broader exposé on Howell Raines and all the crosscurrents of resentments—arguments and counterarguments about fights with other editors and his star system. But that was what a sizable contingent in the newsroom wanted." Barry agrees. "We weren't looking to effect regime change," he says. "And we didn't harbor any personal animus for Gerald and Howell. In my case, at least, those two men treated me well."

"We all in some way love the institution," says Barstow. "It's a complicated love, but there was a sense that the best service we could do here was use all of our combined skills to do the most complete job we could humanly do.

"I remember thinking before that the great lesson in American history is that the cover-up is worse than the crime. We wanted this work to represent the fullest picture possible. I was astonished at what had happened to [the accounting firm] Arthur Andersen—here's this great institution, and it is no more because of shredded documents. We wanted to make sure that didn't happen here."

THE *TIMES'S* REPORT

On Saturday, May 10, Catherine Mathis was at her weekend home in New Jersey. Mathis, the *Times*'s relentlessly cheery spokeswoman, openly admits she has "drunk the Kool-Aid" when it comes to *The New York Times*. Unlike previous *Times* spokespeople, Mathis doesn't treat media reporters as if they are an annoyance, and she doesn't act as though she's doing favors when she parcels out information.

Like the rest of the media world, Mathis was waiting for the *Times*'s story on Jayson Blair to hit. At 1:00 p.m. that Saturday, pieces of the *Times* report began to be posted on the Web. The completed version, posted soon after, clocked in at 7,102 words, or two full pages of the Sunday paper. Two more pages and another 6,439 words were spent correcting errors in Blair's stories.

"A staff reporter for The New York Times committed frequent acts of journalistic fraud while covering significant news events in recent months," the main piece began. It went on:

The widespread fabrication and plagiarism represent a profound betrayal of trust and a low point in the 152-year history of the newspaper. The reporter, Jayson Blair, misled readers and Times colleagues with dispatches that purported to be from Maryland, Texas and other states, when often he was far away, in New York. He fabricated comments. He concocted scenes. He lifted material from newspapers and wire services. . . .

Every newspaper, like every bank and every police department, trusts its employees to uphold central principles, and the inquiry found that Mr. Blair repeatedly violated the cardinal tenet of journalism, which is simply truth. . . .

The Times inquiry also establishes that various editors and reporters expressed misgivings about Mr. Blair's reporting skills, maturity and behavior during his five-year journey from raw intern to reporter on national news events. . . .

The investigation suggests several reasons Mr. Blair's deceits went undetected for so long: a failure of communication among senior editors; few complaints from the subjects of his articles; his savviness and his ingenious ways of covering his tracks. Most of all, no one saw his carelessness as a sign that he was capable of systematic fraud.

Mr. Blair was just one of about 375 reporters at The Times; his tenure was brief. But the damage he has done to the newspaper and its employees will not completely fade with next week's editions, or next month's, or next year's.

"It's a huge black eye," said Arthur Sulzberger Jr., chairman of The New York Times Company and publisher of the newspaper, whose family has owned a controlling interest in The Times for 107 years. "It's an abrogation of the trust between the newspaper and its readers."

The piece was an excoriation of the Jayson Blair saga as well as an explanation, but at its heart the *Times* story was a great yarn. It featured massive fraud, a charismatic con man, and a powerful institution brought to its knees. The piece also would serve as a road map for much of what was to come. It flicked at the problems that had arisen since Howell Raines took over the *Times*, touched on Boyd and Blair's perceived relationship, and addressed the widespread frustration of midlevel editors at the *Times*.

Catherine Mathis's home phone began ringing almost immediately. Reporters from *Time*, *Newsweek*, *The Washington Post*, and the *Los Angeles Times* called. *The Wall Street Journal* was doing a story for Monday. The TV networks wanted someone to go on the air. Was there any circumstance under which Howell Raines would resign? Was the *Times* going to cover the story further? Mathis wasn't sure of the answer to many of the questions she was facing. Like many in the *Times*'s newsroom, she had learned that Howell Raines didn't much enjoy taking advice from others, nor did he always share his intentions with others. Mathis struggled along the best she could.* No, she said, Raines wasn't planning on resigning. And the story would be covered if there were important new developments.

Although Dan Barry and David Barstow had written most of the main story, there was no front-page byline. Instead, the story included a credit box on its inside pages that read, "This article was reported and written by Dan Barry, David Barstow, Jonathan D. Glater, Adam Liptak and Jacques Steinberg. Research support was provided by Alain Delaqueriere and Carolyn Wilder." This absence of a byline on the paper's front page contributed to the sense that the *Times* report was an institutional response to an internal crisis. Unlike, say, David Shaw's Staples Center report in the *Los Angeles Times*, or the ombudsman's report in *The Washington Post* following the Janet Cooke fiasco, there was no explanation of how the report evolved or who in the newsroom was allowed to see it before publication.

On Sunday, May 11, the media storm erupted. Many of the major dailies across the country wrote about Blair; many focused on the *Times*'s claim that the Blair scandal was a "low point" in the paper's

---

* In his May 2004 *Atlantic* article, Raines would claim that he hadn't bothered to read the story when it was first available on the Internet on Saturday, nor had he bothered to read it in that evening's bulldog print edition of the *Times*. Instead, he wrote, he read the piece on Sunday, "in sections" while on a shad-fishing excursion on the Delaware River.

152-year history. That Sunday, *The Denver Post*, the *San Francisco Chronicle*, and *The Tennessean* all ran items on fraudulent Blair stories that they had run after getting them from the *Times*'s newswire. (The coverage was not without its unintentional humor. The *Orlando Sentinel* ran a breathless editorial titled "Squander Credibility and All Is Lost." Earlier in the paper, the *Sentinel* had run an item on Blair—who had had errors in less than 20 percent of his articles for the *Times*—under this headline: "Most of Reporter's Articles Had Problems, New York Times Says.")

By Monday morning, the *Times*'s report and rumors about the mood inside the paper were dominating New York's media world. Reaction in the newsroom was mixed. Some felt the four-page examination hadn't attached sufficient blame to Raines and Boyd; others felt the entire exercise had been one of solipsistic overkill; many didn't know what to think. Outside the *Times*, pundits eagerly tried to poke holes in the *Times*'s account, usually without taking into consideration the reporting team's assigned mission or its intense time constraints.

Considerable attention was also paid to the role of race in the Jayson Blair affair. Partisans on both sides of the debate immediately began to use the incident to further their agendas, with some African American journalist associations proclaiming Blair's race had nothing to do with his ascension at the paper, and opponents of affirmative-action programs blaming the entire incident on a misguided effort to diversify. The reality wasn't so simple. Blair's career at the *Times* had undeniably been shaped by his race—he'd initially been recruited into a minority internship program—but the vagaries of his career under Howell Raines's tenure had more to do with the favoritism and factionalism that had gripped the paper.

Whatever people's reactions, it was clear the story would become the most talked about subject of the day. The *Times*'s report had been published in one of the first truly quiet news cycles since September 11: The attack on Iraq had concluded, the situation on the ground had not yet descended into chaos, and the next year's presidential campaign had not yet moved into high gear. There was no national drama like the sniper case. Raines, and the *Times*, moved into that vacuum, if only for a week or two. Still, for all the speculative frenzy, there was almost no discussion about whether or not Raines would step down. He was seen as too powerful, his Pulitzer sweep too recent.

On Monday, after being prompted by one of his editors, Howell Raines came by the fourth-floor training room the reporting team had been using as its headquarters and perfunctorily thanked the team for the job they did. Boyd also came by and shook the reporters' hands. "We were very proud of the piece," says Liptak. "And at the same time we probably weren't sufficiently sensitive to the fact that all sorts of people had wanted it to be about Howell, or they wanted it to talk about race—I don't think they read it for itself." The team quickly discovered the extent to which their reactions to Blair's deceptions, and to the newsroom culture that enabled them, were out of sync with the rest of the newsroom; the reporters had had, after all, a full week to make sense of the details in the piece, details their colleagues were just now beginning to process.

At the same time, the team was wondering about their futures. Says Barstow, "We were all half waiting for the time when we'd be told, 'We really need a seasoned journalist to lead the resurrection in the Westchester Weekly section. That's really the paper's highest priority right now, and you're our guy. And by the way, you start on Monday.' " Raines was, after all, known to hold grudges. "We were sort of wondering," says Liptak, "who was going to end up at large-type weekly."

Barstow remembered all too well what happened to Tim Golden, a onetime investigative reporter who butted heads with Raines: One day, Golden came in to work and was told he would be reassigned to the *Times*'s website. Instead, he quit. And, of course, Kevin Sack's byline was no longer appearing in the *Times*.

Before they could get too nervous about their futures, however, Raines said he wanted to meet with the five reporters individually. Adam Liptak went first. Did Liptak, Raines asked, have anything else he wanted to talk about? Liptak started talking about how closer monitoring of the paper's expense reports could not only help keep track of reporters but might also give a sense of whether or not a particular story was worth the expenditure. Raines's eyes glazed over.

Then Liptak said that Raines needed to address his troops. Raines said that he'd be doing that in the coming days. "I've made the decision as a leader that the best way I can manage this is in small groups," he said. Liptak cut him off. "I remember feeling a little surprised at myself that I had the nerve to say this to him. He can be a scary man," Liptak says. "I said, 'No, Howell, you need to get out there in front of every-body.' He just said he had made his decision."

That afternoon, Raines called Joyce Purnick, Clyde Haberman, and Floyd Norris, three of the newsroom's most senior members, and asked to meet them for dinner so they could discuss the mood at the paper. Purnick wrote the paper's "Metro Matters" column. She had served as the paper's metro editor before Landman and was married to Max Frankel, a former *Times* executive editor. Like Purnick, Haberman has also worked at the *Times* for a quarter century, most recently as the au-thor of "NYC," one of the paper's biweekly metro columns. Norris had spent the least amount of time on the paper—he'd been at the *Times* for fourteen years and was the paper's marquee business columnist. Norris and Purnick had both worked with Raines on the editorial board, and Haberman and Raines had known each other since the 1970s, when they both covered the Carter campaign, Haberman for the *New York Post*, Raines for the *St. Petersburg Times*.

That afternoon, Norris walked around the newsroom talking to re-porters. "I thought I should get some feel for what the newsroom atti-tude was," Norris says. "I was surprised. People had read some of the preexisting critiques of the Raines management into that piece—that he played favorites or didn't pay sufficient attention to his subordi-nates."

Norris was doing just the kind of pulse taking that Raines, the life-long political reporter, seldom did as executive editor. During his time on the editorial board, Raines made a point of keeping in contact with members of the newsroom, asking key people to lunch once or twice a year. Once he got to the newsroom, Raines generally stayed secluded in his corner office. "There's a famous line attributed to Jack Kennedy, that the White House is not a good place to make new friends," Norris says. "It occurred to me that that was also an issue for executive editors." "Howell never worked the room," says Haberman. "And he was starting without any roots."

Before he left for dinner, Raines sent out an e-mail to the paper's staff. It was more than two pages long and single-spaced. "I have not written or spoken directly to you in the last week because I wanted our reporting and editing team to have the time and freedom to do this valuable work," Raines wrote. He then announced the formation of a committee to examine the Jayson Blair fiasco and recommend changes, to be led by Al Siegal. "It will shape its own agenda," Raines wrote, and Siegal himself would choose the members.

Raines also said he wanted to talk to his staff. "I will try to meet with every interested member of the newsroom staff, in groups of several dozen at a time, on the 11th floor. The collective wisdom of these groups helped prepare me for the enormous challenges of my first 18 months on the job. Now I ask you for the same kind of input and support as we repair the damage inflicted on us and broaden our goals for the future."

That night, Raines and the three columnists went to Esca, a seafood restaurant on Forty-third Street, two blocks west of the Times building. It was one of Raines's regular spots, and the chef came over to greet the group. But it was not a happy meal. "We hit [Raines] pretty squarely with a bill of particulars," Haberman says.

The next day, Raines met with David Barstow. Barstow was already upset with Raines's reaction to the story. "There was a sense that he just didn't get it," Barstow says. "Small group meetings are one of the worst forums for candid discussion. They're designed more for him to talk than listen. This was already crisis management." Barstow walked into Raines's office around eleven o'clock on Tuesday morning, four days after he and Barry had had their final interview with him.

"His whole demeanor had completely changed," Barstow says. "He was more slumped in his posture. He just looked rocked." Raines,

Barstow thought, was looking for a way to move forward, but for the first time in his tenure he felt unsure about his footing. "It was upsetting. On the one hand to see him so unsure, and on the other hand he still had to come to grips with what this was. He had to have good information."

"I wish I had good news for you," Barstow said. "But I don't." Just as he had on Friday, Barstow brought in a yellow legal notepad. This time, he would show Raines what he was writing. The first two words were "losing newsroom."

Barstow had long admired Raines—both men were veterans of the *St. Petersburg Times*, and when Barstow joined *The New York Times*, Raines invited him to lunch. But now, says Barstow, "too many people were tiptoeing around the guy and not telling him what they really thought. I wanted to walk into his office and hit him over the head with a two-by-four and make him understand what was going on." Barstow went through his list: People thought Raines was more interested in getting buzz than being right; reporters were convinced good stories were doled out on the basis of personal relationships; senior editors were afraid to speak up. Raines took notes in a black-and-white marble-faced notebook.

Barstow also told Raines he needed editors who were willing to stand up to him, and he needed editors in his inner circle who had more experience with investigative reporting. Raines, Boyd, and Andrew Rosenthal, the newsroom's top three editors, all came from a political reporting background. "That's a different thing from covering law enforcement at a high level," Barstow said. "When Jayson came up with five anonymous sources in less than a week, that should have rung a bell." Raines and Barstow were both sitting at a small, circular table in front of the executive editor's desk, and as Barstow went on, Raines seemed to physically shrink into his chair.

Barstow also told Raines he had to meet with the staff as a group. "When we won seven Pulitzers, we celebrated as a group in this newsroom," Barstow said. "That was a high point. This is a low point, and it needs a symmetrical response. You need to take advantage of one of your real gifts—you can be a great speaker."

Raines asked whether it was too late, whether the toothpaste could be put back in the tube.

"I don't know," Barstow said.

After about forty-five minutes, Raines said he had to attend to something. Barstow left. Twenty minutes later, Raines called Barstow back into his office.

"What are my strengths?" Raines asked. "What do people like about me?"

Barstow told Raines he was a great journalist. He reminded Raines of the blistering, emotional editorial he had written when Robert McNamara had published his memoir. "You have a voice, and people need to hear that voice now," Barstow said.

"I like the guy," Barstow says. "I like his passion for journalism. I like his balls, I like his guts. And I liked the basic idea of going like hell after the big stories. . . . What I was saying was not said to stick it to him, it was said because I wanted to see him survive. To do that, he needed good information, and I didn't think he was getting it. And if this pissed him off or if he took offense, I didn't give a fuck."

That afternoon, at 2:31 p.m., Raines sent out another staffwide e-mail message:

As mentioned in yesterday's memo, I have spent much of the last two days conferring with the reporters and editors who wrote the story on Jayson Blair in the Sunday paper. Their advice and those of some of our senior reporters made it clear that we need a meeting of our entire staff, rather than the series of smaller meetings announced yesterday. With apologies for the lateness of this message, I am canceling the meetings we had scheduled for this afternoon. Arthur, Gerald and I have decided to have a town hall meeting tomorrow at a time and place to be announced as soon as a venue is secured.

Writing about this period of time for *The Atlantic*, Raines said he knew, following the publication of the May 11 report, that he would probably lose his job. "I knew at that point," he wrote of his reaction after initially reading the piece, "that I was unlikely to survive."* If this was true, it wasn't the impression he was giving any of the people he was speaking with, and his frenzied activity over the next several weeks did not feel to anyone who encountered him like that of a man resigned to his fate.

---

* Raines went on to fault the article's authors for his likely demise: "The article did not pursue the one area of reporting that might have worked in my favor—how and why critical information about Jayson never reached me," he wrote, showing once again a total lack of understanding about the depth of anger and frustration in the *Times*'s newsroom.

A Fateful Gathering

The town hall meeting on Wednesday, May 14, 2003, was another in a long series of unprecedented events for *The New York Times*. Because the meeting was scheduled so hastily and on a Wednesday—the traditional day for matinee performances—the company wasn't able to secure one of the Broadway theaters it usually borrowed for companywide gatherings. Instead, the *Times* rented out the Loews Cineplex Astor Plaza movie theater (bumping the afternoon showing of the John Cusack–Ray Liotta thriller *Identity*), located at 1515 Broadway, around the corner from the paper's headquarters. Unlike theaters, movie houses don't have stage entrances, and Arthur Sulzberger, Howell Raines, and Gerald Boyd were forced to endure what became a sort of perp walk for photographers and TV crews, as they came in through the theater's front door. All three men smiled grimly for the cameras. Boyd, wearing a dark suit and tie, looked uncomfortable and stiff—"like an undertaker," one *Times* executive quipped. Raines and Sulzberger, both of whom were tieless, strove for a common touch.

Here, finally, was the irresistible visual that television had been lacking. Up to this point, TV news reports on the scandal tended to feature a single stock photo of Blair, recycled footage of Sulzberger and Raines, or still shots of the *Times*'s May 11 front page to illustrate the story. Now there was a farcical mob scene to record. By 2:00 p.m., a half hour before the meeting was scheduled to begin, the sidewalk in front of the theater was jammed with dozens of reporters, photographers, and news cameras. Two pairs of uniformed security guards manned the theater's front doors, checking employees' identification badges as they entered—every *Times* employee was invited, and the paper's dozens of bureaus listened in by speakerphone. Sheila Sharkey, a tourist from Northern Ireland, walked over to check out the scrum as she was making her way through Times Square. "You're kidding," she said when told what was going on. "These aren't movie stars?" A protester wearing a mask of Mohammed Saeed al-Sahaf—the Iraqi information minister known as "Baghdad Bob"—held up a sign that read FORMER NEW YORK TIMES REPORTER WILL LIE FOR FOOD. "Hi, my name is Howell, and I'm a liar," he chanted as each new wave of employees marched by. As if all this weren't humiliating enough, the day before, the *Times* had confirmed that the U.S. Attorney's Office for the Southern District of New York had requested details about Blair's deceptions to determine whether "[Jayson Blair's] reporting conduct violated the law."

No outside reporters were allowed in the Loews theater that day, and the *Times* brass stressed that the forum should be considered a private affair. Even Jacques Steinberg, who would write an account of the meeting for the next day's *Times*, was forced to remain outside the theater along with the rest of the media reporters covering the event. (Lorne Manly, who would edit Steinberg's piece, was allowed inside.) But the traditional solicitude the *Times*'s employees felt about the paper—or at least their usual fear of openly defying their bosses' wishes—had disappeared. *Times* reporters, including one former metro editor, furiously scribbled notes, not only to relay to Steinberg but also for media reporters around the country. At least one person tape-recorded the meeting. Al Siegal, a symbol of the *Times* establishment if there ever was one, took care to sit next to a young African American reporter. "I wanted to show solidarity with a class of people in the newsroom who had real reason to be concerned about their career prospects," he says. The meeting had been called to clear the air about the deceptions of Jayson Blair, but the presence of Raines, Boyd, and Sulzberger onstage, facing more than five hundred of the paper's employees, created an us-versus-them atmosphere.

For years, Sulzberger had been criticized for failing to convey an appropriate level of seriousness and gravitas in just these types of large employee forums. A decade earlier, onstage at another companywide meeting, he had told a forty-year-old employee who was concerned about the company's 401(k) plan, "You're too young to be worried about that," a comment that did nothing to placate the anxious employee but did advance the notion that Sulzberger was cut off from both his employees and the real world. From the onset of the May 14 meeting, the staff was both restless and craving reassurance: It wouldn't take much to tip them in either direction. Sulzberger, who for years had struggled to make his jokes seem funny without veering into the nasty or inappropriate, didn't get off to an auspicious start. He began the meeting by taking a small stuffed moose out of a bag and tossing it over to Raines, who seemed embarrassed by his boss's awkward gesture. The moose, Sulzberger explained, was an old *Times* symbol, signifying a commitment to talking about the obvious, and obviously uncomfortable, issues on the table. Then Sulzberger summed up his feelings about the past several weeks. "If we had done this right, we wouldn't be here today," he said. "We didn't do this right. We regret that deeply. It sucks." The stuffed moose, coupled with what many saw as Sulzberger's inappropriately breezy tone, didn't make anybody feel better. "He's leading the newspaper," one editor later recalled. "We deal in words. We're professionals. And the best he can come up with is, 'It sucks'? Well, he's right: He sucked."

When it was Raines's turn to speak, he did his best to push the discussion beyond the turmoil of the past two weeks. "I've received a lot of advice on what to say to you today, all of it well intended," Raines said. "The best came from reporters who told me to speak to you from my heart. So the first thing I'm going to tell you is that I'm here to listen to your anger, wherever it's directed. To tell you that I know our institution has been damaged, that I accept my responsibility for it and I intend to fix it."

Raines went on to tick off what David Barstow, Clyde Haberman, Joyce Purnick, and Floyd Norris had told him over the past two days. "You view me as inaccessible and arrogant," he said. "I heard that you were convinced there's a star system that singles out my favorites for elevation. Fear is a problem to such an extent, I was told, that editors are scared to bring me bad news." Raines also talked about diversity. "Where I come from, when it comes to principles on race, you have to pick a ditch to die in. And let it come rough or smooth, you'll find me in the trenches for justice." Jayson Blair, Raines said, seemed to be a promising young minority reporter. "Does that mean I personally favored Jayson? Not consciously. But you have a right to ask if I, as a white man from Alabama with those convictions, gave him one chance too many by not stopping his appointment to the sniper team. When I look into my own heart for the truth of that, the answer is yes."*

Raines was trying to defuse the criticism that he was already hearing, criticism that Jayson Blair was favored because he was a sycophant or because Raines and Boyd had been trying to stick it to Jon Landman and Jill Abramson by championing a young reporter they didn't trust. But in trying to do that, Raines made some of the paper's black staffers feel as if they had all been unfairly placed under a cloud of suspicion— as if they, too, were the beneficiaries of a privileged white man's guilt. Gerald Boyd, the man Raines had so proudly appointed as the highest-

---

* Raines, in his *Atlantic* piece, wrote that the real reason he gave Blair extra chances was his history of drug and alcohol abuse: "Whatever slack I was cutting Jayson had nothing to do with his accuracy problems. I thought I was giving this apparently talented and engaging young man a second chance based on a different problem that had been brought to my attention around the end of 2002. That was when Gerald had informed me that Jayson had told him that he had gone to the *Times*'s Employee Assistance Program and requested treatment for alcohol and drug abuse." Not only does that rendering not make sense—why would Boyd have told Raines about Blair's substance abuse problems but not his performance record?—but it also differs from what Raines told the reporting team when it was preparing its May 11 report, when he said that he had been unaware of Blair's drug and alcohol abuse before May 2003.

ranking African American on the paper's editorial staff, seemed particularly uncomfortable in his seat on the stage.

When it was his turn to talk, Boyd was defensive. Echoing a theme he had returned to time and again in the past two weeks, he stressed his lack of involvement with Jayson Blair's career. "Did I pat him on the back?" Boyd asked. "Did I say, 'Hang in there'? Yes, but I did that with everybody." Boyd again refused to accept responsibility for appointing Jayson Blair to the sniper team. Finally, Raines stepped in and said that as executive editor, he accepted the ultimate responsibility for Blair.

The public crow eating continued. Landman, Raines said, had been "right all along" about Blair. Boyd admitted he had never told national editor Jim Roberts about Blair's warnings or track record.

Then the questions began. It quickly became clear that a year and a half's worth of anger and resentment was about to come pouring out. Alex Berenson, a business reporter, stood up and asked what he'd ask any other leader in that situation: Would Raines resign? It was an obvious question, but a shocking one all the same. "My plan is to have this job and perform it with every fiber in my body," Raines said, "as long as [Sulzberger]" will allow it. The publisher jumped in: "If he were to offer his resignation, I would not accept it."

Shaila Dewan, a woman on the paper's metro staff, spoke up. "I've been at the *Times* for three years," she said. "I was hired the same year as Jayson. And my grief over this situation has only shown me how much I have invested in this institution." Then Dewan lit into the paper's leaders. "I have heard no comment on the message inherent in this saga for young reporters. The message is that we would do better to spend our time nominating editors for national awards and chatting about basketball than doing our work. And since we're all being so honest"—here Dewan alluded to Marc Santora, a rookie reporter who had been stationed in Iraq after a stint as Maureen Dowd's assistant— "I'll go ahead and say that some of us might have surmised that we would have been smarter to pursue a job as a columnist's assistant than spending our time getting newsroom experience."

Dewan wasn't finished. "For women, the message is particularly surreal. Apparently it is possible to assemble a team of eight *Times* staffers to investigate Jayson Blair, and report their findings to the executive editor, and have it consist of all men. And that is not the first time such a team has been assembled in my brief tenure at the *Times*. Were there no hungry reporters without Jayson Blair's record who could have been steered to the understaffed national desk [to cover the sniper shootings]? What will you do to restore faith that there is at least a modicum of fairness in the advancement process at the *Times*?"

The longer the questions went on, the more evident it became that the Jayson Blair controversy—at least for the men and women of *The New York Times*—wasn't about Jayson Blair at all. It was about Howell Raines and Gerald Boyd, and the staff was virtually united in its frustration and anger. At one point, Jon Landman clarified something about his now infamous "stop Jayson" memo. He was roundly applauded.

The afternoon's most galvanizing moment came when Joe Sexton, one of Landman's deputy editors, stood to speak. "I believe at a deep level you guys have lost the confidence of many parts of the newsroom," Sexton said. "I do not feel a sense of trust and reassurance that judgments are properly made. People feel less led than bullied." Sexton went on to ask Raines why no one had asked about Blair's sources on the sniper stories. At one point, Sexton, who has a notoriously foul mouth, swore.

At that, Raines, who had been so careful to remain calm, erupted. "Don't demagogue me," he shouted, and reprimanded Sexton for cursing in a public forum. And with that, any small steps toward conciliation Raines had managed to make were erased. "It felt like everything up to that was just a show," a reporter said later that day. "And here was the real Howell once again." Raines, perhaps realizing his mistake, quickly apologized for "acting prickly," explaining, "I've been under a lot of stress lately."

More than two hours after it began, the meeting broke up and hundreds of *Times* staffers made their way back across Broadway. The meeting, almost everyone agreed later, had been an ill-conceived nightmare. "When I was suggesting he talk to the staff, I assumed he would do it in the newsroom," says Barstow. "I wasn't suggesting a movie theater." Even Punch Sulzberger told friends that the meeting had likely been a mistake, creating an opening for more staff unrest and critical outside coverage.

That night, Howell Raines walked out into the newsroom as the evening coffee cart was being pushed around. For one of the first times in his tenure, he was walking the floor, but it was clear that perfunctory meanderings through the newsroom weren't going to heal the rift. The next day's local newspapers featured descriptions of the staff meeting and Raines's apparent effort to appear more accessible, as well as what seemed to be the staff consensus: Howell Raines was failing.

Jack Rosenthal, Raines's predecessor as editorial-page editor and the current head of the Times Company's charitable foundation, says the staff united against Raines in that meeting. "The fascinating thing," Rosenthal says, "is when the hard questions were asked of Raines, like 'Will you resign?' the room exploded with applause. What the applause said to me was this staff wants to protect people for exposing themselves to danger. They were saying, 'We're one.' "

"It only became scary to me at the staff meeting," says Al Siegal. "The sense of a pure, deep dysfunction, with a level of personal animus that was getting in the way of our journalism, became clear there. And I still haven't quite recovered. The depth of the pessimism, the depth of the anger, was just unbelievable."

Even readers were lining up to take their whacks. On Friday, the *Times* ran a letter from Francis W. Rodgers from Rensselaer, New York. "Closing The Times's 'town-hall-style' meeting to news coverage was ironic," Rodgers wrote. "The newspaper now joins those who were urged by The Times to be more open; remember Vice President Dick Cheney's energy meetings and the final Senate deliberations on the Clinton impeachment. . . . Publication of a transcript of the meeting would have been appropriate."

Indeed, so intense was the furor over Raines that even Jayson Blair had been consigned to a supporting role. Blair spent the day of the meeting conferring with his literary agent, trying to figure out if there was a way to monetize his newly found infamy. He seemed oblivious to the pain his actions had caused his former colleagues. At 9:45 that night, he sent out an e-mail to people in his computer's address book, including a number of *Times* staffers. "hey folks," Blair wrote, "this is my new email address. feel free to forward it to anyone who asks to reach me. spread the word to those who still care that i am holding up as well as possible and love so many of you. I [*sic*] time will come for more, but it's not here yet. all the best, jayson."

The next weeks brought no relief for the *Times*. On Thursday, May 15, a *Times* spokeswoman grudgingly acknowledged that the paper was looking into other reporters after questions had been raised about their reporting. The Drudge Report briefly posted an item listing Rick Bragg as one of the writers being investigated and then just as quickly took it down.

THE FALLOUT

For media critics as well as the *Times*'s admirers (and enemies), the scandal was nothing short of mesmerizing; I certainly found myself transfixed. I had spent the previous year working as the media writer for *Newsweek* as well as helping to write and occasionally edit the magazine's national affairs section. *Newsweek*'s deadlines are on Saturday evening, and after the *Times*'s four-page report was released on the afternoon of Saturday, May 10, we scrambled to crash two pages into that week's magazine. Both Howell Raines and Gerald Boyd had turned down repeated interview requests all week.

Toward the end of the story, I wrote about Boyd's relationship with Jayson Blair:

> Blair's close mentoring relationship with *Times* managing editor Gerald Boyd, who is also black, was not explored in depth in the paper. Blair wrote Boyd's biographical sketch in the *Times*'s internal newsletter when Boyd was named managing editor. Blair was known

to brag about his close personal relationships with both Boyd and Raines, and the young writer frequently took cigarette breaks with Boyd.

On Monday, Boyd called me and Mark Whitaker, *Newsweek*'s editor. In his conversation with me, Boyd, his deep voice steady, acknowledged that Blair had nominated him for a National Association of Black Journalists Journalist of the Year Award, an honor that Boyd had won, and also said that Blair had, in fact, written a page-long profile of him for the *Times*'s in-house newsletter.* (Howell Raines's bio was written by Maureen Dowd, once one of Raines's closest friends on the paper's staff.) But, Boyd said, he had never had a close mentoring relationship—or any kind of relationship—with Jayson Blair. If I had only bothered to ask, he said, he would have told me this himself. I took notes on the conversation, because I knew it was likely the only chance I'd get to speak with Boyd.

"Gerald, I tried to ask," I said. "I called you a half-dozen times. I left messages with your secretary and with Catherine [Mathis, the *Times*'s spokeswoman]. If you don't come to the phone, I need to use the information I have, and you were described by multiple people as having a mentoring relationship with Jayson."

Boyd said this was all part of Blair's con. "Ask anyone," he said. "I'm a straight shooter. If you have any questions, call." Our conversation ended genially enough, but Boyd never answered or returned another phone call.

On Tuesday, May 13, the day before the *Times*'s town hall meeting, when *Newsweek*'s top editors gathered to discuss the next week's issue, there was talk of making the *Times* story a cover. The other option was a feature on *American Idol*, which was in the midst of crowning either Clay Aiken or Ruben Studdard as its winner. As the week went on and

---

* The Blair-authored profile—a simultaneously sycophantic and confusing piece—referred to Boyd as a man "with the well-known ability to shred a man's ego and tie in the same softly spoken, understated sentence." It ends on this garbled note: "A few years ago, Gerald attended a program called 'Leadership at the Peak,' . . . and there, he says, he learned to redefine success 'in a collage of ways,' including work, life, friends and family. And all that unleashed energy. Pretty picture."

national attention became more frenzied, it became clear we were going to do the *Times*, and Jayson Blair, as our cover story.

It was a sign of how much the scandal had festered in the two weeks since the Blair story broke. At the time, I wrote a weekly online media column for *Newsweek*, and on May 6, five days after Blair's resignation, I filed a piece detailing the lack of national press attention bestowed on the opening of the Stax Museum of American Soul in Memphis. My only mention of Blair was a two-paragraph addendum at the end of the story. "Journalism—and the *Times*—will survive this scandal with their reputations more or less intact," I had written. "We should all hope Jayson can move on as well."

At the time, this seemed like an appropriate response. Now, the story had become all-consuming.

All week, I had been calling Blair on his cellphone, sometimes two or three times a day. On Thursday, May 15, the day after the town hall meeting and two days before we went to press, I sent Blair an e-mail. He and I had met once before, at an impromptu gathering of journalists at a downtown bar. I had heard that he was struggling to stay sober, and I was sympathetic; I had stopped using drugs and alcohol six years before, when I was in my mid-twenties. When the *Times* report first hit, people close to Blair had said they were worried about his mental state. I wrote to Blair:

> First off, I'm glad to hear you're doing as well as possible. I mean that sincerely, and apart from any work related reasons I have for getting in touch. I know that's the standard line—hope you're doing well, blah blah, and now for the pitch. But it's true.
>
> Separate from that, I'm working on a story about you and the Times. It'll likely be our cover this week; right now it's going to be a 9-page package.
>
> A large part of it is going to deal with you, and your history and work trajectory. Obviously right now the only people I'm able to really talk to are outsiders. There are many virtues of talking to a newsweekly, but there are many virtues of talking to anyplace,

really, and many reasons not to talk, also. I just wanted to make sure
I got in touch.

   If I don't hear from you, and I have specific questions, I'll at least
send an email. And if you want to talk on or off the record, let me
know, by calling here, or my cell or my home.

Later that afternoon, Blair e-mailed me back, initiating a background dialogue he and I would maintain for the next several days. At
the time, Blair told me I was the only journalist he was speaking with.
We had several hour-long conversations and exchanged many e-mails.
Blair seemed to alternate between grappling with a numbing realiza-
tion of what he had done and delighting, with a sort of manic glee,
in the attention he was getting. On Friday afternoon, he arranged for
Ed Keating, a former *Times* photographer,* to meet him and Zuza
Glowacka in downtown Manhattan so they could pose for the *Newsweek* story. In between shots, Blair would e-mail me from a public computer at a Kinko's copy shop or call me on his cellphone. He posed for
Keating as a tough guy, cigarette to his lips, eyes slightly narrowed, en-
joying the theatrics of the shoot.

   On Saturday, Blair called to say he was ready to say something on
the record. He had released only a couple of rote comments, and, he
said, he'd give me his word that this would be the only thing he'd say
to any print reporters. He read out his statement:

   I can't say anything other than the fact that I feel a range of emo-
   tions including guilt, shame, sadness, betrayal, freedom and appreciation for those who have stood by me, been tough on me, and have
   taken the time to understand that there is a deeper story and not to
   believe everything they read in the newspapers.

"That's good, right?" Blair asked when he was done. "Don't believe
everything you read in the newspapers, right?" He cackled and got off
the phone.

---

* Keating had been dismissed by the *Times* for allegedly staging a news photograph.

My editor, Tom Watson, and I worked on the 4,500-word story until midnight that night. I'd been covering the *Times* for two years, since Raines was named executive editor of the paper, and I had deep sources, institutional knowledge, and half a dozen *Newsweek* reporters helping me gather anecdotes. My "nut graf," the summary of the story, read:

> This is the story of two men's rise. Howell Raines, the swaggering, smooth-talking Southerner, had transformed the culture of the staid *New York Times* since stepping into the paper's top editorial position in September 2001—elevating the chosen few, pushing his staff with an unrelenting ferocity and, in his first three months on the job, leading the paper to an unprecedented seven Pulitzer Prizes, six of them for the paper's coverage of the September 11 attacks. Jayson Blair, an awkward, overbearing, chain-smoking cub reporter, seemed to intuitively understand this, and was gaming his way to the upper echelon of *Times* reporters—his personal life unraveling even as he was handed ever more prominent and pressure-packed assignments by supervisors who warned him sternly about his problems while continuing to cheer him on. . . . Raines's fondness for anointing young reporters as future stars put the two on a collision course—which destroyed one man's career, seriously sullied the other's and severely tarnished the reputation of an American institution in the process.

The piece broke news about Blair's history of cocaine and alcohol abuse and was critical of both Raines and Blair. The *Newsweek* story also made clear, in ways it would have been impossible for the *Times* to do, the extent to which people in the newsroom felt that Raines had created the problems that were engulfing the paper. "There was all this cordwood lying around," I quoted one reporter as saying, referring to the anger and frustration at Raines's leadership, "and then along came the spark."

The story was posted online on Sunday morning, May 18. The next day, the piece hit newsstands, with a full-page cover shot of Blair sucking on a cigarette. Blair, I found out later from a friend who lived in the area, went from newsstand to newsstand in Park Slope, Brooklyn, stocking up on copies of the issue—mementos of his moment of infamy.

It's safe to say that Howell Raines was not nearly as excited about his time in the spotlight. I made a perfunctory call to Raines, although I suspected he wouldn't answer. I also called Catherine Mathis and was prepared for her to be angry with the extent to which I had laid the Blair fiasco, and the anger in the *Times*'s newsroom, at Raines's feet. To my surprise, Mathis said the story was fair.

I knew then that Howell Raines was truly in serious danger of losing his job.

AFTER MY STORY was published, Blair agreed to speak with Sridhar Pappu, then *The New York Observer*'s media writer, whose 3,400-word article appeared on Wednesday, May 21. Blair used the opportunity to lash out at the *Times*, insult editors by name, and laugh at the paper's troubles—all of it entirely on the record. "I don't understand why I am the bumbling affirmative action hire when [former *New Republic* writer] Stephen Glass is this brilliant whiz kid," Blair told Pappu. "I fooled some of the most brilliant people in journalism."

On Tuesday, May 20, the same day Pappu's interview was posted on the *Observer*'s website, Howell Raines sent out a memo in which he publicly repudiated many of the newsroom changes he had instituted during the past year. Earlier that day, Raines and Boyd had met with the paper's masthead and department heads. During the meeting, many of the frustrations that had been brewing under the surface boiled over, and Raines capitulated across the board. Raines would, he wrote, "push authority on news coverage and staff assignments down to the department heads." The desk heads, not the masthead, "are the managers who will have the first and most direct responsibility for running their departments and shaping their reports." Department heads would "get heard more consistently in our hiring process." Finally,

Raines announced, Arthur Sulzberger had agreed to hire twenty new people for the newsroom. "This," Raines wrote, "is a direct response to what so many of you said so eloquently about your work loads in last week's [town hall] meeting."

Raines had come into his job loudly denouncing the bottom-up management of his predecessor. He'd argued that the "silo management" that was created when desk heads were given autonomy was ruining the *Times*. And he had told Ken Auletta that he refused to be "rattled by the friction of the moment." "You have to set your sights on a beacon that is a journalistic ideal," Raines had said. "It's important not to get knocked off course by those winds of criticism." Now, Raines was being knocked dramatically off course.

But the *Times*'s—and Raines's—saga wasn't over yet. An ongoing internal investigation, started by an anonymous complaint a week earlier, had uncovered at least one egregious offense by Rick Bragg, one of Raines's favorite writers on the paper. The previous June, Bragg had used an uncredited, unpaid stringer for what was essentially a puff feature on oyster fishermen in the Florida Panhandle.

The story, published on the front page of the *Times* on June 15, 2002, was titled "An Oyster and a Way of Life, Both at Risk." The lead read:

> The anchor is made from the crankshaft of a junked car, the hull is stained with bottom muck, but the big Johnson outboard motor is brand new. Chugging softly, it pushes the narrow oyster boat over Apalachicola Bay, gently intruding on the white egrets that slip like paper airplanes just overhead, and the jumping mullet that belly-flop with a sharp clap into steel-gray water.

The piece was infused with the kind of "being there" touches Raines looked for from Bragg. He described a fisherman "rhythmically stabbing at the soft sand." He wrote about the disappearing mores of the Panhandle fishermen: "More and more, life here feels temporary. The water will change. The oystermen cannot control that, although some of them are trying." The piece ended on this grace note: "The people have a toughness in them here. They can bear almost anything. It is only the bay that is fragile." It was one of only three stories Bragg would write in June 2002, a time when the rest of the staff was being pushed to file three and four times per week.*

As it turns out, Bragg hadn't even done the reporting for his story. Instead, he had dispatched J. Wes Yoder, a young reporter who served as a kind of personal stringer for Bragg, to Florida to do the on-the-ground research. Yoder had spent four nights in Apalachicola, Florida, interviewing fishermen and taking notes on the river before giving his notes to Bragg. Before he filed his story, Bragg flew down to Apalachicola, got off the plane, wandered around for a couple of hours, and flew back home. In *Times* parlance, this was referred to as the "toe-touch" dateline: A reporter would do research and interviews on the phone or rely on stringers' notes and then fly in to a city just so the story could begin with the requisite indication that it had been written from the pertinent locale. Toe-touch datelines had become increasingly popular as Raines pushed his staff to cover more and more ground. Never, however, were they used on puff feature stories. On May 23, the *Times* ran an editors' note on the almost year-old story:

> An article last June 15 described the lives and attitudes of oystermen on the Florida Gulf Coast who faced threats to their livelihood from overuse of water farther north. It carried the byline of Rick Bragg, and the dateline indicated that the reporting was done in Apalachicola.
>
> In response to a reader's recent letter questioning where the reporting took place, The Times has reviewed the article. It found that while Mr. Bragg indeed visited Apalachicola briefly and wrote the article, the interviewing and reporting on the scene were done by a freelance journalist, J. Wes Yoder.
>
> The article should have carried Mr. Yoder's byline with Mr. Bragg's.

---

* At the time, Bragg was suffering from a medical condition that made it difficult for him to travel.

The editors' note wasn't entirely fair: Bragg had long pushed for his stringers to get credit for their work; what's more, it was virtually unheard-of for stringers to get bylines. Still, the note caused much snickering in the *Times*'s newsroom, where Bragg, who boasted about how he operated by a different set of rules from everyone else's, was widely reviled. For years, reporters had been keeping track of their favorite Bragg corrections. One infamous story about a small-town Alabama newspaper couple who exposed corruption by a county sheriff was riddled with errors. Bragg wrote that the sheriff's prison sentence was twenty-seven years; it was actually twenty-seven months. The editor who was profiled was fifty-nine, not in his "late 40's." The circulation of the paper in question was 7,125, not 6,000. And the newspaper's investigation—the heart of Bragg's piece—was published *after* the sheriff had repaid county money to buy his daughter an all-terrain vehicle, not before. Another Bragg story lamenting the fact that only two Las Vegas casinos still featured showgirls had later necessitated a correction that noted that, in fact, there were other casinos that continued to feature showgirls.

Later that Friday, May 23, *Times* sources confirmed that Bragg had been suspended from the paper for two weeks. Bragg, however, wasn't going to go down without a fight. On Monday, he gave an interview to *The Washington Post*'s Howard Kurtz. "Most national correspondents will tell you they rely on stringers and researchers and interns and clerks and news assistants," Bragg told Kurtz. In between quoting his own work by heart and saying he was "too mad to whine" about his suspension, Bragg said he had twice tried to quit the paper—once after a disagreement with an editor over a story—and both times Raines had intervened personally.*

---

* Raines, it turned out, had actually been aware of Bragg's unusual working relationship with J. Wes Yoder. In May 2002, Bragg was dispatched to Birmingham, Alabama, to cover the trial of Bobby Frank Cherry, the last defendant in the 1963 church bombing that killed four black teenage girls. Raines had been living in Birmingham at the time of the bombings, but he said he hadn't been "brave enough" to demonstrate at the time. He took an intense interest in the trial, traveling down to Birmingham and taking notes when Bragg needed to leave the courtroom. While in Birmingham, Raines met Yoder, who also took notes for Bragg when he wasn't in the courtroom. Yoder wasn't paid (although Bragg did pay his rent), and he had no official affiliation with the *Times*. At least once, Raines, Yoder, and Bragg ate dinner together.

Kurtz had been at Los Angeles International Airport on Memorial Day when he got Bragg's call. Kurtz had gotten married the day before and was flying back to Washington that day. "I didn't even have a pad with me," Kurtz says. "I'm scribbling on pieces of paper like a madman, and now my wife comes by and says they're starting to board the plane." On the plane, Kurtz wrote out the piece in longhand and then called from an in-flight phone and dictated it to an editor at the *Post*'s office.

Because Kurtz was writing from the air, he didn't call anyone at the *Times* for comment on Bragg's claims that other *Times* reporters relied on stringers and clerks to gather color for feature stories. *Times* reporters do use stringers, but the unwritten rule was that reporting help was used in situations in which a correspondent was unable to get to the scene himself, such as breaking news stories or trend pieces that relied on anecdotes from around the country. It was rare, if not unheard-of, to have stringers do the majority of reporting for color features. None of this explanation made it into Kurtz's piece.

As soon as the *Post* story was published, the *Times*'s national correspondents waited for someone to defend their reporting methods. No one did. "I told Howell that day that he should issue something to rebut [Bragg's accusations]," says Floyd Norris. "He said he was thinking about it." Part of the problem was that Bragg had repeatedly told Raines that because of his ongoing health problems, he was unable to do the type of travel required for his job. Raines had assured his star reporter time and again they'd find a way to work it out. "At that point," says Norris, "I think Howell had gone from a forceful leader who relied upon his own opinions to a man who was hesitant to take decisive action."

On Wednesday, May 28, the paper's reporters took matters into their own hands. That morning, Peter Kilborn, a national correspondent based in Washington, sent an e-mail to more than a dozen national staffers and the section's two top editors. "Bragg's comments in defense of his reportorial routines are outrageous," he wrote. "I hope there is some way that we as correspondents, alone or with the support of the desk, can get the word out there, within The Times and outside, that we do not operate that way. Blair lies, cheats, and steals. We don't. Bragg says he works in a poisonous atmosphere. He's the poison." Within minutes, the e-mail had been forwarded to me.

"I was really offended," Kilborn said that day. "I bust my ass chasing facts and I go to weird places I've never been and I have to root around to get the story. The whole idea [of using stringers to do the bulk of the reporting] is anathema to decent journalism."

In his e-mail, Kilborn also voiced some of the resentment at Raines. "In the last couple of years, especially, I've bitched about being pushed into corner-cutting jams," he wrote. "However intense the heat recently because of understaffing and demands to produce, we don't take short cuts, and we don't fake it."

"We've been understaffed on the national desk," Kilborn said to me. "That means everybody's got to work harder and faster when there are important developments. And there's Bragg sitting in New Orleans and doing dick, not getting out of town. I certainly resented it."

Within minutes, other correspondents began responding to Kilborn's message. "The problem is we've had a two-tier system that has allowed Bragg to carve out one system for him (cutting corners, using a huge stringer network, telling people he can't be edited) and another for everyone else," wrote national correspondent Timothy Egan. "Also, it's long been an open joke among national staffers that anything Bragg wrote . . . gets on page one, automatically, while everyone else has to earn their way out front." Todd Purdum, based in Washington, added, "Rick Bragg's method is not typical. It's aberrant and repellent. Some of our colleagues have known this for years. Now the world knows it, and we're all the poorer."

As the national correspondents were writing one another, other reporters were sending open letters to Jim Romenesko's website, a one-stop shop for media-industry news and gossip. At 2:00 p.m., David Firestone, who had been a national correspondent in Atlanta before being moved to Washington, wrote, "The reporters that I know don't simply beautify the notes of stringers, interns, news assistants and clerks; they take most of those notes themselves, and they take pride and pleasure in doing so. They want to see the faces of the people they interview. For Tuesday's *Washington Post* story to present such an un-challenged picture does a disservice to an immensely talented staff of hard-working reporters." Just before 5:00 p.m., the *Times*'s New York City Hall bureau chief, Jennifer Steinhauer, wrote: "If my colleague, Rick Bragg, feels compelled to tell any reporter who will listen that he is being punished for engaging in standard practices of stringer abuse at *The New York Times*, that is his constitutional right. But I for one am not going to sit by and let those statements go unchecked." And at 5:15 p.m., Alex Berenson, the reporter who had asked Howell Raines at the staff-wide meeting if he was going to resign, added his thoughts. "I wish I didn't feel the need to get caught up in this mess," Berenson wrote to Romenesko. "But if Rick Bragg is going to impugn the repu-tation of every reporter at the Times, some of us are going to have to respond."

Bragg, meanwhile, was growing more incensed, according to friends. He'd told several people close to him that immediately after his sus-pension, Arthur Sulzberger had called him personally and thanked him for "taking one for the team." Now, instead of dealing with the contin-ued vitriol of the paper's staff, he quit.

At 7:32 that night, Howell Raines sent out a three-sentence message from Al Siegal's e-mail account. This one was addressed "to the staff." "Rick Bragg has offered his resignation, and I have accepted it," Raines wrote. "We know this has been a difficult period. We have full confi-dence in our staff and we will be talking with you more in short order."

The next morning, Raines and Boyd sent out a longer message to the staff. "In the last several days, we have all been seeing our great corps of correspondents . . . depicted unfairly in various news ac-counts," they wrote. In regards to Bragg's claims that many *Times* staffers relied on stringers for their reporting, Raines and Boyd wrote, "We didn't believe, and we don't believe now, that the facts can sustain an 'everybody does it' attitude." The two editors also said they wanted to "thank our staff for being worthy of our confidence and our readers' trust."

IN THE WEEKS following the May 11 report on Blair, Raines had begun meeting again with the paper's top editors, this time to brainstorm about ways to save his editorship. Meanwhile, after a year in which he had remained willfully removed from the turmoil overtaking the newsroom, Arthur Sulzberger rushed in to try to stanch the revolt, sitting in on meetings, orchestrating sit-downs between Raines and people he had made his enemies, and generally trying to find a path out of the paper's seemingly never-ending mess.

The week of the Bragg revelations, there was a meeting in the executive dining room, on the paper's eleventh floor. At one point, members of the masthead, one by one, told Raines what they viewed as his problems. It was nothing that hadn't been said before, but Raines and Sulzberger were both learning that there was no corner of the paper that didn't feel abused and overworked by Raines.

Raines bristled at the meetings. He thought assistant managing editor Soma Golden Behr was trying to organize people against him. "He said he was afraid of me," says Behr. "I think it's 'My way or the highway' for him, and I'm not like that. I'm gonna go in and tell him what I think is wrong, and I want to be listened to. Because otherwise, what am I doing with my life? I told him at one point, if he felt like [I was working against him], he should get me off the masthead." Finally, in the middle of the meeting, Raines stood up and stormed out of the room.

"Howell, Howell, come back here," Sulzberger cried out. Raines came back in. "Nobody hates you. We all really value you. But I think a lot of people are angry at you right now."

"We all know what this is about," Raines said. "This is about one man trying to destroy me for the last two years, and that man is Jon Landman."

The masthead was nonplussed. Raines launched into a litany of the paper's accomplishments, each one preceded by "I." "I won seven Pulitzer Prizes," "I led the paper on the September 11 coverage."

Mike Oreskes, the assistant managing editor in charge of the paper's television and Internet divisions, cut in. "I actually agree with how impressive those accomplishments are, except for five words: 'I, I, I, I, I,' " he said. "It's '*us*.' "

As bleak as things were inside the newsroom, it was in public that the embarrassment was most acute. On May 29, Arthur Sulzberger, Howell Raines, and Gerald Boyd gamely trekked uptown for the annual Pulitzer luncheon at Columbia University. When the Pulitzers had been announced in early April, the *Times* found itself the winner of only one award, the investigative prize for a series on state housing of the mentally ill; the *Times*'s main rivals, *The Washington Post* and the *Los Angeles Times*, had won three apiece. Adding insult to injury, Kevin Sack, the man Raines had drummed out of the paper's national staff the previous spring, was in town with Alan C. Miller to collect the award they had won for work they did for the *Los Angeles Times*.

Times Op-Ed page columnist William Safire and *Dallas Morning News* editor-at-large Rena Pederson, the co-chairs of the Pulitzer board, spoke to the assembled crowd. Both alluded to the troubles at the *Times*. "I would also like to add a special congratulations to the winning journalists today," Pederson said from the stage of Columbia's Low Library, "for upholding standards of integrity at a time when journalistic standards are being challenged, challenged by personnel scandals as well as increasing corporate pressures that too often sacrifice quality for the bottom line." Safire began his talk by addressing what he called "Topic A" in the world of journalism: "The subject of trust. Trust among reporters and editors. Trust among newspapers and their readers."

From their table, where they were joined by Jon Landman, the editor of the *Times*'s winning entry, Raines, Boyd, and Sulzberger looked grim and pained. "It wasn't a happy place," says another journalist who was at the luncheon. "There was a perverse interest in watching their reactions—every time anyone made reference to the scandal, all eyes kind of immediately shifted over to their table. It was like a deathwatch."

———

ON FRIDAY, MAY 30, Arthur Sulzberger asked Jill Abramson to come to New York to meet with him and Raines. Before their meeting with Sulzberger, Raines and Abramson met for breakfast.

Earlier that week, Abramson, in an effort to purge herself of her anger toward Raines, had bought his fly-fishing book. "You're going to be surprised at what I'm reading," Abramson said. When she told Raines she was reading his book, he asked, "What did you learn?"

Abramson told Raines she had been struck by Raines's evolution from being a self-described subscriber to the "redneck way" of fishing, where the fisherman tries to pull in as many fish as humanly possible, to being someone who cared more about the craft of fishing than the result.

"I took that as a heartening message," Abramson said. "If you could learn not to fish the redneck way, then maybe you can change."

"We had a friendly breakfast," says Abramson. At eleven o'clock that morning, Raines and Abramson sat with Sulzberger and discussed what they'd both need to move forward. Raines said he needed Abramson to stop talking behind his back and fomenting discontent among the Washington bureau staff. "I thought that was a fair criticism, and it was a fair thing to need from me," Abramson says. She told Raines she needed Pat Tyler removed from the Washington bureau. "I needed to be his bureau chief," Abramson says. "We couldn't go on with this shadow chief anymore."

The meeting went well, and both editors agreed the other one had made valid points. At the end of the day, before she went back to Washington, Raines asked Abramson to come to his office.

"He closed the door and hugged me," says Abramson. Recounting the episode the following April in the lobby of the Charles Hotel in Cambridge, Massachusetts, Abramson starts to cry. "He said, 'I know I haven't always been good to you. I know I've sometimes treated you badly. And I apologize.'

"I thought we were actually moving to an okay place," Abramson says, wiping the tears from her eyes.

But in all likelihood, the die had already been cast. Lorne Manly had heard enough rumblings to convince him it was time to ask Jacques Steinberg to start preparing "B matter"—the industry term for supporting material that will be used to round out a breaking news story—for a piece on Raines's resignation. Steinberg was supposed to give a speech in Atlanta on Tuesday, June 3; the day before, he canceled the trip and appeared instead by teleconference. "I knew there was a chance that I was going to need to be here," Steinberg says.

Raines, however, still seemed to have no clue about what the future likely held. After a determined campaign to woo the paper's business executives, he seemed not to realize they had lost faith in him. And after a year and a half in which Raines had studiously avoided taking the temperature in the newsroom, he had no feel for what reporters and editors were looking to hear from their leader. The Blair and Bragg incidents had both served as illustrations for many of the very frustrations the newsroom had been voicing since September 2001, frustrations Raines seemed almost proud of ignoring. "One of the mysteries of Howell is how such a terrific political reporter and writer could be so blind to the politics of the newsroom," says one reporter who worked under Raines. Now, as Raines scrambled to meet with smaller groups of staffers, he didn't even have secure enough relationships in the newsroom to approach people on his own; indeed, if he had, he likely wouldn't have been in this situation in the first place. Sadly, Raines found himself having to rely instead upon emissaries. Once again, he approached Clyde Haberman, Joyce Purnick, and Floyd Norris and asked each to find three reporters for a small group dinner on Monday night, June 2.

That dinner was held in the publisher's dining room on the fourteenth floor. "I tried to get a range of experience, people of different ages and parts of the department, in part because I wanted to get people whose own set of friends was varied enough so you'd have more dissemination of whatever was said," says Norris. "Howell was very open. He said he wanted to explain what had happened. And he wanted advice."

"We were all confused," says Haberman. "It was clear he didn't know what the hell was going on."

"Howell kept promising to change his style," says Al Siegal of the meetings and discussions that occurred during the weeks after the town hall meeting. "He said he was going to be more collegial, less top-down. And it gradually became clear to me that what he was talking about was something that he was not constitutionally capable of doing. He was talking about becoming a different person." Raines during this time reminded Siegal of Peter Sellers's portrayal of Dr. Strangelove in the classic Stanley Kubrick film of the same name. Toward the end of the movie, Strangelove proposes to the U.S. president that they set up an underground bunker populated with a select group of genetically desirable people. As he is speaking, Strangelove's lame right arm involuntarily makes the "Heil, Hitler" salute, and Strangelove tries to force his arm back down to his side. "As you watched him struggle, it became clear that [becoming less autocratic] was alien to him," says Siegal. "He's brilliant, but he's not a nice man."

Arthur Sulzberger, meanwhile, was trying to get intelligence directly from the newsroom instead of having it filtered through his executive editor's lens. On Tuesday, he flew to Washington for a lunch with the paper's bureau. It was an unusually frank discussion, and Sulzberger was told repeatedly that the paper couldn't recover as long as Howell Raines and Gerald Boyd remained in charge. When Sulzberger pointed out that the Washington bureau had complained of feeling disenfranchised for almost as long as the paper had had an office in the capital, David Leonhardt, a New York–based business reporter who was in town for the day, spoke up. Actually, Leonhardt said, the feeling in New York was pretty similar.

"Even I was taken aback by the level of bile that was expressed by my colleagues," says Abramson. "How badly they felt about Pat [Tyler] came pouring out. Everything was blamed on Howell." Sulzberger told the bureau that Raines would be staying on as executive editor, then rushed off to return to New York. That afternoon, Abramson gathered the entire bureau in her office and opened a bottle of wine. She told her staff how she had read *Fly Fishing Through the Midlife Crisis*, how she and Howell had met for breakfast. She said she thought Raines could change and that the bureau had to get "rid of this poison and get through this." People should, Abramson said, heal and move on instead of obsessing over what they all hated about Raines.

"I felt like the lunch had been an unhealthy thing," Abramson says. Sulzberger, Abramson thought, seemed particularly shaken, and

Abramson e-mailed him that night to tell him she thought she could help the bureau move forward more constructively. But it was likely already too late. Before heading to Washington, Sulzberger had called Joe Lelyveld, the man Raines had replaced in September 2001, and asked him if he could return to work for a few months. "[The Washington bureau] seemed to put exclamation points on hints," says Lou Boccardi, a former president of the Associated Press and one of three non-*Times* members of the committee Al Siegal assembled to investigate the Blair fiasco.

What the Washington bureau articulated was the extent to which the implicit contract the *Times* has always had with its reporters and editors—that in return for the long hours and the relatively modest pay, employees would get a sense of ownership at the premier news-gathering operation in the world—had been undone by Raines. "Howell destroyed that," says Jack Rosenthal. It was this, more than questionable news judgments or undeserved promotions, that ended Raines's career.

———

BACK IN NEW YORK, Gerald Boyd was walking in Times Square with another member of the masthead. He seemed to realize he wasn't going to last. For several days he'd been telling people all he was trying to do was survive, and he knew that never worked. Now even he was opening up about his frustrations with Raines. He had tried to tell Raines that he was boxing himself into a corner, Boyd said. He had struggled to let him know that he was isolating the newsroom. But Raines, Boyd said, didn't want to listen. It was one of the few times Boyd had spoken to anyone at the paper about his frustrations with Howell Raines.

"Gerald feels that Howell gave him his big chance," says Soma Golden Behr. "Howell's the guy who made him managing editor. And so Gerald found it extremely difficult to articulate his feelings about this whole thing. He kept his relationship with Howell absolutely private, even though it hurt him in the newsroom. Nobody saw how much he argued with Howell, how much he won and how much he lost. Only Gerald knows about that."

That afternoon, Sulzberger began talking with Raines and Boyd about the possibility that the two men would need to step down. Increasingly, other *Times* employees as well seemed to understand intuitively that this was a possibility. On the third-floor newsroom, Glenn Kramon convened a meeting of his demoralized business staff. There was, Kramon said, a real possibility that Raines wasn't going to survive. But that didn't mean the paper should stop producing great journalism. Gardiner Harris, a reporter who had recently been poached from *The Wall Street Journal*, tried to remind the reporters just how great they were.* "Let's seize the initiative," said Kramon. "We've been worrying about what the masthead was going to dictate. Now we have some space to play with."†

"The business department sees how companies work," Kramon said in an interview at the time. "I was just trying to get attention off of, 'Will he or won't he,' and just move forward." Even Raines himself seemed to be realizing he might not survive. That day, he told some newsroom staffers that his wife would love him whether or not he had the title of executive editor after his name.

---

* A year later, when Kramon was being feted after being named to the paper's masthead, he publicly thanked Harris for helping to buck up his staff.
† That afternoon, after writing about Kramon's meeting with his staff, I received an e-mail on my *Newsweek* account from someone with a Yahoo.com address and the handle "nyt nyt." It read, "When are you going to disclose to your readers (or perhaps your editors) that you begged and pleaded Howell Raines for a job? He didn't give you one. . . . And you're a media 'watchdog'? I don't think so. Can't wait to see the editor's note." In late 2001, after my employer, *Brill's Content*, closed down, I had sent in a cover letter and clips to the *Times* and more than a dozen other newspapers and magazines. I never had a conversation with Howell Raines.

NEW ENDINGS,
OLD BEGINNINGS

On Wednesday afternoon, June 3, Howell Raines canceled a dinner he had scheduled for the following night with a group of reporters. He left the newsroom early, telling colleagues he wasn't feeling well.

The next morning, Arthur Sulzberger asked a group of the paper's top editors to come to the fourteenth floor at 10:00 a.m. Howell Raines and Gerald Boyd, Sulzberger said, were stepping down. At 10:30, an e-mail without a subject line was sent to the paper's staff. It read, "Please gather in the newsroom on the 3rd floor at 10:30 a.m." Everyone knew what the e-mail meant—the surreal nightmare that had begun in late April was coming to an unexpectedly quick conclusion. When he stepped into the elevator that would take him down to the third-floor newsroom, Sulzberger spotted Bill Keller. "I want to talk with you," Sulzberger said. "Sometime soon."

On the third floor, Sulzberger told the hastily assembled crowd that he wanted to "applaud

Howell and Gerald for putting the interests of this newspaper, a newspaper we all love, above their own." He went on, "There is so much to say, but it really just boils down to this: This is a day that breaks my heart, and I think it breaks the hearts of a lot of people in this room."

Raines's and Boyd's wives were in the newsroom, as was Punch Sulzberger, who stood off to one side. Jacques Steinberg stood just behind Arthur Sulzberger Jr. as he spoke, taking notes for the next day's news story. When it came time for Raines to talk, he said, "It's been a tumultuous month, twenty months, but we have produced some memorable newspapers." He appeared calm as he talked of his next ventures. "I set out many years ago to live a life devoted to literature and the arts," he said, "and I return to that calling with a wider set of interests in writing, the study of history, in painting and photography."

"Remember," he added, "when a great story breaks out, go like hell." Raines seemed proud and even a little defiant and maintained the confident style that had marked his entire tenure.

Boyd, on the other hand, appeared deeply shaken, even unsure of exactly what he wanted to say. When he spoke, he said he was leaving "willingly and with no bitterness whatsoever, and in the firm belief that *The New York Times* will be in great hands no matter who leads."

Raines grabbed his panama hat and walked out of the newsroom, making his way through an impromptu receiving line that included a number of veteran reporters as well as Punch Sulzberger. Less than a year before, basking in the glow of the paper's seven Pulitzer Prizes, he had said of the *Times*'s newsroom, "It's my place. It's my home. And these are my people." Now he was walking out for the last time.

After exiting the Forty-third Street headquarters, he got into his car and drove straight to his place in Pennsylvania—the same place he had been when the Jayson Blair story first broke.

The members of the newsroom, many of whom had campaigned publicly to have Raines and Boyd deposed, were in shock. Some wept openly. It was as if the paper's staffers were surprised—even upset—by the effects of their open rebellion. More than one newsroom employee compared the situation to the one in *The Lord of the Flies*.

After Howell Raines and Gerald Boyd had left the building, Sulzberger announced that Joe Lelyveld would step in as interim editor. The next morning, the sleepy-eyed Lelyveld, tieless in a yellow button-down shirt, stood in the same place Raines had stood the day before. Lelyveld had had a reputation for being an awkward public speaker, but on June 5, twenty-one months after Howell Raines had vowed to dust the cobwebs from the Lelyveld era, he disproved that reputation.

"I didn't realize until this minute how much I missed you all," Lelyveld said, smiling slightly, after receiving a sustained ovation. "So as I was saying," he began, gently referring to his previous tenure. Then Lelyveld made a speech that repudiated Howell Raines's leadership and newspapering philosophy even as he defended the paper's staff and his own tenure as executive editor.

> This is not a restoration in any personal sense. But I hope it's a restoration of certain values we need to go on putting out the world's best newspaper. I don't mean that as a slight on the two admirable men who led you day after relentless day through the titanic story of 9/11 and then bravely stood here yesterday to say their goodbyes for the good of the paper and walked out of this place to start their new lives, their own *New York Times* recovery programs. My heart goes out to them and for conspicuous improvements like the way we now use pictures, my gratitude too. Like everyone here, I hope. I honor them for their contributions and truly wish them well.
>
> No, I mean to be talking about us now, not them yesterday. The restoration of values I'm talking about has to do with civility and the way we talk to each other. Thoreau said something like this: It takes two to talk—one to speak and another to hear. The newspaper works best when editors listen, not as a matter just of civility but in a spirit of greedy opportunism. When they listen to the ideas and aspirations of their reporters and help them to get those ideas and aspirations into focus. It works best when we're

not talking about ourselves and venting and backbiting but when we're talking about the world we go out to cover and explore for our readers.

I developed in my days here some old saws, a set of maxims from a sort of Poor Joe's Almanac that I'd haul out too often as some of you will recall all too well. On it went this list: Newspapers don't exist for the satisfaction of journalists. They exist for readers. The satisfaction of journalists is OK. It's a fine thing. We're not opposed to it. In fact, we're strongly in favor of it. But it's not the ultimate. We need to do our job for readers. And part of our job, traditionally, is to help set the news agenda for others . . . help set the agenda for this country. We cover what everyone else is covering competitively, aggressively, and yes with a high and heightened metabolism. But we also break our own stories. We cover what we know is important when others aren't paying attention.

Since I'm not going to be here long, I'm a man in a hurry. There's some tidying up to do. Some of our key departments are severely under budget in staffing. Some are way over. We're going to get back on budget by our own efforts and where we can't because of important new demands like the IHT, we'll make our case to the publisher in an orderly, convincing, even forceful manner.

But mainly I'm going to focus on news and talent. That means I don't intend to get much involved in the work of the committees that the publisher has set in motion to rethink our policies. They'll report to him and your next editor. . . .

The cure for what has ailed us is called journalism. The only way to communicate is to speak up in an atmosphere where outspokenness is sometimes rewarded and never penalized. Wherever you are, whatever you do, take it in faith, you now work in that atmosphere. I need your support in this. It can't work because I say it will. You have to make it true. Starting right now. We'll get the new leadership team up and running as fast as we reasonably can. . . .

My beloved mentor, partner and friend Max Frankel used to end all his meetings, big and small, by saying, "Let's go to work." Let's go to work. Let's really go to work. Thank you.

The newsroom erupted into applause. "When Joe spoke that first morning, it was the closest I ever came to crying in the newsroom," says Clyde Haberman. "That speech was marvelous. It was exactly what people needed to hear." Just as gratifying, Sulzberger was at last indicating that he had learned the lessons of Raines's tenure. "This is a newsroom of over 1,200 men and women," he said in an interview that Friday. "Managing that is a complex task."

"The atmosphere of the place changed radically [as soon as Raines left]," says Roger Wilkins, a former *Times* editorialist and columnist who served on the Siegal committee, an internal group that examined the Blair case. "If you looked at the newsroom the day before [Raines and Boyd] resigned and the day after Joe took over, it just felt like a very different place. It was more relaxed. . . . There was just this exhausted relief that now we can get back to journalism."

Sulzberger still had to choose who would lead the *Times* into the future, and he was rapidly discovering the extent to which Raines and Boyd had run the newsroom in precisely the imperious manner Sulzberger professed to disdain: Years before, speaking of the time he served as an assistant metro editor while A. M. Rosenthal was leading the paper, Sulzberger had said, "We had the entire operation resting on the backs of two people. If you were to remove Abe [Rosenthal] and [deputy managing editor] Arthur Gelb from the equation, the place would have been without any sense of vision." Now, with Raines and Boyd gone, there were no obvious candidates from within the newsroom to take over. There was lingering resentment over the role of Andrew Rosenthal, who had served as a third in command under Raines and Boyd. Jon Landman and Jill Abramson were both popular with their charges, but for Sulzberger to choose one of the editors seen as leading the coup against Raines might have been interpreted as an unacceptable reward for open revolt.

Speculation soon coalesced around three candidates: Bill Keller, who had been passed over for the top job two years earlier; Dean Baquet, managing editor of the *Los Angeles Times;* and Marty Baron, editor of *The Boston Globe.* All three had obvious advantages and disadvantages. Keller had experience running the newsroom as Lelyveld's managing editor, and his stint as an Op-Ed page and *Times Magazine* writer showed he was a nuanced and flexible thinker. Choosing Keller, however, would mean that Sulzberger would have to admit both that Raines had been a mistake from the start and that there had been a better candidate all along.

Then there was Baquet, one of the most popular and successful editors of his generation. He'd been widely respected and admired while national editor at the *Times*, so much so that both Joe Lelyveld and Sulzberger had tried, over a weekend retreat at Lelyveld's vacation house in Maine and a one-on-one lunch with Sulzberger, to convince him to stay when he was offered the Los Angeles job. With John Carroll, the executive editor of the *Los Angeles Times*, Baquet had quickly shored up a struggling paper. What's more, Baquet is black. With Boyd's resignation, the *Times* had lost one of its only high-ranking African American editors, and Sulzberger's firmly held belief that the paper needed to diversify had not been diminished by the Blair scandals.

Baron, who had worked as an associate managing editor under Lelyveld, was coming off a string of enormously successful years editing other papers around the country. In 1999, he was hired away from the *Times* to become executive editor of *The Miami Herald*, a once great paper that had suffered mightily under owner Knight Ridder's cost cutting. In 2001, the *Herald* won a Pulitzer Prize in the breaking news category for its Elián González coverage. On July 2, 2001, Baron was named the editor of the *Globe*, a newspaper owned by the New York Times Company. In 2003, the *Globe* won the public service Pulitzer for its coverage of the sex abuse scandal in the Catholic Church.

Over the next month, Baron and Baquet tried to reassure their staffs they weren't about to bolt, while simultaneously meeting with Sulzberger and other *Times* executives. One afternoon, Baron was seen outside the Times building, a fact that was dutifully disseminated by local media scribes. Not long after, New York's *Daily News* reported that Baquet turned down an offer from Sulzberger to serve as the paper's next managing editor, regardless of who was named executive editor. (That wasn't true: Baquet had merely said he wasn't interested in considering a job as managing editor if and when that became an issue.)

Despite Baquet's and Baron's histories at the *Times*, it would have been unprecedented to appoint someone from outside the newsroom to lead the paper. So it became Bill Keller's time. As June bled into July and the media world's preoccupation with the *Times* dimmed, Sulzberger prepared to announce Keller as the man he'd selected to take hold of his family's newspaper.

Howell Raines, however, wasn't quite ready to cede the stage. On Friday, July 11, after being tipped off that Sulzberger was going to announce Keller's ascension on Monday, Raines asked for time to appear on Charlie Rose's PBS show. That night, he was the hour-long program's only guest. He was brash and arrogant, combative and impetuous. He said that before he took over, the *Times* had been struggling. He refused to apologize for his management—"I've always believed if you are a fastball pitcher, you have to throw heat," he said, apparently not realizing that even a dominating fastball pitcher needs to be able to occasionally throw other pitches well if he wants to have any success. He also told Rose that he had left involuntarily, contrary to what Arthur Sulzberger had been saying. He spoke of himself as a "change agent" sent in to increase the "competitive metabolism" of the newspaper gripped by a "lethargic culture of complacency." He described the paper under his leadership as being embroiled in a kind of civil war, with Raines and his small cadre of adherents striving to make the paper better and struggling against many of the paper's editors and reporters who resisted change because it would require more work. Finally, he said he'd model the rest of his life on William Butler Yeats and Pablo Picasso, great artists who achieved enormous successes after they had turned sixty.

After almost two years in which he could instantly command media attention, Raines's appearance on Charlie Rose's show elicited barely a shrug outside the insular world of the New York media. The attention it did get was almost universally negative. The next week, at a cocktail party hosted by former *New Yorker* and *Talk* editor Tina Brown, several other magazine editors spoke of how they had considered asking Raines to write for them until his appearance on Rose's program. "I felt like I was watching a man unraveled," one editor said to a chorus of assents. "And frankly I'd be scared to trust him with the pages of [the magazine]."

On Monday, July 14, Sulzberger announced that Bill Keller would become the seventh executive editor of *The New York Times* (or the eighth, if you were inclined to count Lelyveld twice). Once again, Jacques Steinberg recorded the scene for the next day's paper. Keller's ascension, Steinberg wrote, was "portrayed by the company's management . . . as a reaffirmation of The Times's core journalistic values."

Standing in the same spot where Raines had made his good-bye speech six weeks earlier, Keller said there was no reason to treat working at the *Times* as "an endless combat mission." He told his staff to "do a little more savoring" of life. "That will enrich you and your work, as much as a competitive pulse rate will." Sulzberger looked on approvingly, and he followed with a direct refutation of the criticisms Raines had laid out on Charlie Rose's show. "There's no complacency here," he said. "Never has been. Never will be."

Keller was only fifty-four years old, younger than Raines (fifty-eight), Lelyveld (fifty-seven), and Frankel (fifty-six) had been when they took over the paper. That meant he potentially had over a decade in which to make his mark, significantly longer than Raines would have had even if he had served out a complete term. In one of his first interviews, with *Newsweek*, he worked to show his staffers that he was on their side.

"I don't want to dwell on my predecessor," Keller told me. "But I will say this: The one thing that made me a little sick watching [Raines's *Charlie Rose* appearance] was the collateral damage. I don't mean me and Joe and the publisher, or even Gerald, who was kind of sideswiped in the course of that. I mean the whole staff of this place, all these people who worked their hearts out for him. There he was saying, 'Before I came on the scene, you were a bunch of slackers.' All the people who covered a couple of Balkan wars and the presidential election and the recount were part of a culture of complacency and lethargy. I thought that was insulting and wrong."

Keller also made sure to say something positive about Raines and about Arthur Sulzberger's decision to name him as the paper's executive editor in 2001. "After the *Times* did what it did on September 11," Keller said, "you would have had to scour the country to find someone who was questioning Arthur's judgment. You can't erase from memory the fact that [Raines] led one of the most prodigious feats of journalism in American history."

Now that Raines was gone, even articulating his legacy seemed difficult. What, exactly, staffers wondered, had he wanted to do? Cover more pop culture? That was a battle that had been fought for decades; for years, it had been common to see stories about teen idols on the front page of the *Times*. Feature lively writing? Raines couldn't claim credit for that, either: The *Times* had been making a concerted effort to hire and promote writers with robust narrative voices since the 1960s. Run more of Rick Bragg's stories on the front page? Joe Lelyveld had also favored Bragg's stories; besides, that hadn't worked out so well.

"Doing a lot of college football coverage is a change, but it's not a profound cultural change," says Jon Landman. "Doing the 'all-known-thought' pieces, that wasn't even really a new genre. What was new was that he routinized them and he liked the sensation of making everybody run around at the last minute to make everybody produce them. The exercise of pulling the puppet strings seemed very important. And bizarre. . . . The problem is the substance [of Raines's changes] was a little obscure. It was change, but from what to what? Moving faster is not a transformation—it's an adjustment. He really greatly exaggerated the level of innovation he put into the place. And unfortunately some of the change really was transformational, but bad."

In the end, the catalog of Howell Raines's systemic contributions to the *Times*—increased coverage of college football; the all-known-thought pieces; a year and a half of advocacy journalism; an exhausted and resentful newsroom—seemed a sad legacy for a man whose tenure had begun with so much hope and enthusiasm. Raines, of course, had also assured his place in history as the executive editor who presided over the paper while it gracefully and compassionately covered the biggest story of his generation. But that was only one part of his legacy. The other part told a vastly different, darker story. Raines's obsession with his own place in history—and his compulsive need to see himself as the central force in the *Times*'s universe—would, in the end, translate to a legacy that was dominated by hubris, narcissism, scandal, and failure.

Part Three

AFTER

"ALL ABOUT HOWELL"

In the wake of Howell Raines's abrupt departure, media pundits and *Times* staffers alike were left struggling to make sense of his brief, chaotic tenure. The answer, they realized, didn't lie within Jayson Blair's troubled psyche; ultimately, the former reporter was little more than a catalyst, the *Times*'s own Gavrilo Princip, the Serb nationalist whose murder of Archduke Franz Ferdinand had set off World War I. The real causes of the tumult that gripped the paper could be found in the ways in which Raines's narcissistic personality had manifested itself in his leadership.

In his twenty-one months atop the *Times*'s masthead, Howell Raines had attempted to centralize power not around the *position* of the executive editor—that had been done before—but around himself personally. Raines loved being the center of attention, loved the entrée his job gave him. He wore an eye-catching white panama hat, even as he rode the subway to work. He was, in all likelihood, the first executive editor ever to have his picture taped up on the mirror of his local hair salon next to cutouts of Elvis and postcards of topless women. He loved seeing his name in boldfaced type in other papers' gossip and society pages. He loved making grand entrances at cocktail parties and book soirees, holding court in a corner in a seersucker suit.

Raines's faintly comical self-aggrandizement might have been tolerable—if distracting—at another company, but the success of *The New York Times* has always depended on a culture in which a majority of employees feel some sense of ownership and responsibility for the company and its mission. "When he was here," says Glenn Kramon, "the staff felt it was always all about Howell." Arguably, for the *Times* to be the *Times*, its employees—at every level—need to be willing to sublimate their own egos to serve a larger, quasi-public good. "My staff is worth a lot more on the open market than I can pay them," Kramon says, and, in the days after the May 14, 2003, town hall meeting, he says, "I needed to find a way to keep them here, to make this something they believed in."

Unfortunately, Raines did more than just temporarily alienate many of the paper's reporters and editors. In his effort to force the *Times* to revolve around him, Raines sought to permanently transform the way in which the newspaper was run. In doing this, he came to personify a shift that had been occurring in America for decades, as daily newspapers started modeling themselves after glossy magazines in a response to increased competition and the ubiquity of the twenty-four-hour news cycle. The *Times* had been aggressively adopting editorial innovations from the magazine world since the 1970s, when it added "service" and "soft news" sections in an effort to compete for readers with outlets like the advertising-rich *New York* magazine, which had itself begun as a weekly supplement to the now defunct New York *Herald Tribune*. By the 1980s, that competitive impulse had transformed the "hard news" pages as well, as CNN put pressure on daily papers to add insight and analysis and, especially, drama to their coverage of breaking news. Even though these innovations were viewed with wariness by journalism traditionalists, they were considered necessary to newspapers' collective survival in an ever more entertainment- and information-saturated culture.

"We are not the first, on any important story, to bring you the news," Max Frankel said more than a decade ago. "What does that mean? Why do you read? . . . The kind of thing that we used to wait a week for the newsweeklies to give us, ideally, we're giving you tomorrow morning. We're going to explain this event and combine in a very artful way a report on what happened and why it happened and who says what happened."

Raines took this evolution to arguably perilous ends. If the country's dailies were adopting more and more of the characteristics of magazines—with the additions of lyrical dispatches, tension-filled narratives, and portentous analyses—then why not go all the way and *run* the *Times* in a manner similar to how New York's celebrity magazine editors, such as Tina Brown or *Vogue*'s Anna Wintour, ran their titles? Not content with merely helping to advance the *Times*'s brand, Raines decided to brand himself. Every page of the *Times* would reflect his unique sensibility, his personal news judgments, his passions and predilections. He'd force out writers and editors he didn't get along with and ignore those he couldn't rid himself of. He'd seek buzz and place more importance on getting the big story than on getting the right story, or even on getting the story right.

Naturally, Raines gravitated toward writers who were willing to help him realize his vision. "In the newspaper world," media columnist Simon Dumenco wrote in discussing Raines's and Blair's careers, "if you think like a magazine editor, if you think like a magazine writer—*drama! glamour! style! narrative!*—you get ahead." Jayson Blair intuitively recognized this, just as he intuitively realized that the path to success under Howell Raines was one that often seemed to prize style over substance. So what if the details of Blair's sniper coverage weren't quite right? His stories were gripping. Who cared if Blair hadn't actually interviewed the characters in his pieces? He'd shown a willingness to produce whatever it was that Raines's team ordered up—unlike some writers, who griped about impossible-to-meet deadlines and ridiculous travel demands.

Not surprisingly, Raines found upon taking over the *Times* that the mechanisms that had been put in place over many decades didn't work for him. When he came to power, he did so preaching the virtues of an empowered masthead, of including more people in the daily decision-making process. After discovering that those people had concerns about his way of doing business, he cut them out of the equation rather than negotiate or compromise. But unlike a typical national magazine, with, say, fifty or a hundred staffers, the *Times* has more than a thousand journalists working for it, and the type of autocratic management that might work at the average glossy is destined to fail miserably at a large, unruly news organization where only a small percentage of the staff can ever hope to get meaningful face time with the boss.

Turner Catledge, the *Times*'s first executive editor (and one of Raines's acknowledged heroes), wrote about the need to delegate authority in his 1971 memoir, *My Life and* The Times. "The *Times* was too big to be bossed by the traditional shirt-sleeved managing editor. Our news staff numbered some eight hundred reporters and editors, in New York and elsewhere, and I could deal with them only through a chain of command. . . . The kind of men I wanted in the top positions at the *Times* were independent, creative men, thoroughbreds, and they were not the sort who could be bossed or browbeaten." Catledge went on to say that he needed subordinates who knew things he didn't: "I considered myself an expert in one subject, national politics, and in other areas I expected initiative and imagination from responsible editors."

In an August 2002 interview with Charlie Rose, Howell Raines paid lip service to this type of approach. "You cannot perform quality journalism without quality management and quality leadership," he told Rose. "No one person can have enough ideas in a day to feed the intellectual engine of *The New York Times* or even a single department in *The New York Times*. . . . Whatever greatness adheres to us, it's from the collective brainpower. So my philosophy of management is to try to get more people being shareholders in that process."

The reality, of course, was much different. Raines ensured that only the select few felt they truly had any influence on shaping the *Times*. In the process, not only had he created a culture in which a sociopath like Jayson Blair was allowed to thrive, he had enabled a series of embarrassing miscues that sullied the most valued brand in journalism. He effectively negated the power of the *Times*'s greatest resource—the pooled intelligence and experience of its many employees. Instead of working for a larger good, employees at the paper were forced to focus on protecting their own hides.

"Everybody felt under siege [under Raines]," says Roger Wilkins, the former *Times* editorialist and columnist who served on the Siegal committee. "The instinct to cooperate and watch your buddy's back is diminished. When Thor is up there throwing thunderbolts, your happiest moments come when those thunderbolts hit someone else." The result was a paper that, at its worst, was considerably less than the sum of its parts.

What's more, Raines seemed intent on twisting the role newspapers have played in contemporary American culture. When he became obsessed with Augusta National's refusal to allow women as members, to cite but one example, he "flooded the zone" in a way that very obviously didn't reflect the reality of the rest of the world's concerns. Instead, it reflected Raines's own preoccupations to an extent that gave the lie to the newspaper's historic mission: to inform the world of each day's top stories "without fear or favor," as Adolph Ochs famously stated in 1896.

For decades, the *Times* has maintained its dominance by being a New York newspaper that also serves the country's media, intellectual, and political elites. Howell Raines, though, tried to make the *Times* wholly his—not his employees', not his readers'. It was a costly mistake.

In doing so, Raines unintentionally highlighted what will be an ongoing challenge for the *Times* as it continues its national expansion during a period when the intense variegation of the media has given rise to more and more outlets (witness Fox News and the recent circulation gains of its corporate sibling, the right-wing tabloid the *New York Post*) that find an underrepresented audience niche and work to fill it. Over the next decades, will the *Times*, and the country's other leading newspapers, be forced to niche-ify themselves in order to target readers in hyperspecific socioeconomic groups or with ever more blatant political affiliations? Will the American press move closer toward the British (and Western European) media industry, in which each daily speaks very particularly to political partisans?

A New Team in Place

More than a year after the resignation of Howell Raines, it is clear that the *Times* has already come some distance toward recovering from his administration. After all, a century's worth of accumulated prestige and loyalty could not be washed away in a bad year or two.

Some of the credit for this can be attributed to the deep eagerness of *Times* employees to return to their normal rhythms. Credit also needs to be given to Bill Keller, who became the *Times*'s new executive editor on July 30, 2003. "What I expected was a place that had suffered a blow to its morale and self-confidence," says Keller. "There was that, although it cleared up pretty quickly. What I didn't foresee was the extent to which the operations of the place had broken down to the point where some were dysfunctional."

Without preaching about a need for wholesale change, Keller moved quickly to set the newsroom's operations back on track. On July 31, he appointed Jill Abramson and John Geddes the paper's new managing editors. Geddes had served as the *Times*'s deputy managing editor since 1997 and had joined the paper as a business editor in 1994; Abramson had been at the *Times* since 1997. It was the first time the paper would have two managing editors, and both Abramson and Geddes were coming to the job with far less experience at the *Times* than any previous person who had held the position. Geddes, who had essentially run the paper while Raines and Boyd were consumed with the Blair scandal, would be in charge of newsroom operations, while Abramson would perform the traditional managing editor's role: organizing and supervising the daily news report.

Over the next year, Keller would oversee the turnover of many of the paper's desk editors and department heads. He promoted Jon Landman to a masthead-level position and named Susan Edgerley, one of Landman's deputies, to be the new metro editor (In the spring of 2004, Landman was put in charge of overseeing the culture department.) Glenn Kramon was appointed to a newly created masthead-level position that would oversee training and career development, and Keller lured Larry Ingrassia away from *The Wall Street Journal* to take over as business editor. Roger Cohen stepped down as foreign editor and was replaced by Susan Chira, who had formerly been in charge of the *Times*'s book projects. *Times Magazine* editor Adam Moss agreed to take the lead on a redevelopment of the paper's culture pages and was succeeded at the magazine by his deputy, Gerald Marzorati. Chip McGrath stepped down as editor of the *Book Review* and was replaced by *Vanity Fair*'s Sam Tanenhaus. Keller persuaded *Fortune*'s Michele McNally to become the *Times*'s new director of photography (Jim Wilson, the paper's previous photo director, had stepped down for personal reasons) and promoted Philip Taubman, the deputy editor of the editorial page, to take over Abramson's old job as Washington bureau chief. Patrick Tyler, meanwhile, was reassigned to London. Keller lured Rick Flaste, an old *Times* editor who had gone to work at the *Los Angeles Times*, back to work as the paper's acting science editor*; Cornelia Dean, who had been editing the paper's science coverage, re-

---

* In July 2004, Laura Chang was named the *Times*'s permanent science editor.

turned to writing and reporting. While Raines, the self-described "change agent," had struggled mightily to pry a league of recalcitrant editors out of their jobs, Keller was able to almost entirely recast the paper's desk editors in a matter of months with only a minimum of fuss.

In fact, many of the changes Raines had hoped to make finally began to happen once the newsroom stopped being preoccupied with intramural politics. Within months of taking over, Tanenhaus had reinvigorated the *Book Review*, adding more topical essays and reported features. Michele McNally's impact on the paper's photo selection was felt immediately. Perhaps most important, the much-discussed reworking of the paper's culture pages that had been initiated under Raines finally began to be implemented in the summer of 2004. "We knew the culture report had to be much more news oriented, and we knew we had to make sure we had the best critics in the country," says Frank Rich, who was persuaded by Raines to help with the section's revamping. It's a role he's stayed in under Keller. "We have to be much faster in reporting news about both high and low culture. We really have to be more aggressive in every area."

The *Times* quickly became more aggressive, pushing daily deadlines back for the arts desk so it could feature breaking news. Arthur Sulzberger moved to show that, like his father, he was willing to pour money back into the editorial side of the newspaper even during tough economic times. In the wake of its 2004 Pulitzer haul, the *Los Angeles Times* was faced with forced layoffs imposed by its corporate parent, the Tribune Company. *The New York Times*, meanwhile, went on a hiring spree. While Raines had lost a number of excellent reporters and editors, including Doug Frantz and Kevin Sack, to the *Los Angeles Times*, Bill Keller—with approval from Sulzberger—began to reverse the flow. In late June, Keller made four prominent hires from the *Los Angeles Times*, poaching film editor Michael Cieply, film critic Manohla Dargis, music industry writer Jeff Leeds, and architecture critic Nicolai Ouroussoff. "I do think Arthur has inherited his father's penchant for demonstrating strength when rivals are tempted to retreat," says Keller. "Hiring in hard times is a way of showing confidence in our fundamental conviction—that quality journalism is good business."

It wasn't entirely smooth sailing, to be sure. Shortly after Moss accepted his new assistant managing editor post, he left the *Times* to edit *New York* magazine, a painful defection that had Arthur Sulzberger scrambling to find some way to keep Moss at the *Times*. Roger Cohen's departure as foreign editor was not harmonious—he was pushed out of his job—and late 2003 saw the paper's Baghdad bureau in turmoil as it was beaten on the ground by *The Washington Post* and roiled by a series of petty internal disputes. And in January 2004, before finally settling on Sam Tanenhaus to replace Chip McGrath, Keller gave an interview to Margo Hammond and Ellen Heltzel, the authors of the "Book Babes" column for the Poynter Institute, a St. Petersburg, Florida–based journalism think tank, in which he discussed the *Book Review*'s future. Keller gave the impression the *Times* would seriously cut back on reviewing new literary fiction. "We'll do the new Updike, the new Roth, the new Jonathan Franzen or Zadie Smith," he said. "But there are not a lot of them, it seems to me." Naturally, Keller's remarks provoked no small amount of hand-wringing among the literary intelligentsia, forcing him to publicly clarify his comments a few days later.

Sure enough, the ambient level of discontent that is a daily presence in any newsroom soon became evident. Keller, staffers grumbled, didn't circulate in the newsroom. Abramson, some said sarcastically, had the listening skills of Howell Raines. Reporters complained about how the paper was getting beaten on big stories; some even said Raines would have dominated the devolving situation in Iraq in a way the current team seemed unable to. But the complaints were, for the most part, halfhearted, another sign that things at 229 West Forty-third Street were settling into their old, pre-Rainesian rhythms.

For the reporters and editors who produced the *Times*'s Blair report, things returned to normal as well. Kramon, of course, began his new post. Lorne Manly was named the *Times*'s chief media writer in June 2004, a job that would have him covering trends "across the range of media," according to the memo announcing the new post. Jonathan Glater says he can't comment on any future assignments, but according to several newsroom sources, he was tapped to work as part of a team preparing a multipart series on class in America, a project reminiscent of the 2000 series on race that Gerald Boyd had helped organize and which had won the *Times* a Pulitzer Prize. Adam Liptak and Jacques Steinberg continued to report on legal affairs and the newspaper industry, respectively, and both writers saw their profiles rise.

Dan Barry and David Barstow, meanwhile, saw their black-humor quips about how their work on the Blair project would affect their careers proven delightfully wrong: In April 2004, Barstow won his first Pulitzer Prize for his project on workplace safety. In 2003, Barry began writing the biweekly "About New York" column, which was created more than half a century ago for the legendary reporter and columnist Meyer Berger. And in the spring of 2004, W. W. Norton published Barry's stirring memoir, *Pull Me Up*, to laudatory reviews.

On May 11, 2004, one year after the publication of their report, the seven men who produced the Blair report met at Blue Smoke, an upscale barbecue joint on Manhattan's East Side run by celebrity restaurateur Danny Meyer (Al Siegal didn't attend). The locale was a nod to the dinners they had scarfed down in the page-one conference room a year earlier; as often as not, their takeout feasts were from Virgil's, a Times Square barbecue restaurant with all the charm of a T.G.I. Friday's. Those meals had been grim and came at the end of exhausting days. This one was much more celebratory. The next day, the *Times* would run a glowing review of Barry's book by the playwright Wendy Wasserstein, who called it "an extraordinarily lyrical look at a mid-20th-century working-class Irish-American family. . . . Mr. Barry has managed to find the richness of heart of a now oddly distant America." Everyone was happy in his job and generally upbeat about the future.

"One of the great things about journalism is that when you're thrown into really difficult stories under tight deadlines, you forge these amazing friendships," says Barstow. "This experience will bond me to these guys forever. We were in a foxhole, and we'll always remember that."

IN THE WEEKS following Jayson Blair's resignation, Raines and Arthur Sulzberger appointed three internal committees charged with investigating how Jayson Blair was allowed to thrive and how to safeguard against similar fraudulent employees in the future. The largest of those groups, the Siegal committee, focused on the specifics of the Blair case and came up with recommendations on how to improve the internal workings of the *Times*. A working group on training and performance management proposed a series of recommendations for making sure newsroom leaders and new hires alike were given extensive training and reviews. And a working group on communications tackled the problem of interdepartmental and hierarchical information sharing.

The three reports, totaling almost one hundred pages, were released to the public in July 2003. They received only a sliver of the attention the *Times*'s May 11 Blair report had, but together these three documents may do more to permanently alter the newsroom culture of *The New York Times*—and in time will likely have a similar effect on the journalistic world at large—than anything else that had happened in the previous two years.

One of the main goals of the committee reports was, not surprisingly, to codify the manner in which newsroom leaders were trained. Journalism tends to reward people who do well while operating as lone wolves. Historically, the farther afield the assignment, the more prestigious it is considered: Working out of far-flung domestic bureaus is a step up from toiling for the metro desk, and landing a foreign posting is more glamorous than writing for the national desk. Finally, when another foreign posting seems redundant, the best correspondents are asked to come back to the home office and serve as editors. The skills that make someone a valuable foreign correspondent include being self-motivated and possessing a healthy ego. A good editor, on the other hand, is someone who gets pleasure out of helping other people do well.

"The most important character quality [to be a good editor] is you have to have reached the point in your life where you are willing to realize yourself through the work of others," Max Frankel said soon after retiring. "If you're still a star, if you still need to be center stage, if you're still a performer, God bless you, go perform. If you want to be an editor, you've got to get your kicks the way a parent does out of children . . . and you've got to nourish them and support them in that task."

Before 2003, remarkably, there was no training program in place at the *Times* to teach enormously successful solo stars how to make the transition to being editors. "When I became foreign editor," says Bill Keller, "nobody ever taught me how to evaluate a writer, how to deal with a budget. When we become foreign correspondents, at least we get basic instructions on benefits and how to rent a car and how to get money wired and all that." In promoting editors from the ranks of foreign bureaus, Keller says, "we were taking people whose job it is one day to go out to a barricade and the next day they're managing people."

While the recommendations that emerged from the committee reports were in many cases vague—one of the stated goals of improved management training was to "create a newsroom culture that values civility, diversity, openness, teamwork, trust and career development"—Arthur Sulzberger agreed to fund several new senior-level positions that were designed to shore up the *Times*'s standards and improve its training. They included an ombudsman—which the *Times* termed a "public editor"—whose full-time job would be to investigate and answer outsiders' concerns about the *Times*'s coverage; a standards editor, to codify the *Times*'s practices on everything from the crediting of stringers to the use of anonymous sources; and a career-development editor. Both the standards editor and the career-development editor would be masthead-level positions.

All three positions had been filled by the end of 2003. Daniel Okrent, a former top editor at Time Inc. (and the inventor of Rotisserie League Baseball), was named the paper's public editor; he signed a nonrenewable, eighteen-month contract. Al Siegal was officially named standards editor, the post he had essentially been filling for years. And Glenn Kramon became the paper's career-development editor.

By March 2004, Kramon had helped oversee a major overhaul of the way the paper trained and evaluated employees and managers alike. Newsroom leaders would be required to take two-day management training programs, which, according to a memo Kramon sent to the newsroom, covered "communicating; writing and delivering annual reviews; ethics, standards and accuracy; recruiting and vetting job candidates; our employee assistance program; managing a budget and more." Annual reviews were made mandatory for everyone in the newsroom. The *Times*'s database editor began working on creating a list of every job at the paper, so staffers could ask to be considered for future openings anywhere from Hong Kong to Broadway.

"This can be a big, scary place," says Kramon. "And there was an attitude that once you were here, you just had to survive." Now, he says, that's changed, hopefully permanently, although he knows it's an uphill struggle to make any reform stick in an environment in which time is always in short supply and it's often easier to fix problems instead of teaching people how to avoid them. For now, at least, new hires at the *Times* get something akin to freshman orientation: There are mandatory sessions to teach new employees about the *Times*'s standards and practices, cocktail parties (including ones at Jill Abramson's and John Geddes's New York apartments), and a prescribed mentoring system. "It used to be, you could be here for years and never get formally introduced [around the newsroom]," Kramon says. No longer.

These changes are being watched carefully and in some cases emulated by the journalism profession. In the spring of 2004, *The Washington Post* appointed longtime reporter and editor Peter Perl to be the paper's director of training and professional management, a newly created post. "This was another of our periodic realizations that we can do a better job in managing people," says Perl. "My whole mission here is to try to improve communication that too often is top-down without there being enough bottom-up."

Another likely long-term result from the turmoil at the *Times* is a new standard of openness by which news organizations will be expected to systematically address their employees' obvious ethical transgressions. Before the *Times*'s Blair report, to be sure, there were examples of news outlets conducting probing investigations of their own workers (*The Washington Post*'s 1981 internal investigation of Janet Cooke, for instance). But there was no generally accepted protocol for how news organizations should address their own journalistic scandals. Sometimes, as was the case with *The New Republic*'s Stephen Glass, the dissection was left mainly to other news organizations. Sometimes, as was the case with the *Times*'s own Blood Brothers dispatch, the scandal was essentially ignored. The *Times*'s response to Jayson Blair likely changed the ground rules forever. From now on, there will be an expectation that when it comes to egregious and self-evident rule breaking, news organizations will investigate themselves with the same prosecutorial zeal they bring to outside institutions.

Consider the case of former *USA Today* reporter Jack Kelley, a Pulitzer finalist in 2002. In late May 2003, in the wake of Blair's resignation from the *Times*, *USA Today* began investigating four stories by Kelley after the paper received an anonymous note from a staffer that questioned whether some of Kelley's work had been embellished. It wasn't until seven months later, on January 13, 2004, that *USA Today* published its first story on the investigation, an 1,800-word piece that ran on page 5A. The piece revealed that Kelley had resigned. It also said the internal investigation was over, without there being any conclusions about what had actually happened: "Left unresolved is the question at the foundation of the inquiry: whether Kelley might have embellished or fabricated stories."

That response didn't satisfy anyone. Media watchdogs cried foul, and *USA Today*'s own staffers felt betrayed. Three days later, on January 16, *USA Today* announced it would appoint a panel to launch "an independent review" of all of Kelley's work at the paper, which dated to 1982. An apologetic editors' note on page 3A explained: "In the days since Kelley's termination, new questions have arisen. They raise enough concerns that we feel we need to vet Kelley's record completely and report the results publicly."

In March, the paper published an interim report on the panel's findings in its pages, saying that "the team of journalists has found strong evidence that Kelley fabricated substantial portions of at least eight major stories, lifted nearly two dozen quotes or other material from competing publications, lied in speeches he gave for the newspaper and conspired to mislead those investigating his work." Within weeks,

Karen Jurgensen, the paper's editor, and Hal Ritter, the paper's managing editor for news, had resigned.

USA Today's eventual reckoning was admirable, as was the *Times*'s account of the Blair fiasco. Surprisingly, however, neither these embarrassing episodes nor the enormous amount of attention paid to media
fallibility during the last several years has sparked any kind of serious effort toward establishing safeguards designed to catch faulty information
before it gets into print. In the last decade, both of the country's leading newsweeklies—*Time* and *Newsweek*—eliminated their fact-checking
departments owing to budget constraints; the recent journalistic scandals have not rectified that. And while a traditional fact-checking process
would obviously be impossible at a daily newspaper—constraints on
time preclude having a team of editorial employees on hand to essentially rereport stories before they run—there *are* several possible safeguards, all of which have been met with almost complete indifference
in the industry.

The first measure would be spot checks on randomly selected stories. These checks would be done either after the story has run or, if
time allowed, before publication. These options have been discussed in
the industry for years but have never gained traction. Nicholas Lemann, the dean of Columbia's Graduate School of Journalism, proposed a system similar to this in his *New Yorker* review of Jayson Blair's
2004 memoir. "God is not going to stop making charismatic maniacs,"
Lemann wrote, "so it falls to newspapers to figure out how to do a better job of apprehending them." In March 2004, a single paper, the Fort
Worth *Star-Telegram*, decided to perform prepublication checks on
several local stories each month. So far, it is the only major daily newspaper in the country to do so.

Another option is random postpublication surveys sent to sources
quoted in stories. Media watchdog Steve Brill (for whom I used to
work) has long employed such a policy at his magazines, including the
now-defunct media publication *Brill's Content*. Brill's surveys were helpful, and not only because they caught reporters intent on fabrication—
they also let reporters know what the subjects thought of the work.
"The whole notion that you can't protect against a reporter who's de-

termined to lie to you is ridiculous," says Brill, whose surveys helped nab a reporter at one of his legal publications who had been faking interviews. "If you have random checks, you *can* protect yourself."

Speaking of the fabricated story Jayson Blair wrote about the family of Jessica Lynch, Brill says, "The only way you'd find out if he made up what her house looked like was if [her family] got a self-addressed, stamped envelope with a survey. Maybe then they would have filled it out and sent it back. They certainly weren't going to call up Howell Raines and complain."

Brill told Arthur Sulzberger about his postpublication surveys, but to no avail. "The consensus here, post Blair, was that [fact-checking] is unlikely to be effective," Sulzberger wrote me in an e-mail. "The most plausible argument FOR spot checking is that if reporters know they might be fact-checked, they'll be more careful. But here, they'd know that the odds are slim of getting fact-checked, and some whole categories (foreign news, intelligence coverage, much diplomatic coverage) would be hard to reliably fact-check. What we have done instead is to try to be much more aggressive about responding to signs of suspicion, areas where questions are raised within the paper, from outside, or through the public editor."

Another standard explanation for the industry's tepid response to such safeguards is that journalism is a field that's built on trust—the trust between a reporter and his source, the trust between a writer and his editor, the trust between a publication and its readers. This is true, just as it's true that there's an obvious code of honor among the overwhelming majority of working journalists: Make your work your own; stick to the facts; don't take people's quotes out of context. But this hardly seems satisfying or reassuring. After all, virtually all of civil society is built on unspoken bonds of trust yet we still have police forces and judicial systems. It's a given that a free and vigorous press is one of the most important hallmarks of a healthy democracy, but with that freedom comes a responsibility to ensure a certain level of quality control. It's up to the journalistic community to begin better policing itself. So why isn't this happening?

"The answer is very simple," says Lemann. "I don't know." Brill is equally confused: "It's mystifying."

COURSE CORRECTIONS

If Jack Kelley's downfall at *USA Today* illustrated one of the ways that the fallout from the *Times*'s Blair report will affect the rest of the industry, what is still less obvious—and what the *Times* itself is struggling with—is how news organizations will address stories that are flawed because of something less nefarious than wholesale fraud. The best example of this type of quandary is the *Times*'s own faulty coverage of both the hunt for weapons of mass destruction (WMD) in Iraq and the supposed ties between Iraq's former leaders and al-Qaeda terrorists. During the last nine months of Howell Raines's tenure, the *Times* seemed to break stories on these subjects both before and during the war in Iraq. On February 6, 2003, before the war began, Patrick Tyler wrote a piece headlined "Intelligence Break Led U.S. to Tie Envoy Killing to Iraq Qaeda Cell," which appeared to outline the connections between Saddam Hussein and the terror network financed by Osama bin Laden. Several months later, Judith Miller began a run of stories that repeatedly took Bush administration and Iraqi exile claims about Hussein's WMD capabilities at face value.

The problem was, those stories and others like them weren't breaking news, they were just plain broken. And they were, of course, pieces that had a tremendous real-world impact, both in guiding the debate as the nation attempted to decide whether or not to send troops into Iraq and in shaping the public's understanding of the Bush administration's rationale for heading to war. This time, there could be no simple explanation for what had happened, no easy narrative encompassing one reporter's psychological meltdown. Throughout 2003 and into the first months of 2004, media critics became more vocal and insistent, picking out Miller's reporting in particular as being dangerously flawed.*

It wasn't until the last week of May 2004, as the anniversary of Raines's departure from the *Times* was approaching, that the paper addressed the subject of its coverage, in an unusual editors' note and a column by the public editor, Okrent. "Over the past year," the May 26 editors' note read, "this newspaper has shone the bright light of hindsight on decisions that led the United States into Iraq. . . . It is past time we turned the same light on ourselves."† The 1,144-word note (which, notably, did not run on the front page but was instead printed on page A10) went on to cite "a number of instances of coverage that was not as rigorous as it should have been," as well as pick out "problematic articles" that "depended at least in part on information from a circle of Iraqi informants, defectors, and exiles bent on 'regime change' in Iraq." Though the editors' note alluded to a year's worth of increasingly insistent criticism that had come to focus on the reporting of Judith Miller, it pointedly refrained from singling out "individual reporters."

"Editors at several levels who should have been challenging reporters and pressing for more skepticism," the note read, "were perhaps too intent on rushing scoops into the paper."

---

* Miller did not respond to e-mails or phone calls asking for comment for this book.
† Privately, some top editors at the *Times* acknowledged one reason they had avoided examining Miller's work even after realizing it was flawed was a desire to avoid the kind of flagellation that occurred after the paper's Blair report.

In his column, Okrent was even more forceful, calling the coverage "credulous" and specifically faulting the "heavy breathing headlines." Okrent did single out both Miller and Tyler by name, but he wrote, "The failure was not individual, but institutional." He went on to write that he thought the editors' note—which had been drafted personally by Bill Keller—got it "mostly" right: "The qualifier arises from [the] inadequate explanation of the journalistic imperatives and practices that led The Times down this unfortunate path."

There was good reason for leaving out these explanations. The *Times*'s flawed Iraq reporting was often directly the result of the manner in which Howell Raines ran *The New York Times*, and Bill Keller took over the paper determined to spend his first year healing the newsroom instead of reminding it of its recent trauma. But the insistent chorus of internal and external criticism—most persistently and eloquently from Slate's Jack Shafer and Michael Massing in *The New York Review of Books*—made ignoring the past impossible. In his column, Okrent cataloged those aspects of the *Times*'s culture that contributed to the paper's failure, listing a "hunger for scoops"; a culture in which flashy, front-page stories were prized; a tendency for "hit and run" journalism whereby skeptical follow-ups were rarely assigned; and an ethos in which prized sources were coddled.

After each clause, Okrent could have added "by Howell Raines." Notably, Raines had treated Miller—like Patrick Tyler and Rick Bragg—like a star. At one point soon after September 11, he personally instructed her to go out and "win a Pulitzer." What's more, Raines had effectively chased investigative editor Stephen Engelberg out of the paper; Engelberg, who had co-authored a book on biological warfare with Miller, was known as the one editor who had the knowledge and background to rein Miller in when she became excitedly insistent about whatever latest supposed scoop had been leaked to her. With Engelberg gone, Raines implicitly and explicitly instructed his staff to get her stories prominently into the paper. In addition, according to half a dozen sources within the *Times*, Raines wanted to prove once and for all that he wasn't editing the paper in a way that betrayed his liberal beliefs, something he was especially intent on conveying after the beating the paper took for both its Augusta reporting and its flawed coverage of Kissinger's position on an invasion of Iraq. "My sense was that Howell Raines was eager to have articles that supported the warmongering out of Washington," former investigative editor Doug Frantz wrote in an e-mail to me. Frantz, who personally edited some of Miller's stories, went on to write, "He discouraged pieces that were at odds with the administration's position on Iraq's supposed weapons of mass destruction and alleged links of Al Qaeda. Because of that, Judy Miller's reporting was encouraged by other senior editors at the newspaper, sometimes over the objections of other editors."

SULZBERGER'S CHALLENGES

Today, eleven floors above the newsroom, Arthur Sulzberger is moving forward with his plans for the New York Times Company, insisting 2003's turmoil has changed neither his nor his paper's long-term goals. "It's postponed things," he says, "because we were caught up in our own under-wear, so to speak, for a while. . . . But the plans have not changed."

Still, questions about Sulzberger himself per-sist. "The *Times* couldn't exist without the Sulzbergers," says James Goodale, a former *Times* executive vice president. "But at some point you have to wonder if the bloodline thins." "It's the question many people on the staff have been ask-ing," says Jack Rosenthal. "Was [Raines] a bet that went wrong, or was it a reflection [of] Arthur's lack of skill in picking people or in recognizing faults in people he picked?"

Shortly after he forced out Howell Raines and Gerald Boyd, Sulzberger—who had initially re-fused to accept any responsibility in the *Times*'s May 11 account of the Blair affair, saying, "Let's not begin to demonize our executives—either the desk editors or the executive editor or, dare I say, the publisher"—finally shouldered some of the blame for the meltdown at his family's newspaper. He told the Siegal committee that he "should have been listening harder to what was happening in the newsroom. I blame myself for that." While Sulzberger apparently never lost the support of the company's board of directors, family members made it clear they were none too happy with the way in which their newspaper's reputation was being sullied. Ultimately, it was the very business executives Raines had so deliberately courted who told Sulzberger the time had come to cut Raines loose.

When Arthur Sulzberger selected Howell Raines to be the sixth executive editor of *The New York Times*, his decision was, to be sure, based partially upon Raines's perceived journalistic and leadership skills. Perhaps even more important was Raines's desire to update significantly the content and operations of the *Times* and his adherence to Sulzberger's fervent belief that the *Times* needed to transform itself from being solely a newspaper to being a multimedia content provider. There were certainly aspects of Raines's sales pitch that made good business sense, such as his promised revamping of the paper's culture section, which was a huge—and editorially neglected—source of advertising revenue.

But Raines—who had spent years flattering Sulzberger*—ultimately had an appeal beyond his promised impact on the bottom line. Both Raines and Sulzberger have said that Raines was hired to serve as a "change agent." In this way, Raines can be seen as a defining appointment for Sulzberger, especially coming on the heels of his occasionally frustrating relationship with Joe Lelyveld, the man Sulzberger felt he had little choice but to appoint in the early 1990s. Unlike Lelyveld, who had at times found the manner in which Sulzberger wanted to achieve his goals—concerning diversity or the *Times*'s foray into the Internet or the company's flirtations with television—either simplistic

---

* In his 2004 *Atlantic* piece, Raines compared the relationship between an executive editor and a publisher to a marriage and described how, when making his sales pitch to Sulzberger to run the paper, he sipped white wine while letting Sulzberger drink a martini, waiting for him to "mellow enough to listen to something he might not want to hear."

or headstrong, Raines had for years been an enthusiastic and vocal supporter of Sulzberger's plans. In choosing Raines to be his executive editor, Sulzberger found himself an employee who shared not only his
vision but also some of Sulzberger's complicated reactions to the paper
itself. For his part, Raines needed to see the future of the *Times* as dis-
tinctly different from its past in order to create a self-fulfilling narrative
in which he played the part of an almost mythical hero, riding in to save
a fading institution from obsolescence.

———

Sulzberger has long been dismissive of those who try to ascribe
Oedipal motivations to his leadership of the *Times*, but his selection of
Howell Raines, coupled with his almost religious devotion to having a
plan of attack for confronting the future, can be seen at least partially
as a reaction against his father.* But if Punch Sulzberger wasn't always
aggressive about the company's strategic development, he did viscerally
recognize that the source of the *Times*'s strength and power stemmed
from the fact that its employees—and he counted himself as one—
viewed the institution as working toward a greater good, a higher purpose, that outstripped the worldly aspirations of any one person.
Sulzberger Jr., in contrast, seems more intent on trying to prove the
Times can reinvent itself as the dominant media company in a new era.

Today, Bill Keller is moving forward with some of the innovations
Sulzberger and Raines had talked about three long years ago, most no-
tably the much-discussed revamping of the paper's culture coverage.
But the outlook for Sulzberger's business plans is more mixed.

One of Arthur Sulzberger's favorite sayings is attributed to Dwight
Eisenhower: "The plan is nothing; planning is everything." It's the
planning of the *Times*'s executive team—Sulzberger; Russ Lewis, the
company's CEO; and Janet Robinson, the chief operating officer and

---

* There is a long history of *Times* publishers portraying their administrations as more business minded
than those of their predecessors. In 1951, Punch Sulzberger's father, Arthur Hays Sulzberger, described his tenure as a transition from the "paternalistic management" of Adolph Ochs. "It became my
task to build a machine, to make an institution," he said.

executive vice president—that has positioned the *Times* as the country's leading national paper. This was done in large part in the mid-1990s, as the *Times* worked its jujitsu on the paper's ad and circulation strategies, moves that enabled the paper to sell itself as a truly national product. Previously, the emphasis of ad salespeople at the *Times* had been the New York metro edition; the national edition was an add-on. "That was backwards," says Robinson. "What we should have been saying was, 'Buy the entire distribution of *The New York Times*, and if indeed you would like to advertise just in the New York region, you can choose to appear in the metro section [which is distributed only in New York, New Jersey, and Connecticut].'" So Robinson instructed the *Times*'s ad sales staff to do just that. By 2004, nearly 90 percent of the paper's advertising ran in all editions of the paper.

"We've moved to the point where now we are the national newspaper for a whole stratum of the American population," says Russ Lewis, who will step down as the Times Company's CEO in late 2004, to be replaced by Robinson. "It could have been *The Washington Post*. It could have been the *Los Angeles Times*. But it isn't. It's us."

Indeed, while convincing advertisers to buy national runs, the *Times* has been continuing to aggressively increase the number of markets in which home delivery is available on a day-of-publication basis. By doing this, the *Times* has managed to buck current business trends: Virtually every paper in the country is facing shrinking circulation.

Then, too, there's the *International Herald Tribune*—what has basically become the foreign edition of the *Times*, following the Times Company's 2002 buyout of the *Washington Post*'s interest in the paper—as an engine of overseas growth. The *IHT*, Sulzberger says, will be a major focus of the Times Company, as will aggressive expansion into television and the Internet. "We can now go to an advertiser and say, 'Okay, we became national, now we're becoming global,' " says Sulzberger. "And most of these companies are global. We can offer them thought leaders in Europe and Asia [through the *IHT*], and we can offer them thought leaders in the U.S. with a single buy. That's one of the great opportunities now that we have one hundred percent control [of the *International Herald Tribune*]."

But the *Times*'s takeover of the *International Herald Tribune* can also be seen in a less rosy light. Peter Goldmark, who had been the chairman and CEO of the *IHT* since 1998, had for years been telling executives at both the *Times* and *The Washington Post* that they needed to explore different ownership options. By keeping the *IHT* as a quasi-independent entity, he argued, the papers were ignoring what could be the *IHT*'s greatest strength: its ability to sell global ad buys to businesses looking to pitch their products to an elite audience on both sides of the Atlantic. But when Sulzberger told *Post* executives they needed to either sell the *IHT* to the *Times* outright or have the *Times* drop out of the joint agreement and start an international paper of its own, he not only angered the Graham family, owners of *The Washington Post*, but shut the door on the possibility of maintaining a joint editorial operation while giving the *Times* control of the *IHT*'s management—and ad sales. "That was no one's finest hour," says Goldmark.

What's more, the *Times* appeared not to have a plan for what to do with the *IHT* once it gained control of the paper. It was unclear the extent to which operations were going to be run out of New York or who, exactly, would lead the Paris-based broadsheet. Even the name of the paper was undecided, as the company debated whether to rename the property as the international edition of *The New York Times* or keep its current moniker. Sulzberger says all that uncertainty is an example of being willing to remain flexible under changing circumstances and cites readership studies that showed a preference for keeping the paper's current name. But outside observers say it seemed more as though the Times Company suddenly had a new toy it had no idea what to do with. "It was amateur hour," says a Wall Street analyst who covers the *Times* and the newspaper industry. "Regardless of whether it ends up being a good long-term strategic decision, the way that thing was handled didn't inspire a lot of confidence in anyone."

"These are our bets," says Sulzberger. "They're well-placed bets. But you know what? If the worst were to happen and they didn't work out, it wouldn't kill us. We'd move on. Because we have the resources to do that. So we pick the bets that, in our heart of hearts, we think are going to work. And we go with it." Russ Lewis is similarly confident.

"When people look at the *IHT*, or at Discovery Times [television] and say, 'What the hell are they doing that for?'—well, those same people were saying that about our national edition. There've always been naysayers," he says.

Sulzberger, of course, deserves credit for helping to steer the *Times* through its last decade of growth and dominance. He also deserves credit for swallowing his personal pride in June 2003 and forcing Howell Raines to step down. But if, as he says, planning is everything, then his track record is clearly mixed. Considering Raines's well-documented managerial problems, Sulzberger could have and should have found some way to institute checks on Raines's autocratic tendencies; indeed, for a person who began his tenure as a publisher preaching a need to eliminate overly hierarchical management systems, his blind faith in Raines now seems outright bizarre. When, throughout 2002, there were innumerable signs that the newsroom and newspaper were spinning out of control—when, indeed, people inside and outside the *Times* came to him to tell him about the dangerous level of dysfunction gripping the paper—Sulzberger should have moved decisively.

In the end, this is what makes the *Times*'s recent saga so sad. What might have happened, what might have been avoided, had Sulzberger not chosen Raines?

POSTSCRIPT

The two men whose names became synonymous with the tumult at *The New York Times* were, not surprisingly, the men whose lives were most affected by the events in 2003. And while they appeared to be as different as two men can be—Howell Raines was a white, successful writer and editor fast approaching the end of his career; Jayson Blair was a black, mildly talented reporter just starting his—both shared a need to create overly ambitious narratives from the raw material of their lives.

We all do this to some extent—the human mind seeks a narrative everywhere—but when the stories these men told about themselves turned out to be greater and grander than anything they were capable of, they fell. The disconnect between Raines's and Blair's self-conceptions and their realities gave them permission, in a sense, to smooth the path to distortion and fabrication in the outside world as well. Jayson Blair saw himself as terminally unique. It was okay, then, if he chose to make up stories about the world he was ostensibly covering. Raines, meanwhile, had imagined himself as a desperately needed savior. From there, it wasn't much of a leap for him to imagine similarly mythic struggles taking place both within the *Times*'s newsroom and in the actual news itself.

In the spring of 2004, both Raines and Blair, unwilling to let the drama they had set in motion move on while they were offstage, tried to muscle their way back into the spotlight. On March 6, Jayson Blair published *Burning Down My Masters' House*, a book that was advertised as a memoir. A month later, Howell Raines made an epic return to print with a twenty-one-thousand-word cover story in *The Atlantic* titled "My Times."*

Blair's book was published by the obscure California-based New Millennium Audio—best known for its quickie books about the O. J. Simpson trial—which is run by an unctuous character named Michael Viner. After New York publishing houses passed on Blair's proposal, Viner agreed in September 2003 (in the same week his company filed for bankruptcy) to publish it.† Blair, Viner said, had an important story to share. What's more, he stressed that the book would be scrupulously fact-checked.

For several weeks before its publication, Blair's manuscript was the subject of intense speculation within the *Times*'s newsroom. Outside media interest was high as well; everyone, it seemed, wanted to talk to the man who had shaken the *Times* to its core and necessitated its very public regime change. Katie Couric arranged to interview Blair for an hour-long special on *Dateline NBC*. Blair would also be featured on the *Today* show; *Hardball*, Chris Matthews's CNBC shout-fest; *The O'Reilly Factor*, Bill O'Reilly's Fox News show; and CNN's *Larry King Live*. *Times* reporters braced themselves for the second Blair media frenzy in less than a year.

But the book's actual release was a massive letdown. Blair, who was a skilled enough liar to fool his editors at the *Times* for months on end,

---

* In the October 2003 issue of *Details*, Raines wrote a piece about his son Jeff, a guitarist in the band Galactic.
† In May 2004, New Millennium was liquidated and its back catalog was sold at auction.

had difficulty sustaining even the semblance of a cohesive narrative, either in his book or on the air. *Burning Down My Masters' House*, rather than being an honest and nuanced discussion of the *Times*'s culture or his own deceit (or even race, despite the inflammatory title), was notable mainly for its sloppiness and continued fabrications. A supposedly verbatim conversation with his girlfriend changes from the book's first pages to its last pages, as does the day of the week the conversation supposedly took place. At one point in the book, Blair talks about how he wanted nothing more than to get off of the sniper case; later, he claims his only goal was to stay *on* the case.

Other times, he seems to make things up entirely. He wrote that Gerald Boyd's mother had died "after a long struggle with drugs." "It shaped much of who he was," Blair wrote, "and I was well aware from my interactions with him . . . of his emotional detachment." Odessa Thomas Boyd actually died at age twenty-nine of sickle-cell anemia. "It is unconscionable that a journalist would write something so hurtful," Boyd wrote in a newspaper column shortly after Blair's book was published. "The truth is that my mother did not drink or smoke, and she certainly never used drugs."

Blair also wrote about how he avoided reading the *Times* for much of Sunday, May 11, the day the paper's report about his deceptions ran on the front page. That night, Blair writes, he went out for a dinner of "barbeque chicken sandwiches with sweet plantains on the side." In the middle of the meal, he headed outside for a smoke. "I walked over to a nearby deli and looked at the front page of the Sunday *Times*," he wrote. "I looked at the top of the story and noticed the names on the byline. . . . I did not have to look past the bylines to know that very few stones had been left unturned, but I took a deep breath and started reading the story." There were, of course, no bylines on the front page of the *Times*'s story about Blair; the authors' names, along with the names of two researchers, were buried deep inside the paper. Less than a year after being drummed out of journalism for making up facts about other people's lives, Blair had resorted to fabricating the circumstances of his own emotional responses.

By the time the book was published, Blair seemed unable to keep track of his own deceptions. In Katie Couric's *Dateline* interview, she stumped him with a question about his own memoir. Couric asked Blair about a conversation with an army staff sergeant he admits in the book to fabricating. "The—I—I'm not sure—actually—one second. I am not sure about that one," Blair answered. Couric paused to allow Blair to page through the book he had just finished writing. "Yeah," Blair said finally.

"Yeah?" Couric asked.

"I remember it," Blair replied.

The book, despite an overwhelming amount of press, sold miserably. As of May 19, BookScan, a company that tracks book sales, reported that Blair's book had sold only 3,300 copies. (This figure does not include book club sales or copies sold at Wal-Mart.) To earn back his reported $150,000 advance, Blair would have had to sell over 40,000 copies of his book. By April, Blair's book tour had been canceled. On April 28, a one-line announcement on his eponymous website read, "Jayson Blair is on hiatus from speaking until this fall. A schedule will be posted shortly."

In mid-March, word leaked out that *The Atlantic* was publishing a lengthy cover story by Raines. The piece, released to the press on March 24, was a seemingly unending excoriation of the *Times*. "My intention here is to perform a final service for the newspaper that I worked for and loved for twenty-five years, by revealing the real struggle that was going on behind the scenes at the *Times* as the Blair scandal played out," Raines wrote early on in the piece. Instead, he sprayed blame like machine-gun fire. Lelyveld, the man who bookended Raines's tenure, came in for the harshest criticism: His paper was dull, Raines wrote, and his leadership uninspired. Raines compared Arthur Sulzberger to Wile E. Coyote and portrayed him as weak, immature, and dishonest. Raines went on a lengthy rant about Arthur Gelb, the paper's former managing editor and one of Raines's onetime mentors at the paper; Raines's bile was occasioned by some moderate criticism he had received in the pages of Gelb's recently published memoir, *City Room*. (Raines wrote in his piece that Gelb called him up, sputtering with criticism over Raines's decision to run the May 11 report on Blair. Gelb says he doesn't remember any such incident.)

Curiously, Raines also got a number of facts wrong. He wrote he had met with the "seven" reporters responsible for the *Times*'s Blair report before deciding to hold the May 14 town hall meeting; in fact, only five reporters were assigned to the project, and he hadn't met with even all of them by that date.

Elsewhere, Raines wrote that he learned of Blair's substance abuse issues "around the end of 2002" and that he viewed Blair's apparent recovery as one reason to give him a chance on the sniper team: "I passed Jayson's desk often after his return, and I saw in him a level of vitality and social engagement that I took to be evidence of recovery," he wrote. But in September 2002, Blair was transferred from the paper's metro department—where his desk was close to the front of the newsroom, situated where Raines would need to pass it en route to and from the elevator—to the sports department, located on the fourth floor. What's more, Raines simultaneously maintains that Gerald Boyd did tell him about Blair's substance abuse problems but that Boyd did not tell him about Blair's performance issues, a rendering that strains credulity.

Indeed, Raines's entire account—which, due to its being mainly a personal account, was not fact-checked in *The Atlantic*'s normal manner—is peppered with inaccurate details and faulty recollections. While boasting about the extent to which he revitalized the paper's culture department, he carried on about how the *Times*, under his leadership, had "beaten New York's hip publications to the punch with a lead story on the rock group White Stripes." The *Times* had, in fact, run an early feature story on the band, but in August 2001, the month *before* Raines took over, in the final days of Joe Lelyveld's regime. It's true, also, that under Raines Arts & Leisure had run a lead story on the band, but that was in April 2003, after it had crossed over to become a mainstream phenomenon. (Jon Pareles, who has been the chief rock critic for the *Times* since the late 1980s, wrote the April 2003 piece.) In this instance, Raines's factual error didn't show a will to deceive so much as a determined blindness to accomplishments that predated his tenure. It was unquestionably true that the paper's cultural coverage was in need of revitalization. It was also true that Raines was an energetic champion of this reworking. Finally, it was true that things weren't as bad as he made them out to be and that he didn't make as much of a difference as he would like to think.

Raines's essay severed most of the few remaining ties he might have had with his former colleagues. *Times* employees e-mailed to one another the American Psychiatric Association's diagnostic criteria for narcissistic personality disorder ("has a grandiose sense of self importance"; "is preoccupied with fantasies of unlimited success, power, brilliance"; "believes that he or she is 'special' and unique"; "requires excessive admiration"), and once silent allies felt newly burned. Some of Raines's former colleagues and friends in the Washington bureau referred to the *Atlantic* essay as "The Passion of the Howell," a reference to Mel Gibson's sadistic Crucifixion epic.

The same afternoon Raines's piece was released to the press, editorial-page editor Gail Collins sent me an unsolicited e-mail. "I bet you're getting lots and lots of input right now," wrote Collins, who had been hired by Raines and was one of his staunchest defenders throughout the spring. "One part of Howell's piece that particularly bothered me was his insinuation that the business side could have taken a bigger hit in expense-cutting to protect the newsroom. In fact, the business side has consistently taken the hit in order to protect the editorial product." Collins, who had had lunch every Wednesday with Sulzberger, Janet Robinson, and Raines, went on to recount a meeting that occurred soon after September 11. "Janet Robinson was giving us all the bad financial news, the result of the combination of our ad base downtown and the national economic slump," Collins wrote. "Then Howell said something along the lines of, 'I'm sorry to hear that because we need another bullet-proof jeep for Afghanistan,' and he went on listing the other stuff he wanted to do to support the coverage overseas. Janet cut him off and said: 'Don't even think about it. We'll find the money. What you're doing now is the reason we all work here. Spend whatever you need to.' And Arthur nodded."

Even those journalists Raines tried to compliment sought to distance themselves from his revisionist history. In his article, Raines had compared his approach to that of Marty Baron, prompting Baron to send a letter to the *Atlantic*: "Having never worked for or with [Raines], I can't speak from experience about his approach to managing a news staff. I imagine our styles differ quite a bit. My model (and mentor) is his predecessor, Joe Lelyveld, who is deplorably mistreated and inaccurately portrayed in Raines's assessment of *The New York Times*."

Raines's *Atlantic* article was, many felt, the final insult. But this time, the employees of the *Times* could choose to ignore Howell Raines's bluster. Overwhelmingly, they did.

Raines's piece even had the effect of turning Gerald Boyd into a sympathetic character. Raines condescended to Boyd in the essay, both by saying his appointment was one prompted by the need to test Boyd's mettle and in simply ignoring his accomplishments. Not long after Raines's piece was published, Bill Keller invited Gerald Boyd into the *Times* newsroom for the paper's annual Pulitzer celebration. He was given one of the biggest ovations of the afternoon.*

Just as the hubbub over his rage-fueled diatribe was dying down, Raines began circulating a proposal for a book titled *Catch and Release*, a sequel to *Fly Fishing Through the Midlife Crisis*.† The book, as Raines described it in a nine-page letter to his agent, would weave an account of an "epic" seven-hour battle Raines fought with a marlin in the South Pacific with reminiscences and observations from Raines's professional life, along with the story of how he met and married his second wife. The proposal was soon leaked to the *Daily News*, whose Paul Colford quoted Raines as writing that the book would feed "into the guiding metaphor of captivity and release that is at the heart of fly fishing and

---

* Boyd is currently writing a memoir for Amistad/HarperCollins, writes a regular column for the United Press Syndicate, and is the director of the case study program at Columbia University's School of Journalism.

† In his proposal, Raines continued to make factual errors that elevated his own importance to the *Times*. The *Times*, Raines wrote, only won the top Pulitzer—the prize for "public service"—three times in a century. Two of those, he wrote, were for work published "in the 20 [*sic*] months I served as executive editor." In fact, the *Times* has won five public service awards since the award was instituted in 1917—in 1918, 1944, 1972, 2002, and 2004.

in each individual's struggle to find happiness by discovering who we really are."

The book, Raines promised, would offer an "inside" look at the *Times*. Colford quoted Raines as saying he would describe "the folkways of the place, the character and personalities of the people I worked with, the steady decline of quality journalism and its traditional values that I've witnessed."

Raines included in his proposal a series of sample chapter titles for sections addressing the *Times* and journalism, including "The War of the Daddies' Boys," which would be about the "Oedipal subtext of succession battles at the *Times*"; "Murdoch and His Hirelings," which would detail efforts to use the media as a weapon of "mass disinformation"; and "The Bear Bryant Rules of Journalism," an attempt to cure the *Times*'s "woeful apathy" about getting beaten on big stories.

Raines's letter-cum-proposal also dwelled at some length, according to Colford, on what it was like to be "caught up in a media hurricane." The version of Howell Raines he read about in "mainstream publications like *Newsweek* or *USA Today*" was not "a person I recognized or wanted to know," Raines wrote, adding that his book would "join imaginatively in the creation of this other Howell's life."

The proposal contains a passage in which Raines imagines this other Howell's life. He imagines him as six feet tall instead of five-eight; wonders if he had been able to transform himself into the athlete the real Raines never was; questions whether this doppelgänger would have had more success with girls in high school; and ponders whether he would have had the willpower to stop drinking after two martinis. "What we're up against here is the mutable nature of truth. . . . The human heart in conflict with itself," Raines wrote. He hoped, he wrote, to examine the difference between the type of recreational lying that is necessary in both fishing and romance and the "permanent alterations in one's life" that take place when one lies for effect. Elsewhere, Raines promised to address "the proper definition of masculinity in our time," as viewed through the lens of the newspaper he once led.

Raines's proposal went out to a handful of Manhattan publishing houses under a strict embargo. Some editors were asked to return their copy of the proposal to Raines's agent. A year after the New York literary world buzzed with the possibility that Raines might score a multimillion-dollar payday for his memoir, many editors decided against bidding on the project, for which Raines was requesting at least $500,000. "We caught it," one editor said, "and we decided to release it. After the *Atlantic* piece, I don't know who has the stomach for that kind of stuff anymore." When a handful of editors told Raines and his agent that they had no interest in his take on the newspaper he once professed to love, Raines recast his project to focus almost exclusively on fishing. The book was eventually sold to Scribner for less than the half-million dollars Raines had been anticipating.

ON APRIL 19, 2004, Howell Raines made one of his first public appearances since his resignation almost a year earlier. The occasion was a reading from *Things Worth Fighting For*, a collection of the late *Atlantic* editor Michael Kelly's work, which was held at an Upper West Side Barnes & Noble. Kelly, one of the most beloved journalists of his generation, had been killed covering the Iraq war, and Raines, Tina Brown, and former *New Republic* editor Hendrik Hertzberg, all of whom had edited Kelly over the years, were on hand to read from Kelly's posthumously published book.

Raines's participation was awkward. During Brown's reading, she spoke of how, as the editor of *The New Yorker*, she frequently had to arbitrate disputes with the magazine's Washington bureau, which at the time was staffed by Kelly and Sidney Blumenthal; Raines, doubtless remembering his own very public battles with the *Times*'s D.C. bureau, forced out an audible, and uncomfortable, bark of laughter. When it was his turn to speak, Raines, on several occasions, referred to the *Times* as "us" or "we." He cracked about the "colorful ways of southern newspapermen, which I found are not as well understood as I thought at the time."

After the reading, as Kelly's two young sons signed copies of their father's book, Raines, trailed by his wife, scuttled off to a spot behind a bookshelf, where Lloyd Grove, a gossip columnist for New York's *Daily News*, briefly buttonholed him. As Raines was walking out, I approached him. Since I had begun working on this book the previous summer, I'd sent Raines letters, left messages with his friends and on his answering machine, and written numerous e-mails. He had never answered.

"I'm Seth Mnookin," I said. "I know this isn't the time to talk, but I just wanted to make sure I introduced myself. I'd love to speak with you under whatever conditions you'd be most comfortable with." I extended my hand.

Raines stood there, his hands folded in front of him. I was stunned; I couldn't remember the last time someone had refused to shake my hand.

"I've received your messages," Raines said. And then he turned and walked away.

I watched him walk toward the store's escalator with his wife. After a few moments, he disappeared from sight. Behind me, Mike Kelly's friends, colleagues, and admirers were chatting happily. They were sharing bittersweet stories of a beloved writer and editor in chief, a man whose career was cut tragically short years before its time.

AFTERWORD

The two years following Howell Raines's resignation as editor of *The New York Times* have been difficult ones for the mainstream media, which has seen its reputation go from occasionally dodgy and unreliable to fundamentally untrustworthy by an ever larger (or more vocal, anyway) segment of the American population. This is not to say that much of the criticism has been unfounded; indeed, less than a year after Jayson Blair's serial deceptions at the *Times*, *USA Today* was forced to admit that its marquee foreign correspondent, Jack Kelley, had apparently been fabricating his reports for years, on everything from Cuban refugees to Palestinian suicide bombers. Then came the spring of 2004, which was thick with depressing revelations about the press's failures in its coverage of the hunt for weapons of mass destruction in Iraq, most prominently in the case of *Times* reporter Judith Miller. With winter came the furor surrounding CBS News's bombshell piece on President Bush's Vietnam-era activities, when Dan Rather went on-air with a report that relied on documents purporting to prove that Bush's inclusion in the National Guard had been brokered by his father's political connections. As it turned out, the documents had been forged, and by the time CBS came out of its defensive crouch and launched its own investigation into the matter, the American press was once again facing charges about its purported political biases, its professional ethics, even its basic competency.

There are many folks on both sides of the political aisle who delight in taking shots at the mainstream media, or "the MSM," as it's simply—and dismissively—referred to by bloggers, who've become the press's most vigilant and irritating bêtes noires. Conservatives, to be sure, have been more adept in this regard, as everyone from Rush Limbaugh to the dial-a-pundits at Fox News has become rich and famous fulminating about the "liberal elite." (Liberals also make an effort to browbeat the media, especially on political and military coverage; they just do it less effectively.) This dissatisfaction, of course, is nothing new: political partisans have been moaning and moping about those myopic meanies in the media for decades. What's different today is that the traditional media—the media elite, as it were—is running scared. Circulation at the country's big-city dailies continues to plummet; daily circulation has declined across the industry every year since 1987. Ratings of the network news shows keep dropping. The nation's newsmagazines struggle desperately to hold on to their dwindling audience, as *Time*'s and *Newsweek*'s core readers literally die off. Even CNN, once a paragon of scrupulously researched foreign reportage, has struggled to find a new identity in the wake of the Fox News channel's successes. (In January 2005, in a bizarre effort to seize the moral high ground, CNN's new president, Jonathan Klein, proudly announced that he was dropping the conservative pundit Tucker Carlson due in no small part to criticism Carlson's signature show, *Crossfire*, had received on-air from Comedy Central's Jon Stewart. Needless to say, Klein's act of bravery impressed few.)

TODAY, the media industry is facing the biggest crisis of its existence, a crisis that will redefine both how Americans get the information they receive and how reliable and accurate that information will be. As the media makes increasingly clear that it will do anything it can to hold on to its audience, the public is using its newfound muscle to dictate the terms of engagement, telling news outlets they're not much interested in reporting and news gathering that challenges their assumptions or that attempts to ask difficult and probing questions about the world. The press is in danger of going from being a guide and a teacher— informing and enlightening readers and viewers about people, places, and ideas—to serving as a mirror. More and more news "consumers" seem to want nothing so much as an ideological pat on the back, and news outlets, from Fox News on one end of the spectrum to Air America on the other, are happy to give it to them. It is the biggest sea change the industry has had to face since *The New York Times* set about redefining what it means to be a top-flight news organization in America more than a hundred years ago, and it is a shift that cannot help feel like an indignity for many in the industry, where journalists were until fairly recently regarded as—well, if not noble, perhaps, at least admirable, and sometimes even heroic. Once-proud reporters have become scared and confused, simultaneously trying to figure out what went wrong and desperately trying to win back prestige and audience. As Nicholas Lemann pointed out in a February 2005 *The New Yorker*, "Journalism that is inquisitive and intellectually honest, that surprises and unsettles, didn't always exist. There is no law saying it must exist forever, and there are political and business interests that would be better off if it didn't exist and that have worked hard to undermine it. This is what journalists in the mainstream media are starting to worry about: what if people don't believe in us, don't want us, anymore?"

As melodramatic as that question may sound, it's one that is causing hand-wringing, as well as real concern (and some, but not enough, late-night debate) among the men and women who report and present the news across all platforms. Unfortunately for them, however, their industry's identity crisis is occurring under the watchful eyes of millions of increasingly emboldened press critics, professional and otherwise. And these critics are definitely being heard. Since I began work on *Hard News* in 2003, I've spoken with many people about the future of American media: publishing executives, magazine editors, television producers. Many of them wonder: Is the very nature of what the news media does becoming outdated? Does the public realize the importance and value of a vigorous and free press? Does anyone even care? Still, there is not a lot of hard thinking about how to confront the future. Depressingly, there's also no shortage of selfish cynicism. I've been astounded at the number of people who've told me (on background, of course) that they've pretty much given up trying to figure out ways to stave off what seems to be the inevitable death of the ideal of objectivity—once the press's greatest, most hard-won ideal—in American media. As one book editor told me, "After all, I'll be gone by the time any of this shakes out." The more idealistic frontline soldiers are struggling, but many, like Lemann, seem uncertain about what approach might work best. After all, journalism is a business, and there's no way to force consumers to buy something they're no longer interested in.

In this landscape, *The New York Times* stands out even more than it did half a century ago. But although the *Times* may, in many ways, represent the industry at its best, not even it is immune to the concerns and pressures of a changing media landscape. Ironically, it was that very awareness that compelled *Times* heir and publisher Arthur Sulzberger Jr. to choose Howell Raines to be his paper's executive editor in 2001. In doing so, Sulzberger thought he was ensuring his paper's survival by choosing someone who would be able connect his paper with an audience that had less free time and more sources of information. That he was wrong has not changed Sulzberger's belief that the *Times* can and must continue to find ways to be on the forefront of journalistic excellence, that it has something close to a responsibility to ensure that top-quality journalism continues to thrive. (One need look no further than the state of affairs at the Tribune-owned *Los Angeles Times* to see just how quickly things can turn sour. In 2003, with *The New York Times* battered and grasping for traction, the *Los Angeles Times* won five

Pulitzer Prizes. Almost immediately afterward, the Tribune Company started cutting the paper's staff and budget.)

Still, believing you're right and being right are two very different things, as Sulzberger now well knows. Today, Sulzberger, along with the *Times*'s top editorial leadership, is attempting to prove that the model the paper has followed for years—reinvesting money in the editorial operations and hoping consumers will continue to buy a weightier, more thoughtful product—still holds true. In a way, this attitude, which is often described as condescending or paternalistic by right-wing critics, gives the reader the benefit of the doubt in a way that news designed to reinforce consumers' preexisting notions of the world never will. Despite all the revelations of the last several years, *The New York Times* is still unquestionably the gold standard in American journalism. But in five or ten years, will anyone care? In today's over-oxygenated political climate, in a world where Fox News is the gold standard for an economically successful news operation, is there room, or desire, for such a quaint notion as a paper of record?

I hope—and most of the time even believe—there is. Sometimes, though, I'm not so sure. Friends of mine in their twenties have little time for newspapers; they pick up their information on the fly, from news zippers or blogs or the free commuter handouts that are cropping up like dandelions in many American cities. In the Manhattan building I live in, only two apartments (out of thirty-six) regularly receive a daily newspaper. Since I began working professionally as a journalist in the mid-1990s, I've been hearing about the death of the news media industry almost every year. Those short-term projections have all proven wrong. I hope this longer-term one is wrong as well.

Corrections

In putting together *Hard News*, I knew that the book would come under intense scrutiny because of the nature of the story. For that reason, and because I hoped readers would not only find the book enjoyable but also might learn something, I tried to be as transparent as possible. I included many source notes and bibliographic entries, and was aided by an extremely dedicated and talented team at Random House. Thankfully, I have had almost no complaints about mistakes.

I did, however, make some errors, and in an effort to continue with this transparency, I'm offering up a relative rarity in the world of book publishing: a correction section.

––––––

IN THE HARDCOVER EDITION OF *HARD NEWS*, in the chapter "The First Signs of Scandal" (p. 105), I incorrectly wrote that one source of frustration on the job for *Times* national editor Jim Roberts was his testy relationship with Jon Landman. The two men, I wrote, "sat next to each other at every afternoon's page-one meeting, but they rarely said so much as hello." This information, which was not credited to any outside source in the notes to the hardcover edition of my book, came from a *New York* magazine cover story on the Blair scandal. (The relevant section of the *New York* article reads: "In the daily front-page meetings, Landman sits next to Jim Roberts, the national editor. . . . Roberts never knew of Blair's history, partly because, sources say, Landman didn't tell him—because Roberts and Landman aren't on speaking terms.")

Jon Landman, who, like Jim Roberts, had been generous enough to meet with me for my project, pointed out the error. "Jim Roberts and I talk to each other all the time and have since we started at the *Times* within a few days of each other in 1987," Landman wrote to me in an e-mail after reading my book. "The sit-next-to-each-other-at-the-page-1-meeting-but-are-not-on-speaking-terms canard started in some magazine during the Blair uproar . . . and got pumped into the Internet media bloodstream, where, through repetition, it metastasized into one of those things that everyone knows to be true." In fact, Landman wrote, while he and Roberts are not "drinking buddies," they are now, and have always been, on speaking terms, and have plenty of mutual trust and respect. What's more, there are no assigned seats at the *Times*'s page-one meetings. (Landman concluded his e-mail by writing, "I thought the book captured what went on here accurately and honestly.")

For the Record

(**Note:** The correct, amended version of the text of this book appears in this paperback edition. The errors listed below are present in the hardcover edition only.)

In "The Agenda": It was Kevin Sack himself who suggested he write a story concerning Mario Cuomo's convention speech; the assignment did not come from Howell Raines (p. 54).

In "Resignation": Clyde Haberman served as a college stringer from the City College of New York, not Columbia University (p. 131).

In "One Week In May": It was actually deputy news editor Paul Winfield, not Al Siegal, who wrote the 96-point headline—U.S. ATTACKED—

that ran atop the *Times* on September 12, 2001 (pp. 158–159). (Because of this error, this bit of *Times* arcana is missing from the paperback edition: September 12, 2001, was only the third time in the history of the paper that such a large type was used for a headline. The other two were when Neil Armstrong walked on the moon in 1969 and when President Richard Nixon resigned in 1974, a fact I learned from Ken Auletta's *New Yorker* article "The Howell Doctrine.")

Also in "One Week In May": John Geddes was the deputy managing editor of the *Times* in the spring of 2003, not an assistant managing editor (p. 170).

In "The Fallout": The executive dining room of the *Times* is on the eleventh, not the fourteenth floor of the paper's headquarters (p. 203).

Also in "The Fallout": Alan C. Miller and Kevin Sack shared a Pulitzer Prize for their work at the *Los Angeles Times*; Sack did not win that award on his own (p. 204).

In the first paragraph of "New Endings, Old Beginnings," I incorrectly wrote that on the morning of June 3, Joseph Lelyveld called his old secretary and asked her if she would be available to come back to work. In fact, on June 4, the same day he began his stint as interim executive editor, Lelyveld called Diane Ceribelli, who had worked with Bill Keller when Keller was the *Times*'s foreign editor, and asked her to work as his temporary assistant (p. 210).

In "A New Team in Place": Danny Meyer is a celebrity restaurateur, not a celebrity chef (p. 233).

Also in "A New Team in Place": Brian Gallagher, the former executive editor of *USA Today*, did not resign in the wake of the Jack Kelley scandal. (Editor Karen Jurgensen and managing editor for news, Hal Ritter, were the two top editors who resigned.) Gallagher did leave the news-gathering side of the paper, and became the editor of the editorial page (pp. 237, 238).

Acknowledgments

Four years ago, I had the good fortune of working with Hanya Yanagi-hara when she was an editor at *Brill's Content*. Since then, she has been my friend, confidante, and supporter. Most recently, she's been a passionate, dedicated, and enormously skilled editor for this book. Hanya put up with too frequent midnight phone calls and remained enthusiastic and cheerful during the many times I had to be convinced not to scrap the entire project and start anew. She helped on every level, and on every level she made this book better. Without Hanya, this book would likely not have been finished.

There are many other people who also vastly improved my work. My mother, Wendy Mnookin, one of the country's best poets (*What He Took* is a good place to start), read my manuscript and provided a much-needed combination of motherly encouragement, visceral hatred of split infinitives and sentences begun with conjunctions, and homemade brownies. My father, Jim Mnookin, was also a careful reader and loving cheerleader.

Had Simon Dumenco, a wonderful friend and a brilliant writer, simply taken the time to read my manuscript, it would have been a blessing; he was, after all, editing a magazine, writing a column, and finishing a book of his own. He also provided me with one of the best edits I have ever received, and with only hours to go before my manuscript was due. Fotini Christia also was a dedicated reader, critic, and friend.

This book grew out of work I did while a writer at *Newsweek*. I was extremely lucky to have the guidance of a wonderful editor, Tom Watson, who worked tirelessly to improve my copy. (The *Times*, Tom, they are a-changin'.) Mark Whitaker and Jon Meacham had faith in my work, and their encouragement meant a lot to this young reporter. Suzanne Smalley, Rebecca Sinderbrand, Martha Brant, Holly Bailey, Pat Wingert, and Brian Braiker provided invaluable reporting assistance for my article "The *Times* Bomb," driving through Maryland subdivisions, haranguing landlords and bartenders, and waiting outside the Times building on the off chance some news happened to break. Susan Szeliga helped with research before, during, and after my *Newsweek* cover package on Jayson Blair.

Caroline and Helmut Weymar offered me my very own Lake Como on the Atlantic in the form of a monthlong stay at "78" on Nantucket. It remains the most wonderful month of this entire process, both because of the mental space my time there afforded me and because of their cherished company and encouragement.

When I returned from Nantucket and was faced with the over-whelming prospect of having to actually write a book, the Shorenstein Center's Alex Jones offered me refuge at Harvard. I'd already looked to Alex for inspiration in the form of the book he co-wrote with Susan Tifft, *The Trust*. Having a haven overseen by Alex and Edie Holway was a true blessing.

Over the nine months I worked full-time on this book, I was lucky to have the help of many astute researchers. Meredith Sadin provided excellent (if occasionally comical) transcription and archival assistance. At Harvard, Shashank Bengali prepared succinct crash courses in the history of American journalism, and Philip Tinari pored over Nexis printouts and newspaper archives to track down whatever specific example I was convinced I needed that minute. My neighbor in Quincy House, Irin Carmon, was a tireless and much-appreciated fact-checker, bibliographer, dining hall partner, and friend. Amit Paley, Jacob Russell, and Michelle Chun also helped with the final heave.

During my months at the Shorenstein Center, I allowed myself one distraction: the Boston Red Sox (and the Sons of Sam Horn). A wise friend once said if you want to do excellent work, you should watch excellence. For that I thank G38, Petey, Manny, Tek, Tizzle, Caveman, and that awe-inspiring grab by Pokey with two on and two out in the top of the seventh on June 13 versus the Dodgers. Thanks, too, to Jose Melendez and his keys to the game.

My two mentors in publishing, Marysue Rucci and Geoff Kloske, have been patient and helpful for years and have always offered advice and reassurance whenever I've needed it. Kurt Andersen has been a personal Yoda; he sagely told me the only reason not to write this book was a fear of failure—and that that was the best reason to move ahead with the project.

At Random House, Dan Menaker was enthusiastic and encouraging about this project from the word go; his support, advice, and editing made this book what it is today. Veronica Windholz ensured that I had a truly inspiring team to work with. Stephanie Higgs was forever patient in dealing with my neuroses, Sona Vogel made the manuscript better with every mark of her red pencil, and Laura Goldin, who in her capacity as my onetime babysitter wouldn't let me eat M&M's before bedtime, has been an excellent lawyer and a careful reader. Gina Centrello has been everything a writer dreams of having in a publisher—warm, supportive, and editorially savvy. Late in the game, the miraculous Timothy Mennel swooped in with a jaw-droppingly astute final read. David McCormick is simply a great agent: tireless, enthusiastic, imaginative, and patient.

Finally, thanks to Pamela Hamer for her always spot-on suggestions and caring support. Thanks to my sister and brother, Abby and Jake Mnookin, and to my grandparents, Si and Marjorie Miller, for their love, friendship, and support. And (take that, Mom!) thanks to Miss Kitty for her enduring companionship and devotion.

As I was preparing to hand in the paperback revisions of *Hard News*, Hunter S. Thompson, the writer who made me decide at age fourteen that I had to be a journalist, shot himself in the head. I met

Hunter back in 1999, when I traveled out to Woody Creek, Colorado, to write about his life and legacy. In the years since, he'd remained an inspiration and had become a friend. As anyone who knew Hunter will tell you, there were few things as maddeningly wonderful as hearing your phone ring at 3 A.M. Inevitably, it would be Hunter, holed up in his kitchen and barking into his speakerphone: "Seth? It's Hunter. I didn't catch you doing anything weird, did I?"

In the months following the publication of my book, Hunter remained what he had always been: kind, generous, supportive, and more than slightly insane. He invited me out to do a reading with him in Aspen—an invitation I will always regret not taking—and generously let me needle him when my Patriots throttled his Colts in this year's play-offs. I'll always do my best to remember: When the going gets weird, the weird turn pro.

A Note on Sources

This is how Janet Malcolm began her classic book *The Journalist and the Murderer:* "Every journalist who is not too stupid or too full of himself to notice what is going on knows that what he does is morally indefensible. He is a kind of confidence man, preying on people's vanity, ignorance, or loneliness. . . ." It's a famous line in the industry, and one I've always found to ring false; writing about the media—and specifically about *The New York Times*—crystallized what has always seemed so wrong to me about Malcolm's formulation. Malcolm's thesis grew out of her work on a specific case—the author Joe McGinniss's fawning subject-author relationship with an accused (and later convicted) murderer named Jeffrey MacDonald, a relationship that soured when McGinniss wrote a damning bestseller about MacDonald and his trial. Like most of her writing, Malcolm's work on MacDonald began as a "one off," a long-form piece for *The New Yorker* in which she immersed herself in the life of her subject over a period of several months and then walked away when her piece was finished, "never to see [him] again."

The majority of journalists—journalists working beats, journalists who write for daily newspapers, journalists who need to return to the same carefully nurtured sources day after day—don't have the luxury of working a con. White House reporters who have a mile-long trail of bylines following them to each news conference and interview would be foolish to try to pretend they're doing anything but angling for a juicy scoop. For a reporter on the media beat, this is doubly true. Other journalists know the tricks of the trade. They also understand that tension and conflict make for compelling stories. In this case, if the subject is convinced that the upcoming profile is going to be wholly flattering, he's the one who is either stupid or full of himself.

For this and many other reasons, writing about *The New York Times* is a unique challenge. The journalists at the paper are naturally wary of being the subjects of another writer's reportage, a wariness made more acute by the intense scrutiny that has long been focused on the *Times*. What's more, writing about people in the industry (as opposed to "civilians," as journos often refer to that segment of the world that doesn't make its living humping deadlines and buttonholing interview subjects) means, inevitably, writing about your peers, your once and future colleagues, and sometimes even your friends. It's a tricky, and often uncomfortable, dance.

———————

THIS BOOK IS THE RESULT of more than a hundred interviews, many of which were with current or former employees of *The New York Times*. I'm grateful to them for the candor, time, and trust they extended to me. Virtually the entire current editorial team leading the *Times* agreed to talk to me despite the fact that they knew the result was likely to be painful for them and for some of their colleagues and friends. This was not, as Malcolm would have it, because these journalists were vain, ignorant, or lonely, but rather because of their belief that an accurately reported story is, in itself, worthwhile. More than one editor at the *Times* told me to "write a good book," by which they meant: Write a fair, accurate, and lasting document of a difficult but fascinating time in the paper's history.

A couple of style points: A quote that was obtained through an interview conducted exclusively for this book is accompanied by a present-tense verb—"says," "remarks," "remembers," "recalls." If it's in the past tense, then the quote is either from my previous reporting—for *Newsweek*, *New York* magazine, or Inside.com—or from outside sources. There are a few exceptions, all of which are indicated in the source notes.

A number of people chose not to speak with me for this project, including Howell Raines, Gerald Boyd, Joe Lelyveld, Max Frankel, and A. M. Rosenthal. Anytime I describe a scene or situation involving one of those men, I'm doing so on the basis of reporting from other sources. For the most part, the specifics of this are explained in the source notes as well, although occasionally you'll find a scene or reminiscence attributed solely to a mysterious "author interview," which is the book version of an anonymous source. I sought multiple sources of confirmation before describing a scene involving any of these former editors—and especially when I dealt with Raines and Boyd. I sent both Raines and Boyd many letters and e-mails over the course of reporting and writing this book, and I also left them phone messages and relayed messages through friends and colleagues. Neither responded.

I also want to make clear that while I did interview Arthur Sulzberger Jr. for this project, our conversations were limited to the *Times*'s business plan and strategies. He did not want to talk about the events of 2003 or his relationship with Howell Raines. As with scenes involving Raines and Boyd, the information used to portray any scene involving Arthur Sulzberger was obtained through other sources.

Finally, given the dozens of off-the-record and background interviews I conducted for this book, I chose not to include as part of the bibliography a list of people interviewed. In cases where I interviewed people on the record and used their quotes, I have included their names in the source notes.

Source Notes

Introduction

xi *The first newspaper printed in America* Frank Luther Mott. *American Journalism: A History of Newspapers in the United States Through 250 Years, 1690–1940.* New York: Routledge, 2000. pp. 43–58.

xii *Joseph Pulitzer and William Randolph Hearst* David Nasaw. *The Chief: The Life of William Randolph Hearst.* Boston: Houghton Mifflin, 2000. pp. 104–6.

xii *Hearst, in his inimitable way* Ibid., pp. 125–30.

xii *in 2004 it thoroughly dominated* "The Pulitzer Board Presents the Pulitzer Prize Winners 2004." Available at www.pulitzer.org/cgi-bin/year.pl?1912,25.

xiii *A 2004 Project for Excellence* The Project for Excellence in Journalism. *The State of the News Media 2004.* Available at www.stateofthemedia.org.

xiv *declined an opportunity to invest* Arthur Sulzberger. Speech to the Joan Shorenstein Center on the Press, Politics and Public Policy. Harvard University. Cambridge, Mass. November 20, 2000.

xiv *Hearst Corporation, by contrast* "Hearst Timeline." Available at the Hearst Corporation's website, www.hearstcorp.com/about.

xiv *almost half the paper's daily circulation* Janet Robinson to author.

xiv *"platform agnostic"* Arthur Sulzberger. Speech to the German Newspaper Publishers Association. Berlin, Germany. September 30, 2003.

xiv *"TV, the Internet, all of that is"* Sulzberger to author.

xv *Some Wall Street analysts* Author interviews.

xv   *the Tribune Company, which today owns*   Available at the Tribune
      Company corporate website, www.tribune.com.

xv   *Abuzz.com*   David Simons, "The NY Times Guarantees VC
      Investment." Available at www.forbes.com/2000/05/03/mu10.html.
      May 3, 2000.

xv   *Discovery Times Channel*   "The New York Times in Television: About
      Us." Available at the New York Times Company corporate website,
      www.nytco.com/subsites/nyttv/about.html.

xv   International Herald Tribune   Jack Shafer. "Art Dumps Don: The *Times*
      Moves the *Post* out of Their Paris Flat." Available at www.slate.com/id/
      2073060. October 23, 2002.

xvi   *What's more, the Graham family*   Author interviews.

xvi   *He found Howell Raines*   The New York Times Company corporate
      website, www.nytco.com/company-executives-hraines.html?
      searchpv=nytco.

xvi   *approximately one thousand editorial employees*   Author interviews.

xvii *"Howell seemed to think"*   Haberman to author.

xviii *According to one recent study*   The Project for Excellence in Journalism.
      The State of the News Media 2004.

xviii Times *policy dictated*   Ken Auletta. "Opening Up The Times." *The New
      Yorker.* June 28, 1993.

xix   *"You know the old slogan"*   Roy Rivenburg. "All the Jokes Fit to Tell." *Los
      Angeles Times.* May 17, 2003. Section 5, p. 1.

xix   *May 2004 episode of* The Simpsons   Robert Levine. "The Season
      Finale That Isn't a Season Finale." *The New York Times.* May 23, 2004.
      Section 2, p. 17.

Part One
BEFORE

April 8, 2002

3   *third-floor newsroom*   Author interviews.

4   *Max Frankel, the retired executive editor*   Auletta, "Opening Up The
    Times."

4   *"necessary proof of the world's existence"*   Gay Talese. *The Kingdom and the
    Power.* New York: World Publishing, 1969. p. 72.

5   *a space was cleared in front*   Ken Auletta. "The Howell Doctrine." *The
    New Yorker.* June 10, 2002. Available at www.kenauletta.com/
    howelldoctrine.html.

5 *about to win seven Pulitzer Prizes* The Pulitzer Prizes. See
www.pulitzer.org/cgi-bin/year.pl?1867,33.

5 *For the first time* Auletta, "The Howell Doctrine."

6 *"the not-Abe"* Max Frankel. *The Times of My Life and My Life with* The
Times. New York: Random House, 1999. p. 428.

6 *"A man deserves his own"* Susan E. Tifft and Alex S. Jones. *The Trust.*
Boston: Little, Brown & Co., 1999. p. 558.

6 *"I was reminded today"* Auletta, "The Howell Doctrine."

7 *"We are ever mindful"* Diego Ibarguen. "N.Y. Times Wins Record
7 Pulitzers." Associated Press. April 8, 2002.

7 *"will be studied and taught"* Shelley Emling and Caroline Wilbert.
"Times Scandal Tests Editor's Leadership." *The Atlanta Journal-
Constitution.* June 1, 2003.

7 *Raines later told Ken Auletta* Auletta, "The Howell Doctrine."

7 *"Howell mentioned a lot of folks"* Ibid.

The Sulzberger Family

8 *founded in 1851* Tifft and Jones, *The Trust*, p. 31.

8 *modern incarnation of the* Times Ibid., p. 38.

8 *Today, the New York Times Company* SEC filings, Annual Report, the
New York Times Company. February 20, 2004.

8 *market capitalization* Per quote.yahoo.com. Ticker symbol NYT, as of
May 26, 2004.

9 *"They're a monarchy"* *The Charlie Rose Show.* "The American Scene."
Interview with Max Frankel. PBS. Air date, April 14, 1994.

9 *"Great newspapers and great families"* Harold Evans. "Beyond the
Scoop." *The New Yorker.* July 8, 1996.

10 *"We don't have trust in government"* Tifft and Jones, *The Trust*, p. 774.

10 *last of four children* Ibid., p. x.

10 *"profit be considered desirable"* Ibid., p. 468.

11 *New York Times Class A stock* Ibid., p. 470.

11 *creating a structure whereby* Ibid., p. 469.

11 *"God [was] our personnel manager"* Ibid., p. 471.

11 *"We didn't have a planning process"* Ibid., p. 470.

12 *predetermined budget* Ibid., p. 384.

12 *stock dropped* Ibid., p. 471.

12 *The fortuitously timed 1971 acquisition* Ibid., p. 472.

12 *"My father, Walter Mattson, Abe Rosenthal"* Sulzberger to author.

12 *"Instead of putting more water"* Clyde Haberman. "Sulzberger Passes

Leadership of Times Co. to Son." *The New York Times*. October 17, 1997. p. A1.

13 *managing editor Turner Catledge*   Tifft and Jones, *The Trust*, p. 384.

14 *"Unpretentiousness is his greatest gift"*   Haberman, "Sulzberger Passes Leadership of Times."

14 *authorized the* Times*'s publication*   Tifft and Jones, *The Trust*, p. 487.

14 *Lord, Day & Lord*   Ibid., p. 490.

15 *"Make a great paper even greater"*   Frankel, *The Times of My Life*, p. 415.

15 *"It was . . . a vehicle"*   Tifft and Jones, *The Trust*, p. 606.

15 *In late 1991*   Ibid., p. 720.

15 *Craig Aronoff, the head*   Ibid., pp. 722–23.

16 *withstood a challenge from Lance Primis*   Ibid., p. 752.

16 *"If you think I'm sitting"*   Haberman, "Sulzberger Passes Leadership of Times."

16 *Sulzberger hired Russ Lewis*   Ibid.

16 *Joseph Lelyveld, the paper's executive editor*   Ibid.

17 *"There are four things"*   Ibid.

17 *"The most important partnership"*   Ibid.

17 *"This place doesn't run"*   Lewis to author.

17 *"His action"*   Haberman, "Sulzberger Passes Leadership of Times."

The Prince

18 *when Prince Charles visited*   Tifft and Jones, *The Trust*, p. 615.

18 *Sulzberger visited Harvard*   Arthur Sulzberger speech. November 20, 2000.

18 *Alex Jones, who, in addition*   "Alex S. Jones Named New Director of the Shorenstein Center." *Harvard University Gazette*. April 20, 2000.

19 *"I'll outlive the bastards!"*   Auletta, "Opening Up The Times."

20 *"We think she is smarter"*   Tifft and Jones, *The Trust*, pp. 554–55.

20 *series of management seminars*   Auletta, "Opening Up The Times."

20 *"Sulzberger . . . is impatient"*   Ibid.

21 *"Some would argue"*   Ibid.

21 *promote the fifty-seven-year-old*   Robert D. McFadden. "Lelyveld Will Succeed Frankel as The Times's Executive Editor." *The New York Times*. April 8, 1994. p. A1.

21 *interview with Charlie Rose*   The Charlie Rose Show, April 14, 1994.

21 *"When you run a desk"*   Behr to author.

22 *Gene Roberts, the retired editor*   Eugene L. Roberts Jr. Curriculum vitae. Available at www.journalism.umd.edu/faculty/groberts/cv.html.

22 *since he retired* The Pulitzer Prizes. See www.pulitzer.org/archive/ archive.html.

22 *"Joe didn't use the masthead well"* Behr to author.

22 *Lelyveld chose Bill Keller* "Times Appoints Managing Editor and 2 Deputies." *The New York Times.* May 23, 1997. p. C1.

22 *he wouldn't turn sixty-six until* Gabriel Snyder. "Raines Succeeds Lelyveld at *Times.*" *The New York Observer.* May 28, 2001. p. 6.

The Making of an Editor

24 *In 1964, after graduating* Auletta, "The Howell Doctrine."

25 *"He always had an air"* Ibid.

25 *Raines left journalism* Ibid.

25 *Raines was hired* Ibid.

25 *"I was looking for"* Jones to author.

25 *During Jones's fourteen years* Ibid.

26 *"Howell was a mentor to Arthur"* Rosenthal to author.

26 *"making life harder"* Howell Raines. *Fly Fishing Through the Midlife Crisis.* Garden City, N.Y.: Anchor Books, 1994. p. 20.

26 *"being piddled away, by me"* Ibid., p. 163.

26 *"We are full of lust"* Ibid., p. 182.

27 *"So here is where I came"* Ibid., p. 299.

27 *Bill Kovach, disappointed* Auletta, "The Howell Doctrine."

27 *Craig Whitney, Kovach's replacement* Ibid.

28 *"He was a damn good"* Behr to author.

28 *autocratic to the point of ridiculousness* Tifft and Jones, *The Trust*, p. 672.

28 *"He could be very combative"* Behr to author.

29 *Raines's winning article* Howell Raines. "Grady's Gift." *The New York Times Magazine.* December 1, 1991.

30 *took over as the editorial-page editor* "The Times Appoints Three Editors to Major Posts." *The New York Times.* September 12, 1992. Section 1, p. 9.

30 *"While we were still in transition"* Rosenthal to author.

30 *"On the job training"* "Reading Mr. Clinton's Lips." Editorial. *The New York Times.* January 28, 1993. p. A20.

30 *"Dobermans"* "Hold Off the Republican Dobermans." Editorial. *The New York Times.* January 30, 1993. p. A20.

31 *"intellectual cupboard"* "Mr. Clinton's Captious Critics." Editorial. *The New York Times.* February 23, 1993. p. A20.

31 *"Does he really care"* "Mr. Clinton, Meet Mr. Gore." Editorial. *The New York Times.* April 20, 1993. p. A28.

31 *"mere assertion with real accomplishment"* "A Dawn of Promise."
   Editorial. *The New York Times*. January 21, 1993. p. A24.

31 *"traditional high road for the gutter"* Howard Kurtz. "Talking Tough at
   The Times: Howell Raines's Editorials Don't Finesse with Politesse."
   The Washington Post. May 10, 1993. p. B1.

31 *"new chief pontificator"* Ibid.

31 *"Howell on the Prowl"* Howard Kurtz. "The Gray Lady's Colorful Chief:
   New Executive Editor Howell Raines Elicits Strong Opinions." *The
   Washington Post*. September 6, 2001. p. C1.

31 *"When you spend a lot of paragraphs"* Kurtz, "Talking Tough at The
   Times."

31 *"We sound like the* New York Post*"* Paul Starobin. "Raines's Reign:
   Thunder from the Times." *National Journal*. April 24, 1993. p. 990.

32 *"did rattle the china"* Frankel, *The Times of My Life*, p. 392.

32 *"I didn't want us to undermine"* Timothy Noah. "The Deadly Dozen."
   George. May 1999.

32 *"He tended to lecture"* Author interview.

32 *"He made that editorial page so exciting"* Collins to author.

33 *"routinely attempt to hide simpleminded"* Timothy Noah. "Howell
   Agonistes." Available at www.slate.com/id/1000276. December 17, 1998.

33 *"Raines would do well"* Michael Tomasky. "His Terrible, Swift Sword."
   The Nation. January 4, 1999.

33 *"To me, it seemed"* Author interview.

33 *"That was a stormy time"* Author interview.

33 *Privately, Raines himself joked* Author interviews.

33 *"[Campaign finance] is the most boring"* Collins to author.

34 *headlines were similar to the point* Editorials from *The New York Times*, in
   order of list: July 30, 2001, p. A16; July 20, 2001, p. A20; July 3, 2001,
   p. A16; March 27, 2001, p. A22; April 3, 2001, p. A18; June 25, 2001,
   p. A16; March 22, 2001, p. A26.

34 *"He would not stop"* Collins to author.

34 *Robert McNamara's 1995 memoir* Robert S. McNamara and Brian
   VanDeMark (contributor). *In Retrospect: The Tragedy and Lessons of the
   Vietnam War*. New York: Crown Publishers, 1995.

34 *"Comes now Robert McNamara"* "Mr. McNamara's War." Editorial. *The
   New York Times*. April 12, 1995. p. A24.

35 *"It was simply beating"* Noah, "The Deadly Dozen."

35 *Bob Semple, another* Times The Pulitzer Prizes. See
   www.pulitzer.org/year/1996/editorial-writing.

35 *"Howell and I talk"* *Washington Journal*. Interview with Arthur

Sulzberger Jr. and Howell Raines by Brian Lamb. C-SPAN1. Air date September 22, 1997, 6:00 p.m.

36 *State of the* Times *talks* Noah, "The Deadly Dozen."

The Competition

38 *"I thought the paper"* Howell Raines. "My Times." *The Atlantic.* May 2004.

38 *broke a story* Raymond Bonner and Josh Barbanel. "Democrats Rue Ballot Foul-up in a 2nd County." *The New York Times.* November 17, 2000. p. A1.

38 *broke news about the controversial* David Barstow and Somini Sengupta. "Judge Who Rebuffed Gore Had Run-ins with Justices." *The New York Times.* December 8, 2000. p. A1.

38 *"our rivals up the road"* Jack Shafer. "The Scoopless *Washington Post.*" Available at www.slate.com/id/1006703. December 18, 2000.

39 *"The period in which it became"* Keller to author.

39 *"The ingrained management habit"* Raines, "My Times."

40 *In February 2001* The New York Times Company corporate website, www.nytco.com/company-executives-jlrobinson.html.

40 *"We had to create a new newspaper"* Sulzberger to author.

40 *"Whether we liked it or not"* Raines, "My Times."

41 *"My wife sometimes refers to me"* Howard Kurtz. "Newsroom Favorite Bill Keller Named Times' Top Editor." *The Washington Post.* July 15, 2003. p. C1.

41 *Raines is a dynamic and forceful* Baquet to author.

41 *"Under Joe, I felt"* Siegal to author.

41 *"There was a feeling"* Behr to author.

41 *"Howell will continue"* "The New York Times Announces Howell Raines to Become Executive Editor." Press Release, the New York Times Company. May 21, 2001.

42 *"My first and foremost responsibility"* Robert D. McFadden. "Times Names Raines as Successor to Lelyveld as Executive Editor." *The New York Times.* May 22, 2001. p. A1.

42 *Under the heading of "I would like to see"* Seth Mnookin. "Bill Keller, Passed Over for Top Spot at New York Times, Has 'Pig-in-Shit' New Gig." Inside.com. June 19, 2001.

42 *"The first lesson of management"* Baquet to author.

The Deputy

44   *"No more Mr. Gruff"*   Seth Mnookin. "Gerald Boyd Named New York Times Managing Editor—First African-American in the Job." Inside.com. June 26, 2001.

45   *he helped found and edit*   Jayson Blair. "Gerald." In *Times Talk*. Internal Newsletter. September 2001.

45   *"He was extremely aggressive"*   David Carr and Janny Scott. "A Formidable Run Undone by Scandal and Discontent." *The New York Times*. June 6, 2003. p. B8.

45   *"Gerald is not your biggest"*   Behr to author.

45   *"He was very proud"*   Sontag to author.

46   *"Gerald really showed me a lot"*   Sack to author.

46   *According to people who worked for and with him*   Author interviews.

47   *"I wanted to see, as Arthur himself"*   Raines, "My Times."

47   *sported an Afro*   Blair, "Gerald."

47   *"There were just two minority reporters"*   Harry Lewis. "NY Times Taps Gerald Boyd as Its New Managing Editor." *St. Louis Post-Dispatch*. July 27, 2001. p. A1.

47   *"I hope tomorrow, when some kid"*   Susan Sachs. "Times Names Gerald Boyd as Its Next Managing Editor." *The New York Times*. July 27, 2001. p. A13.

Race in the Newsroom

48   *"the journalistic profession"*   " 'The Communications Media, Ironically, Have Failed to Communicate': The Kerner Report Assesses Media Coverage of Riots and Race Relations." History Matters: The U.S. Survey Course on the Web. Available at http://historymatters.gmu.edu/d/6553.

48   *Ten years later, in 1978*   Ted Pease. "Minority Job-seekers Don't Fare as Well." *The American Editor*. November 11, 1999. Available at www.asne.org/kiosk/editor/99.oct-nov/pease1.htm.

48   *By 2003, that number had risen*   Jennifer Barrios and April D. Bethea. " 'Snail-Pace' Minority Gains Spur Concern." *The ASNE Reporter*. April 20, 2004. Available at www.asne.org/index.cfm?id=5173.

49   *Another theory—that there are*   Lee B. Becker, Tudor Vlad, Jisu Huh, and Nancy R. Mace. "Annual Enrollment Report: Graduate and Undergraduate Enrollments Increase Sharply." *Journalism & Mass Communication Educator* 58, no. 3 (2003). Available at www.grady.uga.edu/annualsurveys/Enrollment02/enroll02sum.htm.

49 *"The culture is such"* Wilkins to author.

49 *A semiformalized effort* Frankel, *The Times of My Life*, p. 465.

49 *He wrote in his memoir* Ibid., p. 468.

49 *"There was a real problem"* The Charlie Rose Show, April 14, 1994.

50 *"Joe was all for Arthur"* Tifft and Jones, *The Trust*, p. 686.

50 *at the same time that Frankel* Frankel, *The Times of My Life*, p. 466.

51 *a black reporter named Kenneth Noble* Author interviews.

51 *"But Gerald went and visited Ken"* Mathews to author.

51 *"Ken couldn't hack it"* Author interview.

The Agenda

53 *In August 2001* Author interviews.

53 *Sack had been hired* Sack to author.

54 *Raines's staff was preparing* Author interviews.

54 *"Her family is there"* Sack to author.

56 *"We thought our metabolism"* Author interview.

56 *"Please don't make me relive"* Katy Roberts. "Re: New York Times Book Project." E-mail message to author. December 8, 2003. 4:47 p.m.

A New Era

57 *The flagging economy* Philip Shenon. "Bush and Daschle Agree Not to Tap Social Security." *The New York Times*. September 5, 2001. p. A1. Also, Susan Saulny. "New Jobless Centers Offer More Than a Benefit Check." *The New York Times*. September 5, 2001. p. A1.

58 *In one of his first* Seth Mnookin. "Philosopher King Is Out at the New York Times, as Southern Pol Settles In." Inside.com. September 5, 2001.

58 *Raines lined the walls of his office* Auletta, "The Howell Doctrine."

58 *Raines also instituted a 10:30 a.m. meeting* Author interviews.

59 *"I used to spend most"* Bradlee to author.

59 *"indifference to competition"* Raines, "My Times."

60 *Howell Raines lives in* Auletta, "The Howell Doctrine."

61 The New York Times *would dispatch* Ibid.

62 *"There was the enormous stress"* Oreskes to author.

62 *Raines met with investigative editor Stephen Engelberg* Engelberg to author.

63 *"When you empower the desk editors"* Roberts to author.

64 *"Where are these people going?"* Author interview.

64 *"Early on"* Kramon to author.

65 *Alex Berenson detailed how Enron*   Alex Berenson. "Enron's Collapse:
    Selling Energy; Ex-Workers Say Unit's Earnings Were 'Illusory.' " *The
    New York Times*. January 25, 2002. p. A1.

65 *Kurt Eichenwald authored*   Kurt Eichenwald with Diana B. Henriques.
    "Enron's Many Strands: The Company Unravels; Enron Buffed Image
    to a Shine Even as It Rotted from Within." *The New York Times*.
    February 10, 2002. p. A1.

The Washington Bureau

66 *"We don't know who's going"*   Abramson to author.

68 *"Jill Abramson never expressed any frustration"*   Patrick E. Tyler. "Re: New
    York Times Book Project." E-mail message to author. June 4, 2004.
    6:39 a.m.

68 *"The issue of the heavy-handedness"*   Auletta, "The Howell Doctrine."

A Growing Mandate

70 *"This story was so consuming"*   The Charlie Rose Show. "New York Times
    Editor Howell Raines on 9/11 (Part I)." Interview with Howell Raines.
    PBS. Air date, August 6, 2002.

70 *"I felt in the case of Kevin"*   Abramson to author.

71 *"I just thought that was awful"*   Oreskes to author.

71 *"He let Gerald carry all"*   Sack to author.

71 *San Francisco–based Evelyn Nieves*   Seth Mnookin. "Hard Raines." *New
    York*. February 18, 2002.

72 *Raines had insisted Bragg be sent*   Auletta, "The Howell Doctrine."

72 *"It was my dream to do this"*   "Rick Bragg Biography." Available at
    www.bookbrowse.com/index.cfm?page=author&author ID77.

72 *"fill . . . their white trash quota."*   Ibid.

72 *The Pulitzer board agreed*   "The Pulitzer Board Presents the Pulitzer
    Prize Winners 1996." Available at www.pulitzer.org/cgi-bin/
    year.pl?1735,16.

72 *"I stopped reading him"*   Ana Marie Cox. "Bragging Rights." The Antic
    Muse. Online Posting. May 29, 2003, 12:05 p.m. Available at
    www.theanticmuse.com/~anamarie/archives/000098.html.

73 *In 1997, Bragg published*   Rick Bragg. *All Over but the Shoutin'*. New
    York: Pantheon Books, 1997.

73 *"Pakistan Is 2 Worlds"*   Rick Bragg. "Pakistan Is 2 Worlds: One Urbane,
    One Enraged." *The New York Times*. October 1, 2001. p. B1.

73   *"Surrounded by caged birds"*   Rick Bragg. "Seeking Miracles in a Place of
     Cruelty and Beauty." *The New York Times*. October 28, 2001. p. A1.

73   *"What's wrong with putting"*   Auletta, "The Howell Doctrine."

74   *"He's looking for 30-year-olds"*   Mnookin, "Hard Raines."

74   *"I know that inaccurate reports"*   Rosemary Shields for Howell Raines.
     "A note from Howell Raines." E-mail message. February 15, 2002.
     3:01 p.m.

74   *"What seemed to happen"*   Behr to author.

Pushing Back, Moving On

77   *"I didn't know what to do"*   Abramson to author.

77   *"Far from being a shadow"*   Tyler. "Re: New York Times Book Project."

77   *Abramson, on the other hand*   Abramson to author.

78–79   *"A lot of people did"*   Siegal to author.

79   *soon after her lunch*   Abramson to author.

79   *"I'm hearing Abe's back!"*   Auletta, "The Howell Doctrine."

80   *an "unsophisticated" analysis*   *The Charlie Rose Show*. Interview with
     Howell Raines. PBS. Air date, July 11, 2003.

80   *a 2003 national reporting Pulitzer*   Available at
     www.pulitzer.org/year/2003/national-reporting.

81   *"Howell won't mind"*   Author interviews.

81   *The author's bio in Raines's 1977 novel*   Howell Raines. *Whiskey Man*. New
     York: Viking, 1977. Back flap copy.

81   *"boss from hell"*   Stephen Engelberg. "Book Review Lies and the Sly Liar
     Who Tries to Justify Them." *The Oregonian*. March 21, 2004. p. D6.

81   *On November 1, 2001, after polishing off*   William J. Broad, Stephen
     Engelberg, Judith Miller, and Sheryl Gay Stolberg. "Excruciating
     Lessons in the Ways of a Disease." *The New York Times*. October 31,
     2001. p. A1. Also William J. Broad, Stephen Engelberg, and James
     Glanz. "Assessing Risks, Chemical, Biological, Even Nuclear." *The New
     York Times*. November 1, 2001. p. A1.

81   *"This can't work"*   Engelberg to author.

82   *"It was a potentially great job"*   Frantz to author.

83   *a story about the space-shuttle disaster*   Matthew Rose and Laurie P. Cohen.
     "Men in the News: Amid Turmoil, Top Editors Resign at New York
     Times—for Raines, Reporters' Lapses Helped Stoke Friction over
     Management Style—'An Endemic Cultural Issue.' " *The Wall Street
     Journal*. June 6, 2003. p. A1.

84   *"Everybody started to get calls"*   Landman to author.

The Daily Report

85   *"One person quits"*   Raines, "My Times."

86   *"These [all-known thoughts] were"*   Behr to author.

86   *"If the drought drags on"*   Andrew C. Revkin. "Extended Drought Strains Resources Along East Coast." *The New York Times*. April 21, 2002. p. A1.

87   *"He decided we were undercovering"*   Landman to author.

88   *"Every editor and reporter"*   Robert J. Samuelson. "A Liberal Bias?" *The Washington Post*. August 29, 2001. p. A21.

88   *"Leading Republicans from Congress"*   Todd S. Purdum and Patrick E. Tyler. "Top Republicans Break with Bush on Iraq Strategy." *The New York Times*. August 16, 2002. p. A1.

88   *"listening carefully to"*   Elisabeth Bumiller. "President Notes Dissent on Iraq, Vowing to Listen." *The New York Times*. August 1, 2002. p. A1.

89   *"The imminence of proliferation"*   Henry A. Kissinger. "Our Intervention in Iraq." *The Washington Post*. August 12, 2002. p. A15.

89   *"Not since William"*   Charles Krauthammer. "Kidnapped by the Times." *The Washington Post*. August 18, 2002. p. B7.

89   *"I had to tell them"*   Carr to author.

89   *"This is certainly a shift"*   Seth Mnookin. "The Changing 'Times.' " *Newsweek*. December 9, 2002.

89   *"By this time"*   Abramson to author.

90   *"Ms. Spears"*   Laura M. Holson and Alex Kuczynski. "Schoolyard Superstar Aims for a Second Act, as an Adult." *The New York Times*. October 6, 2002. p. A1.

90   *"There's nothing wrong"*   Landman to author.

Augusta

91   *"CBS Staying Silent"*   Alessandra Stanley and Bill Carter. "CBS Staying Silent in Debate on Women Joining Augusta." *The New York Times*. November 25, 2002. p. A1.

91   *"[The Augusta coverage] was just shocking"*   Mnookin, "The Changing 'Times.' "

92   *"Raines is on the verge"*   Mickey Kaus. "Kerry Mystery Contest; Plus: Raines Remains Silent, Day 6!" Online Posting. Kausfiles. www.slate.com. November 26, 2002.

92   *"At some point"*   Jack Shafer. "The *New York Times*' Augusta Blog: Stop Me If You've Read This Story Before." Available at www.slate.com/id/2074599. November 25, 2002.

92 *"We're* The New York Times" Sulzberger to author.

92 *"I remember being surprised"* Okrent to author.

92 *"The Masters story"* Kramon to author.

92 *Paul Colford, reported* Paul D. Colford. "Times Editors Kill 2 Columns in Augusta Rift." New York *Daily News*. December 4, 2002. p. 50.

93 *"Howell and I believe"* Gerald Boyd. "NYT M.E. Gerald Boyd's memo re Augusta." Online Posting. Poynter Online—Forums, "Memos Sent to Romenesko." December 4, 2002. 4:45:56 p.m. Available at www.poynteronline.org/forum/default.asp?id=32127.

95 *"If Boyd's memo"* Mickey Kaus. "The *NYT* Buckles." Online Posting. Kausfiles. www.slate.com. December 5, 2002.

95 *"Gerald's memo was totally"* Haberman to author.

95 *"I guess it was because"* Alan Shipnuck. *The Battle for Augusta National: Hootie, Martha, and the Masters of the Universe.* New York: Simon & Schuster, 2004. p. 141.

95 *"There was a very strong"* Ibid., p. 143.

95 *"I think Gerald"* Ibid., p. 145.

96 *"prompted critical commentary"* Felicity Barringer. "2 Rejected Sports Columns to Be Printed by The Times." *The New York Times*. December 7, 2002. p. A17.

96 *"I was appalled"* Author interview.

96 *"If there's ever a revolt"* Ibid.

97 *Raines wed his longtime girlfriend* Sridhar Pappu and Anna Jane Grossman. "My Big Fat Times Wedding." *The New York Observer*. March 17, 2003. p. 1.

Part Two
SPRING 2003

The First Signs of Scandal

101 *On Saturday, April 26* Rivard to author.

101 *The headline read* Jayson Blair. "Family Waits, Now Alone, for a Missing Soldier." *The New York Times*. April 26, 2003. p. A1.

102 *stories about a suspect* John MacCormack. "Missing & Presumed Dead." *San Antonio Express-News*. December 28, 1999. p. A1.

102 *The* Express-News *story* Macarena Hernandez. "Valley Mom Awaits News of MIA Son." *San Antonio Express-News*. April 18, 2003. p. A1.

103 *"Jayson was always"* Hernandez to author.

103 *"Instead of going to the Times"* Macarena Hernandez. "What Jayson Blair

Stole from Me, and Why I Couldn't Ignore It." *The Washington Post*. June 1, 2003. p. B5.

103 *"Juanita Anguiano points"* Blair, "Family Waits, Now Alone, for a Missing Soldier."

104 *the Anguianos' Martha Stewart* Macarena Hernandez. "National Betrayal." *San Antonio Express-News*. June 1, 2003. p. H1.

104 *"Since someone at the* Times" Rivard to author.

104 *"By the time I got there"* Roberts to author.

106 *"At that time, he hadn't decided"* Kurtz to author.

Jayson Blair

107 *"just another black man"* Jayson Blair. *Burning Down My Masters' House*. Beverly Hills, Calif.: New Millennium, 2004. p. 95.

107 *"They are the finest people"* Latt to Holly Bailey for *Newsweek*. Seth Mnookin et al. "Times Bomb." *Newsweek*. May 26, 2003.

108 *"He just bounced in one day"* Cahill to Patrice Wingert for *Newsweek*. Mnookin et al., "Times Bomb."

108 *The yearbook index lists* Centreville High School yearbook.

109 *Blair seems to have faked* Chris Mergerson. "God Attracts 62 Students and 4 Teachers." *Centreville Sentinel*. September 22, 1993. p. 2.

109 *"Jayson attached [my name]"* Mergerson to author.

110 *Blair enrolled at Liberty University* David Folkenflik. "The Making of Jayson Blair." *Baltimore Sun*. February 29, 2004. p. F10.

110 *"He was easy to pick out"* Callahan to Martha Brant for *Newsweek*. Mnookin et al., "Times Bomb."

110 *"When Jayson was initially hired"* Newman to Rebecca Sinderbrand for *Newsweek*. Mnookin et al., "Times Bomb."

113 *"All of us were ambitious"* Author interview.

113 *"He tried to undermine our efforts"* McMenamin to Brian Braiker for *Newsweek*. Mnookin et al., "Times Bomb."

113 *Another intern says Blair frequently tried* Author interview.

113 *"I've seen some who like to abuse"* Dan Barry, David Barstow, Jonathan D. Glater, Adam Liptak, and Jacques Steinberg. "Times Reporter Who Resigned Leaves Long Trail of Deception." *The New York Times*. May 11, 2003. p. A1.

113 *Joyce Purnick, then the metro editor* Blair, *Burning Down My Masters' House*, p. 106.

114 *According to Arthur Sulzberger* Adrienne P. Samuels. "Black Journalists Discuss 'Blair Affair.' " *St. Petersburg Times*. August 10, 2003.

115 *"I told him that he needed to find"* Barry et al., "Times Reporter Who Resigned Leaves Long Trail of Deception."

115 *"He always struck me as"* Author interview.

115 *Gerald Boyd headed the committee* Barry et al., "Times Reporter Who Resigned Leaves Long Trail of Deception."

116 *"It was clear that Gerald"* "The Siegal Committee Report; Report and Recommendations of the Working Group on Training and Performance Management; Recommendations and Thoughts of the Communications Subcommittee." July 28, 2003. p. 39. Available at www.nytco.com/committeereport.pdf.

116 *"To say now that his promotion"* Barry et al., "Times Reporter Who Resigned Leaves Long Trail of Deception."

116 *the* Times *ran the following correction* Jayson Blair. "A Rousing Rock Show for a Wounded City." *The New York Times*. October 21, 2001. p. B10. Correction appended October 23, 2001.

117 *negative review* "Siegal Committee Report," p. 38.

117 *"There's big trouble"* Barry et al., "Times Reporter Who Resigned Leaves Long Trail of Deception."

117 *"You have enormous promise and potential"* Author interviews.

118 *not "inclusive"* Auletta, "The Howell Doctrine."

118 *Blair took two personal leaves* Barry et al., "Times Reporter Who Resigned Leaves Long Trail of Deception."

118 *two of Blair's supervisors* "Siegal Committee Report," p. 39.

119 *"In a weird way"* Blair to author.

119 *"It was real filth"* Landlord to Suzanne Smalley for *Newsweek*. Mnookin et al., "Times Bomb."

119 *"He was just spinning out"* Author interview.

Sniper Time

121 *"This guy's hungry"* Barry et al., "Times Reporter Who Resigned Leaves Long Trail of Deception."

121 *Jayson Blair broke out of the pack* Jayson Blair. "Retracing a Trail: The Investigation; U.S. Sniper Case Seen as a Barrier to a Confession." *The New York Times*. October 30, 2002. p. A1.

121 *"We had sources waving us away"* Abramson to author.

121 *"When I read that first story"* Barstow to author.

122 *Within days,* The Washington Post See, for example, Susan Schmidt and Katherine Shaver. "Muhammad Interrogation in Dispute; U.S.

Attorneys Cut Off Talks, Local Prosecutor Alleges." *The Washington Post*. October 31, 2002. p. A1.

122 *"The* Post *got beat"* Erik Wemple. "Sniping Coverage." *Washington City Paper*. November 8, 2002.

122 *"Jayson," Raines wrote* Linda Conte for Howell Raines. "From Howell re: Wednesday's great scoop." E-mail message. November 1, 2002. 11:05:52 a.m.

122 *"I interpreted it as, 'Fuck you,'"* Abramson to author.

122 *"I can't imagine accepting"* Barry et al., "Times Reporter Who Resigned Leaves Long Trail of Deception."

123 *Boyd walked by the* Times's *metro desk* Author interviews.

123 *In a December 22 front-page story* Jayson Blair. "Teenager's Role Tangles Case Against Older Sniper Suspect." *The New York Times*. December 22, 2002. p. A1.

123 *business reporter Gretchen Morgenson* Laurie P. Cohen and Matthew Rose. "Amid Turmoil, Top Editors Resign at New York Times." *The Wall Street Journal*. June 6, 2003. p. A1.

123 *"I couldn't throw it away"* Kramon to author.

123 *"Zuza [Glowacka] encouraged me"* Blair, *Burning Down My Masters' House*, p. 273.

124 *In college, while writing* Jayson Blair. "Media Right to Expose Wrong." *The Diamondback*. May 7, 1999.

124 *"fully psychotic"* Blair, *Burning Down My Masters' House*, p. 287.

124 *he was writing from inside* Barry et al., "Times Reporter Who Resigned Leaves Long Trail of Deception."

124 *"He did not seem to have"* Roberts to author.

125 *Blair's April 26, 2003, front-page story* Blair, "Family Waits, Now Alone, for a Missing Soldier."

Resignation

126 *"I was still wondering"* Roberts to author.

127 *"Many people in my newsroom"* Rivard to author.

127 *"We believe your Houston reporter"* Robert Rivard. Letter to Bill Keller. March 30, 1999.

127 *"Having reported for a couple"* Bill Keller. Letter to Robert Rivard. April 7, 1999.

127 *"It's not quite plagiarism"* Howard Kurtz. "New York Times Story Gives Texas Paper Sense of Déjà Vu; San Antonio Editor Cites 'Damning' Similarity." *The Washington Post*. April 30, 2003. p. C1.

128 *Wemple, who had written* Wemple, "Sniping Coverage."

128 *"The first words out of his mouth"* Kurtz to author.

128 *Wemple's story indicated* Erik Wemple. "Repeat Performance." *Washington City Paper*. May 2, 2003.

128 *"Dear Bob"* Author interview.

129 *"He just seemed nervous"* Williams to author.

131 *"I said I was an expert"* Haberman to author.

131 *Haberman, who had been banned* Elizabeth Kolbert. "Tumult in the Newsroom." *The New Yorker*. June 30, 2003. See also Talese, *The Kingdom and the Power*, pp. 377–81.

131 *Gerald Boyd got hold of* Roberts to author.

132 *Blair sent a letter* Sridhar Pappu. "Off the Record." *The New York Observer*. May 12, 2003.

132 The New York Times *ran its first* Jacques Steinberg. "Times Reporter Resigns After Questions on Article." *The New York Times*. May 2, 2003. p. A30.

132 *"I have been struggling"* Tara Burghart. "Former New York Times Reporter Apologizes." Associated Press. May 2, 2003.

132 *"trouble with basics"* Paul D. Colford. "Times to Probe Reporter's Stories." New York *Daily News*. March 3, 2003. p. 17.

133 *"this was a promising"* *Reliable Sources*. Hosted by Howard Kurtz. CNN. Air date May 4, 2003. Transcript available at www.cnn.com/transcripts/0305/04/rs.00.html.

133 *who himself had been snookered* Jack Shafer. "The Jayson Blair Project: How Did He Bamboozle the *New York Times*?" Available at www.slate.com/id/2082741. May 8, 2003.

134 *Jacques Steinberg had arrived* Steinberg to author.

134 *Reston's career at the* Times James Reston. *Deadline*. New York: Random House, 1991.

135 *Lorne Manly, the* Times's Manly to author.

135 *"It was suggested to me"* Steinberg to author.

136 *Blair, she said, was covering* Williams to author.

137 *"I keep trying"* Manly to author.

137 *"No, no, no, he didn't come"* Steinberg, "Times Reporter Resigns After Questions on Article."

137 *"David Shaw treatment"* David Shaw. "A Business Deal Done—a Controversy Born." *Los Angeles Times*. December 20, 1999. p. V1.

137 *"I was thinking about Reston"* Steinberg to author.

137 *"We both knew there was more"* Manly to author.

A Team Assembled

139   *"I had no idea"*   Liptak to author.

140   *The whole time he was practicing*   Glater to author.

141   *one of his more amusing*   Jonathan Glater. "Adultery May Be a Sin, but It's a Crime No More." *The New York Times*. April 17, 2003. p. A16.

141   *"Well, at least you went"*   Glater and Liptak to author.

143   *a follow-up to a three-part*   David Barstow and Lowell Berman. "At a Texas Foundry, an Indifference to Life." *The New York Times*. January 8, 2003. p. A1.

143   *"On his best day"*   Barstow to author.

144   *"You're suddenly looking"*   Steinberg to author.

144   *"It was similar to a litigation"*   Liptak to author.

144   *"He couldn't believe"*   Steinberg to author.

144   *"Fairly early on"*   Liptak to author.

145   *"He had a kind of mental rigor"*   Siegal to author.

145   *"I had never worked with Jayson"*   Kramon to author.

145   *"It became clear that we could not"*   Steinberg to author.

146   *The closest parallel to the team's endgame*   A. H. Raskin. "The Strike: A Step-by-Step Account." *The New York Times*. April 1, 1964. p. A1.

147   *Blood Brothers, a black youth gang*   Junius Griffin. "Anti-White Harlem Gang Reported to Number 400." *The New York Times*. May 6, 1964. p. A1. Also, Junius Griffin, "N.A.A.C.P. Assails Reports of Gang." *The New York Times*. May 11, 1964. p. A27.

147   *published a profile*   Fox Butterfield and Mary B. W. Tabor. "Woman in Florida Rape Inquiry Fought Adversity and Sought Acceptance." *The New York Times*. April 17, 1991. p. A17.

147   *calling the Bowman piece a "mistake"*   Anna Quindlen. "A Mistake." *The New York Times*. April 21, 1991. Section 4, p. 17.

148   *a defensive editors' note*   Editors' Note. *The New York Times*. April 26, 1991. p. A3.

148   *an unbylined story*   "On Names in Rape Cases." *The New York Times*. April 17, 1991. p. A17.

148   *asked Marty Baron*   Marty Baron. "Re: Lewinsky story sourcing." Memo to Joe Lelyveld and Bill Keller. February 15, 1998.

149   *"Joe wanted me to just examine"*   Jones to author.

149   *They commissioned an editors' note*   "The Times and Wen Ho Lee." Editors' Note. *The New York Times*. September 26, 2000. p. A2.

150   *Jones was no longer under contract*   Jones to author.

151   *a dispatch from Hunt Valley, Maryland*   Jayson Blair. "Watching, and

Praying, as a Son's Fate Unfolds." *The New York Times*. March 24, 2003. p. B1.

151 *one from April 7 in Cleveland* Jayson Blair. "For One Pastor, the War Hits Home." *The New York Times*. April 7, 2003. p. B1.

151 *In the middle of the meeting* Steinberg to author.

151 *From Portland, Barstow asked* Barstow to author.

151 *By Friday evening, the paper's top* Kramon to author.

152 *"It was a good story"* Barry to author.

152 *"Anytime you're doing a project"* Landman to author.

One Week in May

153 *"We had no idea how deep"* Barstow to author.

154 *"It was starting to sink in"* Liptak to author.

154 *"That day, I remember my shoulders"* Glater to author.

155 *"We just bawled like babies"* Jayson Blair and Douglas Jehl. "Rescue in Iraq and a 'Big Stir' in West Virginia." *The New York Times*. April 3, 2003. p. A1. Also, "Family of Rescued Soldier Rejoices." Associated Press. April 2, 2003.

155 *Haraz Ghanbari was a freelance photographer* Barry et al., "Times Reporter Who Resigned Leaves Long Trail of Deception."

156 *Late on Sunday, May 4* Barstow, Manly, Siegal, Barstow, Barry, Steinberg, and Glater to author.

158 *April 2002 e-mail from Jon Landman* Barry et al., "Times Reporter Who Resigned Leaves Long Trail of Deception."

159 *"They half begged and half demanded"* Siegal to author.

160 *"[Later that week] I interviewed"* Barstow to author.

160 *"None of the reporters took glee"* Barry to author.

161 *"It was excruciating"* Steinberg to author.

161 *"I'd walk around"* Barry to author.

161 *"That night, I couldn't sleep"* Glater to author.

161 *"We were seeing indications"* Steinberg to author.

162 *"It was an amazing story"* Barstow to author.

162 *"the level of journalistic crime"* Barry to author.

162 *Manly reported to Al Siegal* Manly to author.

163 *"[Monday, May 5] was the one time"* Kramon to author.

163 *Everyone froze* Manly to author.

163 *"We knew they wanted us"* Liptak to author.

164 *"I just went and said"* Barry to author.

164 *"When we were talking"* Glater to author.

164 *Had he been the one* Liptak to author.

165 *"I was calling him"* Steinberg to author.

165 *"I have a story"* C. J. Chivers. "Re: far from home." E-mail message. March 1, 2003. 12:51:06 a.m.

166 *"My shirt was getting rancid"* Barstow to author.

167 *"I get to the front desk"* Barry to author.

167 *The Westin had recently introduced* Available at Westin Hotels & Resorts company website, www.starwood.com/westin/service/reservations_service.html.

168 *the last time they would talk* Barry and Barstow to author.

169 *"Clearly, if you're putting a story"* Siegal to author.

170 *Raines appeared on PBS's* NewsHour *The NewsHour with Jim Lehrer.* "The Search for Truth." Reported by Terence Smith. PBS. Air date, May 9, 2003. Transcript available at www.pbs.org/newshour/bb/media/jan-june03/blair_05-09.html.

171 *"I said to the other guys"* Steinberg to author.

171 *"It was pretty palpable"* Barstow to author.

171 *"We weren't looking"* Barry to author.

171 *"We all in some way love"* Barstow to author.

The *Times*'s Report

173 *"drunk the Kool-Aid"* Mathis to author.

173 *pieces of the* Times *report* Barry et al., "Times Reporter Who Resigned Leaves Long Trail of Deception."

176 *That Sunday,* The Denver Post "Writer's Work Published in the Denver Post." *The Denver Post.* May 11, 2003. p. A10. Also, "The Chronicle Ran 3 of Blair's Stories." *San Francisco Chronicle.* May 11, 2003. p. A1. Also, "At Least One Story by Jayson Blair That Was Published in The Tennessean Contained Errors Corrected Yesterday by The New York Times." *The Tennessean.* May 11, 2003. p. 16A.

176 *The* Orlando Sentinel *ran* Manning Pynn. "Squander Credibility and All Is Lost." *Orlando Sentinel.* May 11, 2003. p. G3. Also, "Most of Reporter's Articles Had Problems, New York Times Says." *Orlando Sentinel.* May 11, 2003. p. A22.

176 *Reaction in the newsroom was mixed* Author interviews.

177 *"We were very proud of the piece"* Liptak to author.

177 *"We were all half waiting"* Barstow to author.

177 *"We were sort of wondering"* Liptak to author.

178 *Norris walked around the newsroom* Norris to author.

179 *Raines sent out an e-mail* Howell Raines. "A Message to the Staff by Howell Raines." E-mail message. May 12, 2003. 5:40:08 p.m.

179 *"We hit [Raines] pretty squarely"* Haberman to author.

179 *"There was a sense"* Barstow to author. Also, Jacques Steinberg. "Editor of Times Tells Staff He Accepts Blame for Fraud." *The New York Times.* May 15, 2003. p. A31. Also, Howard Kurtz. "To the Editors: How Could This Happen?; N.Y. Times Staff, Execs in 'Painful and Honest' Meeting over Plagiarism Fiasco." *The Washington Post.* May 15, 2003. p. C1.

181 *Writing about this period* Raines, "My Times."

A Fateful Gathering

184 *Sheila Sharkey, a tourist* Paul D. Colford et al. "Times Chief Says He's Not Quitting." New York *Daily News.* May 15, 2003. Also, Josh Getlin. "As N.Y. Times Struggles with Scandal, Editor Insists He'll Stay." *Los Angeles Times.* May 15, 2003.

184 *the* Times *had confirmed* "New York Times: Ex-Reporter Faces Fraud Inquiry." Available at www.cnn.com/2003/US/Northeast/05/13/ ny.times.investigation. May 13, 2003.

185 *"I wanted to show solidarity"* Siegal to author.

185 *"You're too young"* Tifft and Jones, *The Trust,* p. 655.

185 *"I've received a lot of advice"* "Dark Days for the Gray Lady." Associated Press. May 15, 2003.

186 *"Does that mean I personally"* "Profile of Howell Raines." Associated Press. June 5, 2003.

186 *"Whatever slack I was cutting"* Raines, "My Times."

187 *"Did I pat him on the back?"* Kurtz, "To the Editors."

187 *Shaila Dewan* Author interview.

189 *Jack Rosenthal, Raines's predecessor* Rosenthal to author.

189 *"It only became scary to me"* Siegal to author.

189 *"Closing The Times's"* Francis W. Rodgers. "Jayson Blair: Fallout Goes On." Letter to the Editor. *The New York Times.* May 16, 2003. p. A26.

190 *he sent out an e-mail* Mnookin et al., "Times Bomb."

The Fallout

192 *The Blair-authored profile* Blair. "Gerald."

192 *Howell Raines's bio* Maureen Dowd. "Howell." In *Times Talk.* Internal Newsletter. September 2001.

193 *I filed a piece detailing* Seth Mnookin. "A Week to Remember in Memphis." Newsweek.com Web Exclusive. May 6, 2003.

195 *My "nut graf"* Mnookin et al., "Times Bomb."

196 *Blair agreed to speak* Sridhar Pappu. " 'So Jayson Blair Could Live, The Journalist Had to Die.' " *The New York Observer*. May 26, 2003. p. 1.

196 *Howell Raines sent out a memo* Howell Raines and Gerald Boyd. "A note from Howell and Gerald." E-mail message. May 20, 2003. 5:30:24 p.m.

197 *"silo management"* Raines, "My Times."

197 *And he had told Ken Auletta* Auletta, "The Howell Doctrine."

197 *The story, published on the front* Rick Bragg. "An Oyster and a Way of Life, Both at Risk." *The New York Times*. June 15, 2002. p. A1.

199 *One infamous story* Rick Bragg. "Small Alabama Newspaper Prevails in Crusade to Expose Corrupt Sheriff." *The New York Times*. June 1, 1998. p. A10.

199 *the fact that only two* Rick Bragg. "The Era of Showgirls Is Leaving Las Vegas." *The New York Times*. March 22, 2001. p. A1.

199 *On Monday, he gave an interview* Howard Kurtz. "Suspended N.Y. Times Reporter Says He'll Quit; Rick Bragg Decries 'Poisonous Atmosphere.' " *The Washington Post*. May 27, 2003. p. C1.

200 *Kurtz had been at* Kurtz to author.

200 *Peter Kilborn* Seth Mnookin. "Firestorm in the Newsroom: The Times's National Staff Defends Their Reporting Methods." Newsweek.com Web Exclusive. May 28, 2003.

201 *"I was really offended"* Kilborn to author.

201 *David Firestone, who had been* David Firestone. "NYT National Desk Isn't Built on Stringers." Online Posting. Poynter Online—Forums. "Letters Sent to Romenesko." May 28, 2003. 1:59:33 p.m. Available at www.poynter.org/forum/default.asp?id=letters.

202 *Jennifer Steinhauer, wrote* Jennifer Steinhauer. "This NYT-er Won't Let Bragg's Claims Go Unchecked." Online Posting. Poynter Online—Forums. "Letters Sent to Romenesko." May 28, 2003. 4:54:18 p.m. Available at www.poynter.org/forum/default.asp?id=letters.

202 *Alex Berenson, the reporter* Alex Berenson. "Not Everyone Does It 'the Bragg Way.' " Online Posting. Poynter Online—Forums. "Letters Sent to Romenesko." May 28, 2003. 5:17:37 p.m. Available at www.poynter.org/forum/default.asp?id=letters.

202 *sent out a three-sentence message* Howell Raines. "A Message to the Staff." E-mail message. May 28, 2003. 7:32:34 p.m.

202 *sent out a longer message to the staff* Rosemary Shields for Howell Raines.

"A note from Howell and Gerald." E-mail message. May 29, 2003. 11:47:40 a.m.

203 *"He said he was afraid"* Behr to author.

204 *"I would also like to add"* Rena Pederson. "Remarks at Pulitzer Prize Luncheon." May 29, 2003. Available at www.pulitzer.org/resources/pederson_speech.html.

204 *Safire began his talk* William Safire. "Remarks at Pulitzer Prize Luncheon." May 29, 2003. Available at http://www.pulitzer.org/resources/safire_speech.html.

204 *"happy place"* Author interview.

205 *Earlier that week, Abramson* Abramson to author.

206 *"I knew there was a chance"* Steinberg to author.

206 *"I tried to get a range"* Norris to author.

206 *"We were all confused"* Haberman to author.

206 *"Howell kept promising"* Siegal to author.

207 *he flew to Washington* Cohen and Rose, "Amid Turmoil, Top Editors Resign at New York Times."

207 *"Even I was taken back"* Abramson, Boccardi, Rosenthal, and Behr to author.

208 *"Gerald feels that Howell"* Behr to author.

209 *On the third-floor newsroom* Seth Mnookin. "A Sorry Sight." Newsweek.com Web Exclusive. June 4, 2003.

209 *I received an e-mail* "nyt nyt." E-mail message to author. June 4, 2003. 3:54 p.m.

New Endings, Old Beginnings

210 *At 10:30, an e-mail without a subject line* E-mail message to *New York Times* newsroom. 10:30:36 a.m.

210 *"I want to talk with you,"* Seth Mnookin. "Read All About It." *Newsweek*. June 16, 2003. p. 34.

211 *"It's been a tumultuous"* Jacques Steinberg. "Times's 2 Top Editors Resign After Furor on Writer's Fraud." *The New York Times*. June 6, 2003. p. A1.

211 *"I set out many years ago"* Paul D. Colford et al. "Times Is Paper of Wreckage." New York *Daily News*. June 6, 2003.

211 *grabbed his panama hat* Author interviews.

212 *"I didn't realize"* Transcribed in newsroom for author.

214 *"When Joe spoke that first morning"* Haberman to author.

214 *"This is a newsroom"* Mnookin, "Read All About It." p. 35.

214 *"The atmosphere of the place"* Wilkins to author.

214 *"We had the entire operation"* Tifft and Jones, *The Trust*, p. 568.

214 *soon coalesced around three candidates* Mnookin, "A Sorry Sight."

215 *In 2001, the* Herald *won* Available at www.knightridder.com/papers/pulitzer/pulitzer_year.html.

215 *In 2003, the* Globe *won* Available at bostonglobe.com/newsroom/awards/pulitzers.stm.

215 *was seen outside the Times building* Keith J. Kelly. "Boston Globe's Baron at Times as Contest for Editor Heats Up." *New York Post*. July 10, 2003. p. 35.

215 *New York's* Daily News *reported* Paul D. Colford. "Times Wish-List May Be One Short." New York *Daily News*. June 20, 2003. p. 70.

216 *asked for time to appear* Howard Kurtz. "Raines Says He Was Asked to Resign at N.Y. Times." *The Washington Post*. July 12, 2003. p. C1.

216 *great artists who achieved* Joe Hagan. "Raines Talk Show Is Deconstructed by Times Staff." *The New York Observer*. July 21, 2003. p. 1.

217 *Once again, Jacques Steinberg* Jacques Steinberg. "Bill Keller, Columnist, Is Selected as The Times's Executive Editor." *The New York Times*. July 15, 2003. p. A1.

217 *one of his first interviews* Seth Mnookin. " 'Let's Move On.' " Newsweek.com Web Exclusive. July 16, 2003.

218 *"Doing a lot of college football"* Landman to author.

Part Three
AFTER

"All About Howell"

224 *"When he was here"* Kramon to author.

225 *"We are not the first"* *The Charlie Rose Show*, April 14, 1994.

225 *"In the newspaper world"* Simon Dumenco. "The Birth of Frankenblair," *Folio:*. July 17, 2003. p. 7.

226 *"The* Times *was too big"* Turner Catledge. *My Life and* The Times. New York: Harper & Row, 1971. pp. 187–88.

226 *"You cannot perform quality journalism"* *The Charlie Rose Show*, August 6, 2002.

227 *"Everybody felt under siege"* Wilkins to author.

A New Team in Place

229 *Bill Keller, who became* Steinberg. "Bill Keller, Columnist, Is Selected as
The Times's Executive Editor."

229 *"What I expected"* Keller to author.

229 *appointed Jill Abramson and John Geddes* Jacques Steinberg. "2 Are
Appointed at The Times to Managing Editor Positions." *The New York
Times*. August 1, 2003. p. A18.

230 *He promoted Jon Landman* "Times Names Metropolitan Chief as
Assistant Managing Editor." *The New York Times*. September 26, 2003.
p. A18.

230 *named Susan Edgerley* "The New York Times Chooses New Editor for
the Metro Section." *The New York Times*. October 17, 2003. p. B3.

230 *Glenn Kramon was appointed* "New Appointments for 2 Editors at
Times." *The New York Times*. October 29, 2003. p. A16.

230 *lured Larry Ingrassia away* "Business Editor Is Appointed by the Times."
The New York Times. January 15, 2004. p. C2.

230 *Roger Cohen stepped down* "Times Names Susan Chira Foreign Editor."
The New York Times. January 14, 2004. p. A8.

230 *Adam Moss agreed to take the lead* "Times Names Editor to New Post for
Features." *The New York Times*. August 6, 2003. p. A15.

230 *succeeded at the magazine by his deputy* "The Times Names New Editor of
Magazine." *The New York Times*. September 3, 2003. p. A15.

230 *Chip McGrath stepped down* "Times Appoints Editor for Book Review."
The New York Times. March 11, 2004. p. E7.

230 *Keller persuaded* Fortune's *Michele McNally* "The Times Appoints
Photography Director." *The New York Times*. April 29, 2004. p. A23.

230 *promoted Philip Taubman* David Carr. "The Times Names a New Chief
of Its Bureau in Washington." *The New York Times*. August 7, 2003.
p. A5.

230 *lured Rick Flaste* Tom McGeveran. "After Moss Departure, Times
Starting Over on Book Review Boss." *The New York Observer*. March 1,
2004. p. 1.

231 *"We knew the culture report"* Rich to author.

231 *the* Los Angeles Times *was faced with forced layoffs* "Los Angeles Times
Cuts About 160 Jobs." *Los Angeles Times*. June 22, 2004. p. C2.

231 *Keller made four prominent hires* Nikke Finke. "Invasion of the Body
Snatchers Part *Deux*." *LA Weekly*. Web Exclusive Update. July 2, 2004.

231 *"I do think Arthur"* Keller to author.

232 *left the* Times *to edit* New York *magazine* David Carr. "New York

Magazine Names an Editor from The Times." *The New York Times*. February 12, 2004. p. C14.

232 *roiled by a series of petty* See, for example, Sridhar Pappu. "Times Stars Spar: Reporters Rock Baghdad Bureau." *The New York Observer*. January 19, 2004. p. 1.

232 *Keller gave an interview* Margo Hammond and Ellen Heltzel. "The Plot Thickens at the New York Times Book Review." Online Posting. Poynter Online—Book Babes. January 21, 2004. Available at www.poynter.org/column.asp?id=57&aid=59576.

232 *forcing him to publicly clarify* See, for example, Paul Harris. " 'Betrayal' by Literary Bible." *The Observer* (London). February 8, 2004. p. 20.

232 *Keller, staffers grumbled* Author interviews.

232 *can't comment on future assignments* Glater to author.

233 *"One of the great things"* Barstow to author.

234 *came up with recommendations* "Siegal Committee Report."

234 *"The most important character quality"* *The Charlie Rose Show*, April 14, 1994.

235 *"When I became foreign editor"* Keller to author.

235 *"create a newsroom culture"* "Siegal Committee Report." p. 4.

235 *All three positions had been filled* Jacques Steinberg. "The Times Chooses Veteran of Magazines and Publishing as Its First Public Editor." *The New York Times*. October 27, 2003. p. A19. Also, Jacques Steinberg. "Times Names First Editor for Standards." *The New York Times*. September 10, 2003. p. A20.

236 *a memo Kramon sent* Glenn Kramon to newsroom. "Career Development Update." March 11, 2004. 6:30 p.m.

236 *"This can be a big, scary"* Kramon to author.

236 *"This was another of our periodic"* Perl to author.

237 The New Republic*'s Stephen Glass* Ann Reilly Dowd. "The Great Pretender." *Columbia Journalism Review*. July–August 1998. Available at http://archives.cjr.org/year/98/4/glass.asp. Also, Buzz Bissinger. "Shattered Glass." *Vanity Fair*. September 1998. pp. 176–190. Also, Editors' Note. *The New Republic*. June 1, 1998. Also, Howard Kurtz. "Stranger Than Fiction: The Cautionary Tale of Magazine Writer Stephen Glass." p. 8. *The Washington Post*. May 13, 1998. p. A1.

237 *the* Times*'s own Blood Brothers dispatch* Griffin. "Anti-White Harlem Gang Reported to Number 400." Also, Griffin, "N.A.A.C.P. Assails Reports of Gang."

237 *former* USA Today *reporter* Blake Morrison. "USA Today Reporter Resigns After Deception." *USA Today*. January 13, 2004. p. 5A.

237   USA Today *announced*   Peter Johnson. "USA Today to Review All of
      Reporter's Work." *USA Today*. January 16, 2004. p. 3A.

237   *the paper published an interim report*   Blake Morrison. "Ex–USA Today
      Reporter Faked Major Stories." *USA Today*. March 19, 2004. p. 1A.

238   *Karen Jurgensen, the paper's editor*   David Folkenflik. "USA Today's
      Culture Aided Reporter's Deception, Panel Finds; 2 More Top Editors
      Resign After Plagiarism Scandal." Baltimore *Sun*. April 23, 2004. p. A1.

238   *both of the country's leading newsweeklies*   Liza Featherstone. "Chucking
      the Checkers." *Columbia Journalism Review*. July–August 1997. Available
      at http://archives.cjr.org/year/97/4/checkers.asp.

238   *"God is not going to stop"*   Nicholas Lemann. "The Wayward Press." *The
      New Yorker*. March 15, 2004. p. 136.

238   *In March 2004, a single paper*   David House. "Yanking Up the Weeds of
      Journalism." Fort Worth *Star-Telegram*. March 28, 2004. p. 1E.

238   *"The whole notion"*   Brill to author.

239   *"The consensus here, post Blair"*   Arthur Sulzberger. "Re: Final Question."
      E-mail message to author. June 4, 2004. 1:51 p.m.

239   *"I don't know"*   Lemann to author.

Course Corrections

240   *Patrick Tyler wrote a piece headlined*   Patrick E. Tyler. "Threats and
      Responses: Terror Network." *The New York Times*. February 6, 2003. p. A1.

241   *editors' note and a column*   "From the Editors: The Times and Iraq." *The
      New York Times*. May 26, 2004. p. A10. Also, Daniel Okrent. "Weapons
      of Mass Destruction? Or Mass Distraction?" *The New York Times*.
      May 30, 2004. Section 4, p. 2.

241   *Privately, some top editors*   Author interviews.

242   *most persistently and eloquently*   See, for example, "The *Times* Scoops That
      Melted: Cataloging the Wretched Reporting of Judith Miller." Available
      at www.slate.com/id/2086110. July 25, 2003. Also, "Miller Time (Again):
      The *New York Times* Owes Readers an Explanation for Judith Miller's
      Faulty WMD Reporting." Available at www.slate.com/id/2095394.
      February 12, 2004. Also, "Surrender, Judith Miller! Knight Ridder Has
      the Goods on You." Available at www.slate.com/id/2100747. May 24,
      2004. Also, Michael Massing. "Now They Tell Us." *The New York Review
      of Books*. February 26, 2004. p. 43. Also, Judith Miller et al. " 'Now They
      Tell Us': An Exchange." Letters to the Editor. *The New York Review of
      Books*. March 25, 2004. p. 45. Also, and Michael Massing. "Unfit to
      Print?" *The New York Review of Books*. June 24, 2004. p. 6.

242   *Engelberg, who had co-authored a book*   Judith Miller, Stephen Engelberg, and William J. Broad. *Germs: Biological Weapons and America's Secret War.* New York: Simon & Schuster, 2001.

243   *"My sense was that Howell Raines"*   Doug Frantz. "RE: Times book/Miller." E-mail message to author. May 20, 2004. 3:57 a.m.

Sulzberger's Challenges

244   *"It's postponed things"*   Sulzberger to author.

244   *"The* Times *couldn't exist"*   Goodale to author.

244   *"It's the question"*   Rosenthal to author.

245   *"should have been listening harder"*   "Siegal Committee Report," p. 43.

245   *"his 2004* Atlantic *piece"*   Raines, "My Times."

245   *"change agent"*   "Siegal Committee Report," p. 43. Also, Raines, "My Times."

246   *There is a long history*   Meyer Berger. *The Story of* The New York Times *1851–1951.* New York: Simon & Schuster, 1951. p. vi.

246   *One of Arthur Sulzberger's favorite*   Sulzberger to author.

247   *"That was backwards"*   Robinson to author.

247   *nearly 90 percent of the paper's*   Sulzberger, Robinson, and Lewis to author.

247   *"We've moved to the point"*   Lewis to author.

247   *Virtually every paper in the country*   See, for example, Jacques Steinberg. "Newspaper Circulation Continues Overall Decline." *The New York Times.* May 4, 2004. p. C4.

247   *"We can now go"*   Sulzberger to author.

248   *had for years been telling executives*   Peter C. Goldmark. "Statement of Peter C. Goldmark Jr., Chair and CEO of the International Herald Tribune, to the IHT Staff, Paris, January 20, 2003." Poynter Online—Journalism Junction. Available at www.poynter.org/column.asp?id=54&aid=17777.

248   *"That was no one's finest hour"*   Goldmark to author.

248   *"It was amateur hour"*   Author interview.

248   *"These are our bets"*   Sulzberger to author.

249   *"When people look at the* IHT*"*   Lewis to author.

Postscript

252   *"Raines wrote a piece about his son"*   Howell Raines. "If Your Kid Says He Wants to Be a Rock Star . . . Let Him." *Details.* October 2003.

252 *Blair's book was published* Hillel Italie. "Jayson Blair, Former New York Times Reporter, Has Book Deal." Associated Press. September 10, 2003.

252 *After New York publishing houses passed* Cesar G. Soriano. "Blair Signs Book Deal." *USA Today*. September 11, 2003. p. D2.

252 *the same week his company filed* David D. Kirkpatrick. "Hollywood Publisher Seeks Bankruptcy After Losing Suit." *The New York Times*. September 11, 2003. p. C5.

252 *New Millennium was liquidated* Paul D. Colford. "Publisher's Story Ends." New York *Daily News*. May 13, 2004. p. 64.

253 *A supposedly verbatim conversation with his girlfriend* Blair, *Burning Down My Masters' House*, pp. 3, 295.

253 *"after a long struggle with drugs"* Ibid., p. 212.

253 *"It is unconscionable that a journalist"* Gerald Boyd. "Blair's Lies Spread Beyond Journalism." Universal Press Syndicate. March 21, 2004.

253 *"barbeque chicken sandwiches"* Blair, *Burning Down My Masters' House*, p. 53.

254 *Katie Couric's* Dateline *interview* *Dateline NBC*. Interview with Jayson Blair by Katie Couric. NBC. Air date, March 5, 2004. NBC News Transcripts.

254 *"Jayson Blair is on hiatus"* See www.jayson-blair.com/appearances.html. Update dated April 28, 2004.

254 *"My intention here is to perform"* Raines, "My Times."

255 *doesn't remember any such incident* Author interviews.

255 *"beaten New York's hip"* Joe Hagan. "Hurling Your Basic Rock at the Arty Crowd." *The New York Times*. August 12, 2001. Section 2, p. 25.

255 *had run a lead story* Jon Pareles. "White Stripes: Same Old Colors." *The New York Times*. April 6, 2003. Section 2, p. 1.

256 *diagnostic criteria for narcissistic* *Diagnostic and Statistical Manual of Mental Disorders*. 4th ed. Washington, D.C.: American Psychiatric Association, 1994.

256 *"The Passion of the Howell"* Author interview.

256 *sent me an unsolicited e-mail* Gail Collins. E-mail message to author. March 24, 2004. 6:10:45 p.m.

257 *"Having never worked for"* Martin Baron. Letter to the Editor. *The Atlantic*. July–August 2004. p. 20.

257 *the* Times *has won five public service awards* See www.pulitzer.org/archive/archive.html.

257 *The book, as Raines described it* Howell Raines. Letter/book proposal to Mark Reiter, datelined Henryville, Penn.

257 *The proposal was soon leaked*   Paul D. Colford. "Raines to Update His Times at Times." New York *Daily News*. July 2, 2004. p. 42.

259 *"We caught it"*   Author interview.

259 *The book was eventually sold to Scribner*   Paul D. Colford. "Scribner to Publish Raines Tale." New York *Daily News*. July 7, 2004. p. 54.

Afterword

262 *Circulation at the country's*   Ahrens, Frank. "Hard News: Daily Papers Face Unprecedented Competition." *The Washington Post*. February 20, 2005. p. F01.

262 *In January 2005, in a bizarre*   Carter, Bill. "CNN Will Cancel 'Crossfire' and Cut Ties to Commentator." *The New York Times*. January 6, 2005. p. c5.

263 *As Nicholas Lemann pointed out*   Lemann, Nicholas. "Fear and Favor: Why Is Everyone Mad at the Mainstream Media?" *The New Yorker*. February 14–21, 2005. pp. 168–176.

Selected Bibliography

Ahrens, Frank. "Hard News: Daily Papers Face Unprecedented Competition." *The Washington Post.* February 20, 2005. p. F01.

"Alex S. Jones Named New Director of the Shorenstein Center." *Harvard University Gazette.* April 20, 2000. Available at www.hno.harvard.edu/gazette/2000/04.20/shorenstein.html.

"At Least One Story by Jayson Blair That Was Published in The Tennessean Contained Errors Corrected Yesterday by The New York Times." *The Tennessean.* May 11, 2003. p. 16A.

Auletta, Ken. "Opening Up The Times." *The New Yorker.* June 28, 1993. pp. 55ff.

———. "The Howell Doctrine." *The New Yorker.* June 10, 2002. pp. 48ff. Available at www.kenauletta.com/howelldoctrine.html.

Barack, Lauren, and Keith J. Kelly. "Top Writer on Ice in New Times Scandal." *New York Post.* May 24, 2003. p. 6.

Barber, Phil. "A Brief History of Newspapers." Available at www.historicpages.com/nprhist.htm.

Barringer, Felicity. "Resign or Not to Resign? Question That Weighs on Editorial Writers." *The New York Times.* September 18, 1998. p. A24.

———. "Taking a Stand; Why Newspapers Endorse Candidates." *The New York Times.* November 5, 2000. Section 4, p. 1.

———. "2 Rejected Sports Columns to Be Printed by The Times." *The New York Times.* December 7, 2002. p. A17.

Barrios, Jennifer, and April D. Bethea. " 'Snail-Pace' Minority Gains Spur Concern." *The ASNE Reporter.* April 20, 2004. Available at www.asne.org/index.cfm?id=5173.

Barry, Dan. *Pull Me Up.* New York: W. W. Norton & Co., 2004.

Barry, Dan, David Barstow, Jonathan D. Glater, Adam Liptak, and Jacques Steinberg. "Times Reporter Who Resigned Leaves Long Trail of Deception." *The New York Times.* May 11, 2003. p. A1.

Barstow, David, and Lowell Bergman. "At a Texas Foundry, an Indifference to Life." *The New York Times.* January 8, 2003. p. A1.

Barstow, David, and Somini Sengupta. "Judge Who Rebuffed Gore Had Run-ins with Justices." *The New York Times.* December 8, 2000. p. A1.

Becker, Lee B., Tudor Vlad, Jisu Huh, and Nancy R. Mace. "Annual Enrollment Report: Graduate and Undergraduate Enrollments Increase Sharply." *Journalism & Mass Communication Educator* 58, no. 3 (2003): 273–300. Available at www.grady.uga.edu/annualsurveys/Enrollment02/enroll02sum.htm.

Berenson, Alex. "Enron's Collapse: Selling Energy; Ex-Workers Say Unit's Earnings Were 'Illusory.' " *The New York Times.* January 25, 2002. p. A1.

Berger, Meyer. *The Story of* The New York Times *1851–1951.* New York: Simon & Schuster, 1951.

Bissinger, Buzz. "Shattered Glass." *Vanity Fair.* September 1998. pp. 176–90.

Blair, Jayson. "Media Right to Expose Wrong." *The Diamondback.* May 7, 1999.

———. "Gerald." In *Times Talk.* September 2001.

———. "A Rousing Rock Show for a Wounded City." *The New York Times.* October 21, 2001. p. B10.

———. "Retracing a Trail: The Investigation; U.S. Sniper Case Seen as a Barrier to a Confession." *The New York Times.* October 30, 2002. p. A1.

———. "Teenager's Role Tangles Case Against Older Sniper Suspect." *The New York Times.* December 22, 2002. p. A1.

———. "Watching, and Praying, as a Son's Fate Unfolds." *The New York Times.* March 24, 2003. p. B1.

———. "For One Pastor, the War Hits Home." *The New York Times.* April 7, 2003. p. B1.

———. "Family Waits, Now Alone, for a Missing Soldier." *The New York Times.* April 26, 2003. p. A1.

———. *Burning Down My Masters' House.* Beverly Hills, Calif.: New Millennium, 2004.

———. Personal Website. Available at www.jayson-blair.com.

Blair, Jayson, and Douglas Jehl. "Rescue in Iraq and a 'Big Stir' in West Virginia." *The New York Times.* April 3, 2003. p. A1.

Bonner, Raymond, and Josh Barbanel. "Democrats Rue Ballot Foul-up in a 2nd County." *The New York Times.* November 17, 2000. p. A1.

Boyd, Gerald. "Blair's Lies Spread Beyond Journalism." Universal Press Syndicate. March 21, 2004.

Bragg, Rick. *All Over but the Shoutin'*. New York: Pantheon Books, 1997.

———. "Small Alabama Newspaper Prevails in Crusade to Expose Corrupt Sheriff." *The New York Times*. June 1, 1998. p. A10.

———. "The Era of Showgirls Is Leaving Las Vegas." *The New York Times*. March 22, 2001. p. A1.

———. "Pakistan Is 2 Worlds: One Urbane, One Enraged." *The New York Times*. October 1, 2001. p. B1.

———. "Seeking Miracles in a Place of Cruelty and Beauty." *The New York Times*. October 28, 2001. p. A1.

———. "An Oyster and a Way of Life, Both at Risk." *The New York Times*. June 15, 2002. p. A1.

Brat, Ilan. "Blair Scandal Doesn't Bog Down Boyd." *The Arizona Republic*. October 14, 2003.

Broad, William J., Stephen Engelberg, and James Glanz. "Assessing Risks, Chemical, Biological, Even Nuclear." *The New York Times*. November 1, 2001. p. A1.

Broad, William J., Stephen Engelberg, Judith Miller, Sheryl Gay Stolberg. "Excruciating Lessons in the Ways of a Disease." *The New York Times*. October 31, 2001. p. A1.

Bumiller, Elisabeth. "President Notes Dissent on Iraq, Vowing to Listen." *The New York Times*. August 1, 2002. p. A1.

Burghart, Tara. "Former New York Times Reporter Apologizes." Associated Press. May 2, 2003.

"Business Editor Is Appointed by The Times." *The New York Times*. January 15, 2004. p. C2.

Butterfield, Fox, and Mary B. W. Tabor. "Woman in Florida Rape Inquiry Fought Adversity and Sought Acceptance." *The New York Times*. April 17, 1991. p. A17.

Carr, David. "The Times Names a New Chief of Its Bureau in Washington." *The New York Times*. August 7, 2003. p. A5.

———. "New York Magazine Names an Editor from The Times." *The New York Times*. February 12, 2004. p. C14.

Carr, David, and Janny Scott. "A Formidable Run Undone by Scandal and Discontent." *The New York Times*. June 6, 2003. p. B8.

Carter, Bill. "CNN Will Cancel 'Crossfire' and Cut Ties to Commentator." *The New York Times*. January 6, 2005. p. c5.

Catledge, Turner. *My Life and* The Times. New York: Harper & Row, 1971.

CBS News Sunday Morning. "Hooked: New York Times Editor Howell Raines an Avid Fly Fisherman." Reported by Charles Kuralt. CBS. Air date, December 5, 1993.

———. "Our Times; History, Operations and Views of *The New York Times*." Hosted by Terence Smith. CBS. Air date, June 30, 1996.

"Changes in Senior Staff Are Made by The Times." *The New York Times.* December 6, 1986. p. A16.

The Charlie Rose Show. "The American Scene." Interview with Max Frankel. PBS. Air date, April 14, 1994.

———. Interview with Max Frankel. PBS. Air date, April 5, 1999.

———. "New York Times Editor Howell Raines on 9/11 (Part I)." Interview with Howell Raines. PBS. Air date, August 6, 2002.

———. Interview with Howell Raines. PBS. Air date, July 11, 2003.

"The Chronicle Ran 3 of Blair's Stories." *San Francisco Chronicle*, May 11, 2003. p. A1.

Cohen, Laurie P., and Matthew Rose. "Amid Turmoil, Top Editors Resign at New York Times." *The Wall Street Journal.* June 6, 2003. p. A1.

Colford, Paul D. "Times Editors Kill 2 Columns in Augusta Rift." New York *Daily News.* December 4, 2002. p. 50.

———. "Times to Probe Reporter's Stories." New York *Daily News.* March 3, 2003. p. 17.

———. "The Times Probing 'All the Fiction Fit to Print.' " New York *Daily News.* May 9, 2003. p. 48.

———. "Times Wish-List May Be One Short." New York *Daily News.* June 20, 2003. p. 70.

———. "Publisher's Story Ends." New York *Daily News.* May 13, 2004. p. 64.

———. "Raines to Update His Times at Times." New York *Daily News.* July 2, 2004. p. 42.

———. "Scribner to Publish Raines Tale." New York *Daily News.* July 7, 2004. p. 54.

Colford, Paul D., et al. "Times Chief Says He's Not Quitting." New York *Daily News.* May 15, 2003. p. 7.

———. "Times Is Paper of Wreckage." New York Daily News. June 6, 2003. p. 5.

" 'The Communications Media, Ironically, Have Failed to Communicate': The Kerner Report Assesses Media Coverage of Riots and Race Relations." History Matters: The U.S. Survey Course on the Web. Available at www.historymatters.gmu.edu/d/6553.

Conconi, Chuck, and Edwin Diamond. "Will Roberts Produce Harder Times?" *The Washingtonian.* May 1994.

Corry, John. *My Times.* New York: Putnam, 1993.

Cox, Meg, and Alix M. Freedman. "New York Times Selects Outsider as a Top Editor." *The Wall Street Journal.* April 8, 1994. p. B1.

"Dark Days for the Gray Lady." Associated Press. May 15, 2003.

Dateline NBC. Interview with Jayson Blair by Katie Couric. NBC. Air date, March 5, 2004. NBC News Transcripts.

"A Dawn of Promise." Editorial. *The New York Times*. January 21, 1993. p. A24.

"Democrats and the Fourth Estate, Cont." *National Journal's Congress Daily*. February 26, 1993.

Diagnostic and Statistical Manual of Mental Disorders. 4th ed. Washington, D.C.: American Psychiatric Association, 1994.

Dowd, Ann Reilly. "The Great Pretender." *Columbia Journalism Review*. July–August 1998. p. 14. Available at http://archives.cjr.org/year/98/4/glass.asp.

Dowd, Maureen. "Howell." In *Times Talk*.

Dumenco, Simon. "The Birth of Frankenblair." *Folio:*. July 17, 2003. p. 7.

Editors' Note. *The New York Times*. April 26, 1991. p. A3.

Editors' Note. *The New Republic*. June 1, 1998. p. 8.

Editors' Note. *The New York Times*. April 14, 2002. Section 6, p. 16.

Eichenwald, Kurt, with Diana B. Henriques. "Enron's Many Strands: The Company Unravels; Enron Buffed Image to a Shine Even as It Rotted from Within." *The New York Times*. February 10, 2002. p. A1.

Emling, Shelley, and Caroline Wilbert. "Times Scandal Tests Editor's Leadership." *The Atlanta Journal-Constitution*. June 1, 2003. p. 15A.

Engelberg, Stephen. "Book Review Lies and the Sly Liar Who Tries to Justify Them." *The Oregonian*. March 21, 2004. p. D6.

Evans, Harold. "Beyond the Scoop." *The New Yorker*. July 8, 1996. pp. 9–10.

"Family of Rescued Soldier Rejoices." Associated Press. April 2, 2003.

Featherstone, Liza. "Chucking the Checkers." *Columbia Journalism Review*. July–August 1997. Available at http://archives.cjr.org/year/97/4/checkers.asp. p. 12.

Fermino, Jennifer, Keith Kelly, and Todd Venezia. "Scandal-Broadsheet Boss: My Editor Stays—Angry Journalists Put Newspaper's Execs on Hot Seat." *New York Post*. May 15, 2003. p. 4.

Finke, Nikke. "Invasion of the Body Snatchers Part *Deux*." *LA Weekly*. Web Exclusive Update. July 2, 2004.

Flannery, Pat. "News Editors Take Notes on Fixing Credibility." *The Arizona Republic*. October 17, 2003. p. 3B.

Folkenflik, David. "Times' Editors Gather Staff to Apologize for Inaction." *Baltimore Sun*. May 15, 2003. p. D1.

———. "The Making of Jayson Blair." *Baltimore Sun*. February 29, 2004. p. F10.

———. "USA Today's Culture Aided Reporter's Deception, Panel Finds; 2 More Top Editors Resign After Plagiarism Scandal." *Baltimore Sun*. April 23, 2004. p. A1.

Frankel, Max. *The Times of My Life and My Life with* The Times. New York: Random House, 1999.

"From the Editors; The Times and Iraq." *The New York Times*. May 26, 2004. p. A10.

Gardner, Mike. "NY Times Claims Kent State Football Attendance Miscounted; Angers Many." *Daily Kent Stater* (via University Wire, Nexis). December 26, 2002.

Gelb, Arthur. *City Room.* New York: Putnam, 2003.

Getlin, Josh. "As N.Y. Times Struggles with Scandal, Editor Insists He'll Stay." *Los Angeles Times.* May 15, 2003. p. A1.

Glater, Jonathan D. "Adultery May Be a Sin, but It's a Crime No More." *The New York Times.* April 17, 2003. p. A16.

Glionna, John M. "Inmate Didn't Get Life, So He Chose Death at 92." *Los Angeles Times.* July 11, 2002. p. A1.

"Globe Completes Review; Backs Columnist Barnicle." *The Boston Globe.* June 21, 1998. p. A28.

Goldmark, Peter C. "Statement of Peter C. Goldmark Jr., Chair and CEO of the International Herald Tribune, to the IHT Staff, Paris, January 20, 2003." Poynter Online—Journalism Junction. Available at www.poynter.org/column.asp?id=54&aid=17777.

Gould, Jennifer, and Keith J. Kelly. "Blair's Pal Also Leaves Newspaper." *New York Post.* May 14, 2003. p. 4.

Greenberg, Paul. "Is Press Biased? Are You Kidding?" *The Commercial Appeal.* August 22, 1996. p. A13.

Greene, Bill. "Janet Cooke: The Players . . ." *The Washington Post.* April 19, 1981. p. A12.

Greene, Leonard, Keith J. Kelly, and Todd Venezia. "Times Change—Editor Ripped Boston 'Plagiarist' Paper." *New York Post.* May 16, 2003. p. 7.

Griffin, Junius. "Anti-White Harlem Gang Reported to Number 400." *The New York Times.* May 6, 1964. p. A1.

———. "N.A.A.C.P. Assails Reports of Gang." *The New York Times.* May 11, 1964. p. A27.

Haberman, Clyde. "Sulzberger Passes Leadership of Times Co. to Son." *The New York Times.* October 17, 1997. p. A1.

Hagan, Joe. "Hurling Your Basic Rock at the Arty Crowd." *The New York Times.* August 12, 2001. Section 2, p. 25.

———. "The Blair Pitch Project." *The New York Observer.* May 26, 2003. p. 1.

———. "Raines Talk Show Is Deconstructed by Times Staff." *The New York Observer.* July 21, 2003. p. 1.

Hammond, Margo, and Ellen Heltzel. "The Plot Thickens at The New York Times Book Review." Online Posting. Poynter Online—Book Babes. January 21, 2004. Available at www.poynter.org/column.asp?id=57&aid=59576.

Hancock, Noelle. "Fake Newsman Speaks Truth." *The New York Observer.* May 19, 2003. p. 3.

Hardball. Interview with Jayson Blair by Chris Matthews. MSNBC. Air date, March 11, 2004. Transcript no. 031100cb.461. Available at www.msnbc.msn.com/id/4514639.

Harris, Leon. "Howell Raines Discusses Introspection in Fly Fishing." CNN. December 3, 1993.

Harris, Paul. " 'Betrayal' by Literary Bible." *The Observer* (London). February 8, 2004. p. 20.

Harwood, Richard. "Incivility: Sparks Fly in Debate over Propriety of 'Civic Journalism.' " *The Ledger.* March 12, 1996. p. A9.

Haslanger, Phil. "Tales of Fishing and Aging." *Capital Times.* May 13, 1994. p. 7A.

Henry, William A. "A Head of the Times." *Time.* April 18, 1994. p. 66.

Hernandez, Macarena. "Valley Mom Awaits News of MIA Son." *San Antonio Express-News.* April 18, 2003. p. A1.

———. "National Betrayal." *San Antonio Express-News.* June 1, 2003. p. H1.

———. "What Jayson Blair Stole from Me, and Why I Couldn't Ignore It." *The Washington Post.* June 1, 2003. p. B5.

Hirschhorn, Larry. "The Fall of Howell Raines and *The New York Times:* A Study in the Moralization of Organizational Life." Lecture given to the Organisation for Promoting Understanding of Society (OPUS) Conference. London, November 21, 2003.

Hoagland, Edward. "Happily Casting for the One That Will Get Away." *The New York Times.* October 5, 1993. p. C17.

"Hold Off the Republican Dobermans." Editorial. *The New York Times.* January 20, 1993. p. A20.

Holson, Laura M., and Alex Kuczynski. "Schoolyard Superstar Aims for a Second Act, as an Adult." *The New York Times.* October 6, 2002. p. A1.

House, David. "Yanking Up the Weeds of Journalism." Fort Worth *Star-Telegram.* March 28, 2004. p. 1E.

"Howell Raines and the New York Times." Editorial. *The New York Observer.* May 26, 2003. p. 4.

Hubler, Shawn. "A Fight Is Brewing: Effort to Make 'Politically Correct' Coffee Berkeley's Only Choice Has Caused Quite a Stir." *Los Angeles Times.* July 3, 2002. Section 5, p. 1.

Ibarguen, Diego. "New York Times Bars Free-lance Author." Associated Press. February 21, 2002.

———. "N.Y. Times Wins Record 7 Pulitzers." Associated Press. April 8, 2002.

Italie, Hillel. "Jayson Blair, Former New York Times Reporter, Has Book Deal." Associated Press. September 10, 2003.

Johnson, Peter. "Times' Execs Address Blair Scandal: Questions of Favoritism, Dishonesty at Closed Meeting." *USA Today.* May 15, 2003. p. 7D.

———. "USA Today to Review All of Reporter's Work." *USA Today.* January 16, 2004. p. 3A.

———. "Panel to Review Former USA Today Reporter's Work." *USA Today.* January 30, 2004. p. 3A.

Jones, Alex S. "Journal Says a Reporter Is Under S.E.C. Inquiry." *The New York Times.* March 30, 1984. p. D1.

Jurkowitz, Mark. "Admitting Fabrications, Globe Columnist Resigns." *The Boston Globe.* June 19, 1998. p. A1.

Kalb, Marvin. *One Scandalous Story.* New York: Free Press, 2001.

Kaus, Mickey. Blog entries, November 2002–July 2003. Online Postings. Kausfiles. Available at www.slate.com.

Keller, Bill. "Mr. Diversity." *The New York Times.* June 28, 2003. p. A15.

Kelly, Keith J. "A Blair Tell-All Could Net $1M." *New York Post.* May 14, 2003. p. 34.

———. "Times Gal: I Didn't Aid Beau Blair." *New York Post.* May 17, 2003. p. 4.

———. "Sulzberger Holding D.C. Staff Summit." *New York Post.* June 3, 2003. p. 35.

———. "Interim Boss Vows: Times a-Changin'." *New York Post.* June 7, 2003. p. 9.

———. "Keller an Inside Fave to Run Times Newsroom." *New York Post.* June 11, 2003. p. 32.

———. "Media Critic McGowan Cashes in with Blair Book Project." *New York Post.* June 27, 2003. p. 46.

———. "Times Brass Puts Leash on Miller." *New York Post.* June 29, 2003. p. 29.

———. "Inside Scoop Has Keller Winning Exec Editor Job." *New York Post.* July 6, 2003. p. 27.

———. "Boston Globe's Baron at Times as Contest for Editor Heats Up." *New York Post.* July 10, 2003. p. 35.

———. "Book and Boss; Blair Tome Deal, Editor Pick May Hit at Same Time" *New York Post.* July 13, 2003. p. 33.

———. "The Worst of Times: In-House Report Blasts Management Culture." *New York Post.* July 31, 2003. p. 31.

Kelly, Keith J., and Dan Mangan. "All the News Not Fit to Print—Times in Mutiny over Bosses' 'Whitewash.' " *New York Post.* May 13, 2003. p. 4.

———. "Times Weighs Correction to Mega Apology." *New York Post.* May 28, 2003. p. 38.

———. "Will Pulitzer Winner Brag in His Walking 'Paper'?" *New York Post.* June 6, 2003. p. 46.

———. "Pinch on the Spot: Times Publisher Faces Wrath of Family Staff." *New York Post.* June 7, 2003. p. 21.

Kelly, Keith J., Dan Mangan, and Todd Venezia. "The Times Madman: Colleagues Blast Blair's Q&A Insults." *New York Post.* May 22, 2003. p. 5.

————. "Blair Says 'Sorry' as His Ex-Bosses Fall." *New York Post.* June 6, 2003. p. 4.

————. "Times Up for Raines' Reign: Top Editor & No. 2 Quit amid Story-Fake Scandal." *New York Post.* June 6, 2003. p. 5.

Kirkpatrick, David D. "Hollywood Publisher Seeks Bankruptcy After Losing Suit." *The New York Times.* September 11, 2003. p. C5.

Kissinger, Henry A. "Our Intervention in Iraq." *The Washington Post.* August 12, 2002. p. A15.

Kolbert, Elizabeth. "Tumult in the Newsroom." *The New Yorker.* June 30, 2003. pp. 42ff.

Koningsberg, Eric. "*Times* Pulpit: More Taste, Less Filling." *The New York Observer.* July 26, 1993.

"Konrad Kujau." *The Times* (London). September 14, 2000. Features.

Kosterlitz, Julie. "The Times's Prescription." *National Journal.* January 9, 1993. p. 82.

Krantz, Michael. "Still Setting America's Agenda; Special Report; Newspapers." *MediaWeek.* April 25, 1994. p. 22.

Krauthammer, Charles. "Kidnapped by the Times." *The Washington Post.* August 18, 2002. p. B7.

Kugler, Sara. "New York Times Finds Two Errors in Wider Probe of Free-lance Author's Stories." Associated Press. April 15, 2002.

Kurtz, Howard. "Talking Tough at The Times: Howell Raines's Editorials Don't Finesse with Politesse." *The Washington Post.* May 10, 1993. p. B1.

————. "Parting Shot." ("Media Notes.") *The Washington Post.* June 28, 1993. p. B1.

————. "Outsiders with the Inside Edge." *The Washington Post.* January 6, 1994. p. C1.

————. "Roberts Rules; Hard Driving Times Editor Collides with Entrenched Ways." June 30, 1995. p. D1.

————. "N.Y. Times Names Keller to Top Post." *The Washington Post.* May 23, 1997. p. B4.

————. "Stranger Than Fiction: The Cautionary Tale of Magazine Writer Stephen Glass." *The Washington Post.* May 13, 1998. p. A1.

————. "Under Pressure, Boston Globe Keeps Barnicle." *The Washington Post.* August 12, 1998. p. D1.

————. "As The Globe Turns." *The Washington Post.* August 25, 1998. p. C1.

————. "The Gray Lady's Colorful Chief: New Executive Editor Howell Raines Elicits Strong Opinions." *The Washington Post.* September 6, 2001. p. C1.

————. "New York Times Story Gives Texas Paper Sense of Déjà Vu; San Antonio Editor Cites 'Damning' Similarity." *The Washington Post.* April 30, 2003. p. C1.

————. "Reporter Resigns over Copied Story." *The Washington Post.* May 2, 2003. p. C1.

———. "More Reporting by Times Writer Called Suspect; Parents of Two Other Soldiers, Attorney in Sniper Case Say They Never Spoke to Blair." *The Washington Post*. May 8, 2003. p. C1.

———. "Disgraced Reporter's Deceptions Date to '99; As Intern, Blair 'Interviewed' D.C. Mayor." *The Washington Post*. May 10, 2003. p. C3.

———. "N.Y. Times Uncovers Dozens of Faked Stories by Reporter." *The Washington Post*. May 11, 2003. p. A1.

———. "To the Editors: How Could This Happen?; NY Times Staff, Execs in 'Painful and Honest' Meeting over Plagiarism Fiasco." *The Washington Post*. May 15, 2003. p. C1.

———. "Blair Book Proposal Lashes Out at Paper." *The Washington Post*. May 24, 2003. p. C1.

———. "Intra-Times Battle over Iraqi Weapons." *The Washington Post*. May 26, 2003. p. C1.

———. "Suspended N.Y. Times Reporter Says He'll Quit; Rick Bragg Decries 'Poisonous Atmosphere.' " *The Washington Post*. May 27, 2003. p. C1.

———. "Rick Bragg Quits at New York Times; Departure Follows Comments That Roiled Scandal-Shaken Newsroom." *The Washington Post*. May 29, 2003. p. C1.

———. "N.Y. Times Defends Its Reporting Methods." *The Washington Post*. May 30, 2003. p. C4.

———. "Bylines, Datelines and Fault Lines at the N.Y. Times." *The Washington Post*. June 2, 2003. p. C1.

———. "Times Editor's Tough Style Left Him Few Staff Allies." *The Washington Post*. June 6, 2003. p. A12.

———. "Howell Raines's Tenure: It Left a Nasty Mark." *The Washington Post*. June 9, 2003. p. C1.

———. "Raines Says He Was Asked to Resign at N.Y. Times." *The Washington Post*. July 12, 2003. p. C1.

———. "Newsroom Favorite Bill Keller Named Times' Top Editor." *The Washington Post*. July 15, 2003. p. C1.

———. "N.Y. Times to Appoint Ombudsman; Paper Acts After Task Force Decries Newsroom Culture That Helped Foster Scandal." *The Washington Post*. July 31, 2003. p. C1.

———. "Tight-Lipped Editors Irk USA Today Staffers." *The Washington Post*. January 9, 2004. p. C3.

———. "Fear and Lying at USA Today." *The Washington Post*. January 11, 2004. p. A1.

Kurtz, Howard, and Pamela Ferdinand. "Mike Barnicle Forced out at Boston Globe." *The Washington Post*. August 20, 1998. p. B1.

Larry King Live. "Howell Raines on the Art of Aging Gracefully." Interview with Howell Raines. CNN. Air date, November 25, 1993.

———. Interview with Jayson Blair. CNN. Air date, March 9, 2004.

Layton, Charles. "Miller Brouhaha." *American Journalism Review.* August–September 2003. p. 30.

LeDuff, Charlie. *Work and Other Sins.* New York: Penguin, 2004.

Lemann, Nicholas. "Fear and Favor: Why Is Everyone Mad at the Mainstream Media?" *The New Yorker.* February 14–21, 2005. pp. 168–176.

Lemann, Nicholas. "The Wayward Press." *The New Yorker.* March 15, 2004. p. 136.

Levine, Robert. "The Season Finale That Isn't a Season Finale." *The New York Times.* May 23, 2004. Section 2, p. 17.

Lewis, Harry. "NY Times Taps Gerald Boyd as Its New Managing Editor." *St. Louis Post-Dispatch.* July 27, 2001. p. A1.

Lieberman, David. "Changing of the Guard at 'N.Y. Times.' " *USA Today.* April 8, 1994. p. B1.

"Los Angeles Times Cuts About 160 Jobs." *Los Angeles Times.* June 22, 2004. p. C2.

Lyons, Nick. " 'It's Not About Catching Fish.' " *The New York Times Book Review.* September 19, 1993. Section 7, p. 7.

MacCormack, John. "Missing & Presumed Dead." *San Antonio Express-News.* December 28, 1999. p. A1.

Malcolm, Janet. *The Journalist and the Murderer.* New York: Knopf, 1990.

Mangan, Dan. "Former Times Liar Battles Coke: Mags." *New York Post.* May 19, 2003. p. 4.

Martin, Jurek. "Passing the Baton at *New York Times.*" *Financial Times.* April 11, 1994.

Massing, Michael. "Now They Tell Us." *The New York Review of Books.* February 26, 2004. pp. 43ff.

———. "Unfit to Print?" *The New York Review of Books.* June 24, 2004. pp. 6ff.

McFadden, Robert D. "Lelyveld Will Succeed Frankel as The Times's Executive Editor." *The New York Times.* April 8, 1994. p. A1.

———. "Times Names Raines as Successor to Lelyveld as Executive Editor." *The New York Times.* May 22, 2001. p. A1.

McGee, Celia. "For Vet Newsman, The Times Is Right." New York *Daily News.* November 5, 1999. p. 52.

McGeveran, Tom. "After Moss Departure, Times Starting Over on Book Review Boss." *The New York Observer.* March 1, 2004. p. 1.

McNamara, Robert S., and Brian VanDeMark (contributor). *In Retrospect: The Tragedy and Lessons of the Vietnam War.* New York: Crown Publishers, 1995.

Mergerson, Chris. "God Attracts 62 Students and 4 Teachers." *Centreville Sentinel.* September 22, 1993. p. 2.

Miller, Judith, Stephen Engelberg, and William J. Broad. *Germs: Biological Weapons and America's Secret War.* New York: Simon & Schuster, 2001.

Miller, Judith, et al. " 'Now They Tell Us': An Exchange." Letters to the Editor. *The New York Review of Books.* March 25, 2004. p. 45.

Mnookin, Seth. "Bill Keller, Passed Over for Top Spot at New York Times, Has 'Pig-in-Shit' New Gig." Inside.com. June 19, 2001.

———. "Gerald Boyd Named New York Times Managing Editor—First African-American in the Job." Inside.com. June 26, 2001.

———. "Philosopher King Is Out at the New York Times, as Southern Pol Settles In." Inside.com. September 5, 2001.

———. "Hard Raines." *New York.* February 18, 2002. p. 31.

———. "The Times Backs Down: Anderson and Araton Pieces on Augusta Will Be Published This Weekend." Newsweek.com Web Exclusive. December 6, 2002.

———. "The Changing 'Times.' " *Newsweek.* December 9, 2002. p. 46.

———. "A Week to Remember in Memphis." Newsweek.com Web Exclusive. May 6, 2003.

———. "What's Race Got to Do with It?" Newsweek.com Web Exclusive. May 13, 2003.

———. "A Widening Scandal?" Newsweek.com Web Exclusive. May 15, 2003.

———. "A Journalist's Hard Fall." *Newsweek.* May 19, 2003. p. 40.

———. "More Trouble at the Times." Newsweek.com Web Exclusive. May 23, 2003.

———. "Firestorm in the Newsroom: The Times's National Staff Defends Their Reporting Methods." Newsweek.com Web Exclusive. May 28, 2003.

———. "A Sorry Sight." Newsweek.com Web Exclusive. June 4, 2003.

———. "Shake-up at the New York Times." Newsweek.com Web Exclusive. June 5, 2003.

———. "Handicapping the Race at the Times." Newsweek.com Web Exclusive. June 11, 2003.

———. "Read All About It." *Newsweek.* June 16, 2003. p. 34.

———. "New Editor at Times." Newsweek.com Web Exclusive. July 14, 2003.

———. " 'Let's Move On.' " Newsweek.com Web Exclusive. July 16, 2003.

Mnookin, Seth, with Suzanne Smalley, Rebecca Sinderbrand, Martha Brant, Holly Bailey, Pat Wingert, Jonathan Alter, Howard Fineman, and Brian Braiker. "Times Bomb." *Newsweek.* May 26, 2003. p. 40.

Morrison, Blake. "USA Today Reporter Resigns After Deception." *USA Today.* January 13, 2004. p. 5A.

———. "Ex–USA Today Reporter Faked Major Stories." *USA Today.* March 19, 2004. p. 1A.

"Most of Reporter's Articles Had Problems, New York Times Says." *Orlando Sentinel.* May 11, 2003. p. A22.

Mott, Frank Luther. *American Journalism: A History of Newspapers in the United States Through 250 Years, 1690–1940.* New York: Routledge, 2000.

"Mr. Clinton, Meet Mr. Gore." Editorial. *The New York Times.* April 20, 1993. p. A28.

"Mr. Clinton's Captious Critics." Editorial. *The New York Times.* February 23, 1993. p. A20.

"Mr. McNamara's War." Editorial. *The New York Times.* April 12, 1995. p. A24.

Nasaw, David. *The Chief: The Life of William Randolph Hearst.* Boston: Houghton Mifflin, 2000.

Neal, Terry M. "Don't Blame Diversity." Editorial. *The Washington Post.* May 15, 2003. p. A29.

Nelson, Jill. *Volunteer Slavery.* Chicago: Noble Press, 1993.

"New Appointments for 2 Editors at Times." *The New York Times.* October 29, 2003. p. A16.

The NewsHour with Jim Lehrer. "The Search for Truth." Reported by Terence Smith. PBS. Air date, May 9, 2003. Transcript available at www.pbs.org/newshour/bb/media/jan-june03/blair_05-09.html.

"The New York Times Announces Howell Raines to Become Executive Editor." Press Release, the New York Times Company. May 21, 2001.

"The New York Times Chooses New Editor for the Metro Section." *The New York Times.* October 17, 2003. p. B3.

The New York Times Company Website. Available at www.nytco.com.

"New York Times: Ex-Reporter Faces Fraud Inquiry." Available at www.cnn.com/2003/US/Northeast/05/13/ny.times.investigation/index.html. May 13, 2003.

Nielsen, Nancy. "The New York Times Appoints Senior Editors to News and Editorial Posts." *PR Newswire.* September 11, 1992. p. 1.

Nieves, Evelyn. "Freed from Jail Despite His Pleas, 92-Year-Old Is Found Dead in a River." *The New York Times.* July 12, 2002. p. A12.

Noah, Timothy. "Howell Agonistes." Available at www.slate.com/id/1000276. December 17, 1998.

———. "The Deadly Dozen." *George.* May 1999. p. 88.

———. "Two More Cheers for the NYT." Available at www.slate.com/id/1006159. September 28, 2000.

"Now Blair Has Girlfriend Woes." *New York Post.* June 6, 2003. p. 12.

O'Briant, Don. "Raines Reels in the Years." *The Atlanta Journal-Constitution.* October 17, 1993. p. M1.

O'Brien, Sinead. "Secrets and Lies." *American Journalism Review.* September 1998. p. 40.

Okrent, Daniel. "Weapons of Mass Destruction? Or Mass Distraction?" *The New York Times.* May 30, 2004. Section 4, p. 2.

"On Names in Rape Cases." *The New York Times.* April 17, 1991. p. A17.

The O'Reilly Factor. Hosted by Bill O'Reilly. Fox News. Air date, March 10, 2004. Transcript no. 031005cb.256.

Pappu, Sridhar. "Raines Bogeys on 43rd." *The New York Observer.* December 16, 2002. p. 1.

———. "Off the Record." *The New York Observer.* May 12, 2003. p. 1.

———. "The Times on Boil: Was Blair's Crime Worth Hysteria?" *The New York Observer.* May 19, 2003. p. 1.

———. " 'So Jayson Blair Could Live, the Journalist Had to Die.' " *The New York Observer.* May 26, 2003. p. 1.

———. "Jayson Revolt: 43rd St. Petition by Times Tyros." *The New York Observer.* June 2, 2003. p. 1.

———. "Baby, Will Raines Fall?" *The New York Observer.* June 9, 2003. p. 1.

———. "Sulzberger Jr. Vows to Right Times' Course." *The New York Observer.* June 16, 2003. p. 1.

———. "Lelyveld Using Farewell Tour to Retool Times." *The New York Observer.* June 23, 2003. p. 1.

———. "Times Stars Spar: Reporters Rock Baghdad Bureau." *The New York Observer.* January 19, 2004. p. 1.

Pappu, Sridhar, and Anna Jane Grossman. "My Big Fat Times Wedding." *The New York Observer.* March 17, 2003. p. 1.

Pareles, Jon. "White Stripes: Same Old Colors." *The New York Times.* April 6, 2003. Section 2, p. 1.

Pease, Ted. "Minority Job-seekers Don't Fare as Well." *The American Editor.* November 11, 1999. Available at www.asne.org/kiosk/editor/99.oct-nov/pease1.htm.

Pederson, Rena. "Remarks at Pulitzer Prize Luncheon." May 29, 2003. Available at www.pulitzer.org/resources/pederson_speech.html.

"The Pentagon Tests the Press." *Newsweek.* May 6, 1985. p. 29.

"Profile of Howell Raines." Associated Press. June 5, 2003.

The Project for Excellence in Journalism. *The State of the News Media 2004.* Available at www.stateofthemedia.org.

Purdum, Todd S., and Patrick E. Tyler. "Top Republicans Break with Bush on Iraq Strategy." *The New York Times.* August 16, 2002. p. A1.

Pynn, Manning. "Squander Credibility and All Is Lost." *Orlando Sentinel.* May 11, 2003. p. G3.

Quindlen, Anna. "A Mistake." *The New York Times.* April 21, 1991. Section 4, p. 17.

Raines, Howell. *My Soul Is Rested.* New York: Putnam, 1977.

———. *Whiskey Man.* New York: Viking, 1977.

———. "Grady's Gift." *The New York Times Magazine.* December 1, 1991. pp. 50ff.

———. *Fly Fishing Through the Midlife Crisis.* Garden City, N.Y.: Anchor Books, 1994.

———. "Editorial Observer; The High Price of Reprieving Mike Barnicle." *The New York Times.* August 13, 1998. p. A22.

———. "If Your Kid Says He Wants to Be a Rock Star . . . Let Him." *Details.* October 2003. pp. 130–32.

———. "My Times." *The Atlantic.* May 2004. pp. 49ff.

"Raines Didn't Have to Fall." Editorial. *The New York Observer.* June 16, 2003. p. 4.

Raskin, A. H. "The Strike: A Step-by-Step Account." *The New York Times.* April 1, 1964. p. A1.

"Reading Mr. Clinton's Lips." Editorial. *The New York Times.* January 28, 1993. p. A20.

Reibstein, Larry. "It's Back to the Future: The Times Goes for Continuity—and Change." *Newsweek.* April 18, 1994. p. 41.

Reliable Sources. Hosted by Howard Kurtz. CNN. Air date, May 4, 2003. Transcript available at www.cnn.com/transcripts/0305/04/rs.00.html.

———. Interview with Jayson Blair by Howard Kurtz. CNN. Air date, March 21, 2004. Transcript available at www.cnn.com/transcripts/0403/21/rs.00.html.

Reston, James. *Deadline.* New York: Random House, 1991.

Revkin, Andrew C. "Extended Drought Strains Resources Along East Coast." *The New York Times.* April 21, 2002. p. A1.

Rivenburg, Roy. "All the Jokes Fit to Tell." *Los Angeles Times.* May 17, 2003. Section 5, p. 1.

Robertson, Nan. *The Girls in the Balcony.* New York: Random House, 1992.

Rodgers, Francis W. "Jayson Blair: Fallout Goes On." Letter to the Editor. *The New York Times.* May 16, 2003. p. A26.

Rose, Matthew, and Laurie P. Cohen. "Men in the News: Amid Turmoil, Top Editors Resign at New York Times—for Raines, Reporters' Lapses Helped Stoke Friction over Management Style—'An Endemic Cultural Issue.' " *The Wall Street Journal.* June 6, 2003. p. A1.

Rosengarten, Theodore. "We Were There: The Marchers and the Movement." *The Washington Post.* December 25, 1977. p. H1.

Sachs, Susan. "Times Names Gerald Boyd as Its Next Managing Editor." *The New York Times.* July 27, 2001. p. A13.

Samuels, Adrienne P. "Black Journalists Discuss 'Blair Affair.' " *St. Petersburg Times.* August 10, 2003. p. 16A.

Samuelson, Robert J. "A Liberal Bias?" *The Washington Post.* August 29, 2001. p. A21.

Schmidt, Susan, and Katherine Shaver. "Muhammad Interrogation in Dispute; U.S. Attorneys Cut Off Talks, Local Prosecutor Alleges." *The Washington Post.* October 31, 2002. p. A1.

Schrage, Michael. "Arthur Ochs Sulzberger Jr." *Adweek*. June 28, 1999. p. 32.

Shafer, Jack. "The Scoopless *Washington Post*." Available at www.slate.com/id/ 1006703. December 18, 2000.

———. "Art Dumps Don: The *Times* Moves the *Post* out of Their Paris Flat." Available at www.slate.com/id/2073060. October 23, 2002.

———. "The *New York Times*' Augusta Blog: Stop Me If You've Read This Story Before." Available at www.slate.com/id/2074599. November 25, 2002.

———. "Give the *New York Times* a Mulligan: Call Off the Dogs: Its Editors Only Goofed in Spiking the Augusta Columns." Available at www.slate.com/id/2074849. December 4, 2002.

———. "Pity the Poor *New York Times*: A Pitiful, Helpless Giant Has Fallen and Can't Get Up. " Available at www.slate.com/id/2075135. December 6, 2002.

———. "The Jayson Blair Project: How Did He Bamboozle the *New York Times*?" Available at www.slate.com/id/2082741. May 8, 2003.

———. "Defending Howell Raines: He Didn't Catch Jayson Blair. You Didn't Either." Available at www.slate.com/id/2082896. May 13, 2003.

———. "The Tao of Bear: The Paul 'Bear' Bryant Lessons on Leadership Howell Raines Failed to Absorb." Available at www.slate.com/id/2083025. May 16, 2003.

———. "Rick Bragg's 'Dateline Toe-Touch.' " Available at www.slate.com/id/ 2083539. May 23, 2003.

———. "Rick Bragg's Lousy Alibi: The Suspended *New York Times* Reporter Insists—Wrongly—That Everybody Does It." Available at www.slate.com/id/2083607. May 27, 2003.

———. "Dead Man Editing: Sooner or Later, the Beleaguered Howell Raines Will Take a Bullet for His Paper. " Available at www.slate.com/id/2083931. June 3, 2003.

———. "Howell's End: And Then, Like Quicksilver, the New York Times Editor Who Vowed to Stay Was Gone." Available at www.slate.com/id/2084050. June 5, 2003.

———. "Joe Lelyveld Must Go! He's Failed to Deliver Calm, Civility, and Normalcy to the *New York Times*." Available at www.slate.com/id/2084174. June 9, 2003.

———. "The Fabulous Fabulists: Mencken, Liebling, and Mitchell Made Stuff Up Too. Why Do We Excuse Them?" Available at www.slate.com/id/2084316. June 12, 2003.

———. "Correct Me If I'm Wrong: Errors and the Culture of Correction in American Newspapers." Available at www.slate.com/id/2084685. June 20, 2003.

———. "The *Times* Scoops That Melted: Cataloging the Wretched Reporting of Judith Miller." Available at www.slate.com/id/2086110. July 25, 2003.

———. "Miller Time (Again): The *New York Times* Owes Readers an Explanation for Judith Miller's Faulty WMD Reporting." Available at www.slate.com/id/ 2095394. February 12, 2004.

———. "Surrender, Judith Miller! Knight Ridder Has the Goods on You." Available at www.slate.com/id/2100747. May 18, 2004.

Shaw, David. "Media Impact. Why Some Stories Have It—and Others Don't." *Los Angeles Times*. October 27, 1992. p. A1.

———. "A Business Deal Done—a Controversy Born." *Los Angeles Times*. December 20, 1999. p. V1.

Shiflett, Dave. "Winter Reading for the Incompleat Angler." *The Wall Street Journal*. December 13, 1993. p. A5.

Shipnuck, Alan. *The Battle for Augusta National: Hootie, Martha, and the Masters of the Universe*. New York: Simon & Schuster, 2004.

"The Siegal Committee Report; Report and Recommendations of the Working Group on Training and Performance Management; Recommendations and Thoughts of the Communications Subcommittee." July 28, 2003. Available at www.nytco.com/committeereport.pdf.

Simons, David. "The NY Times Guarantees VC Investment." May 3, 2000. Available at www.forbes.com/2000/05/03/mu10.html.

Snyder, Gabriel. "Raines Succeeds Lelyveld at Times." *The New York Observer*. May 28, 2001. pp. 1, 6.

———. "Phony Slave Tales Causes Big Whup at Times Magazine." *The New York Observer*. March 4, 2002. p. 1.

Soriano, Cesar G. "Blair Signs Book Deal." *USA Today*. September 11, 2003. p. D2.

Stanley, Alessandra, and Bill Carter. "CBS Staying Silent in Debate on Women Joining Augusta." *The New York Times*. November 25, 2002. p. A1.

Starobin, Paul. "Raines's Reign: Thunder from the Times." *National Journal*. April 24, 1993. p. 990.

"Statement from Editor and Publisher." *USA Today*. January 16, 2004. p. 3A.

Steinberg, Jacques. "Times Reporter Resigns After Questions on Article." *The New York Times*. May 2, 2003. p. A30.

———. "Editor of Times Tells Staff He Accepts Blame for Fraud." *The New York Times*. May 15, 2003. p. A31.

———. "Times's 2 Top Editors Resign After Furor on Writer's Fraud." *The New York Times*. June 6, 2003. p. A1.

———. "Bill Keller, Columnist, Is Selected as The Times's Executive Editor." *The New York Times*. July 15, 2003. p. A1.

———. "2 Are Appointed at The Times to Managing Editor Positions." *The New York Times*. August 1, 2003. p. A18.

———. "Times Names First Editor for Standards." *The New York Times*. September 10, 2003. p. A20.

———. "The Times Chooses Veteran of Magazines and Publishing as Its First Public Editor." *The New York Times*. October 27, 2003. p. A19.

———. "The Media Business." *The New York Times*. January 14, 2004. p. C4.

———. "A Question of Credibility." *The New York Times*. January 19, 2004. p. C1.

———. "Newspaper Circulation Continues Overall Decline." *The New York Times*. May 4, 2004. p. C4.

Strupp, Joe. "Boyd Says Some at 'NY Times' Are Scared." Editorandpublisher.com Web exclusive. May 13, 2003.

———. "Keller Won the Job, but Lost a Bet: New 'NY Times' Editor Outlines His Vision for Paper." Editorandpublisher.com Web exclusive. July 15, 2003.

"Study Faults Media Coverage of WMD." Editorandpublisher.com Web exclusive. March 9, 2004.

Sujo, Aly. "Times: All News Not Fit to Print If It Disagrees with Us." *New York Post*. December 5, 2002. p. 6.

———. "Good Times Again for Sportswriter." *New York Post*. December 6, 2002. p. 2.

———. "Times to Take a Mulligan." *New York Post*. December 7, 2002. p. 9.

———. "Raines' Hard Fall." *New York Post*. June 6, 2003. p. 40.

Sullivan, Andrew. Blog entries, December 2002–May 2003. Online Postings. Available at www.andrewsullivan.com/index.php?dish_inc=archives/dish_archive.html.

Sulzberger, Arthur. Speech to the Joan Shorenstein Center on the Press, Politics and Public Policy. Harvard University. Cambridge, Mass. November 20, 2000.

———. Speech to the New York Public Library. New York, N.Y. January 10, 2002.

———. Speech to the German Newspaper Publishers Association. Berlin, Germany. September 30, 2003.

Talese, Gay. *The Kingdom and the Power*. New York: World Publishing, 1969.

Thomas, Jack. "Patricia Smith's Betrayal of Trust." *The Boston Globe*. June 22, 1998. p. A19.

Tifft, Susan E., and Alex S. Jones. *The Trust*. Boston: Little, Brown & Co., 1999.

"The Times and Wen Ho Lee." Editors' Note. *The New York Times*. September 26, 2000. p. A2.

"Times Appoints Editor for Book Review." *The New York Times*. March 11, 2004. p. E7.

"Times Appoints Managing Editor and 2 Deputies." *The New York Times*. May 23, 1997. p. C1.

"The Times Appoints Photography Director." *The New York Times*. April 29, 2004. p. A23.

"The Times Appoints Three Editors to Major Posts." *The New York Times*. September 12, 1992. Section 1, p. 9.

"Times Names Deputy in Washington Bureau." *The New York Times*. February 10, 1985. Section 1, p. 26.

"Times Names Editor to New Post for Features." *The New York Times*. August 6, 2003. p. A15.

"Times Names Metropolitan Chief as Assistant Managing Editor." *The New York Times*. September 26, 2003. p. A18.

"The Times Names New Editor of Magazine." *The New York Times*. September 3, 2003. p. A15.

"Times Names Susan Chira Foreign Editor." *The New York Times*. January 14, 2004. p. A8.

Times Talk. Internal Newsletter. September 2001.

Tomasky, Michael. "His Terrible, Swift Sword." *The Nation*. January 4, 1999. pp. 11ff.

Tyler, Patrick E. "Threats and Responses: Terror Network." *The New York Times*. February 6, 2003. p. A1.

Useem, Michael, Jerry Useem, and Paul Asel. *Upward Bound*. New York: Crown Publishers, 2003.

Vaccaro, Mike. "All the News That's Fit to Print? Like Hell!" *New York Post*. December 6, 2002. p. 128.

Von Hoffman, Nicholas. "Times Readers Need a New Decoder Ring." *The New York Observer*. June 16, 2003. p. 4.

Washington Journal. Interview with Arthur Sulzberger Jr. and Howell Raines by Brian Lamb. C-SPAN1. Air date, September 22, 1997, 6:00 p.m.

Wemple, Erik. "Sniping Coverage." *Washington City Paper*. November 8, 2002.

Wemple, Erik, and Josh Levin. "Off Target," *Washington City Paper*. May 9, 2003.

———. "Repeat Performance." *Washington City Paper*. May 2, 2003.

"Wretched Rhymes of Jayson: Jayson Boasts of Fooling Times." *New York Post*. May 21, 2003. p. 10.

"Writer's Work Published in the Denver Post." *The Denver Post*. May 11, 2003. p. A10.

Yardley, Jonathan. "The Führer Fraud: Selling Hitler's 'Diaries.' " *The Washington Post*. April 9, 1986. p. C2.

Young, Noel. "Clash of Titans in Inglorious Black and White." *The Scotsman*. August 13, 1998. p. 23.

Index

PHOTO: KAI REGAN

SETH MNOOKIN is a contributing editor at *Vanity Fair* magazine. He is a former senior writer for *Newsweek*, where he covered media, popular culture, politics, and crime. His work has appeared in *The New York Times Book Review*, *New York* magazine, *The New Yorker*, Slate, Salon, and elsewhere. A 2004 Joan Shorenstein Fellow at Harvard's Kennedy School of Government, he lives in New York City. For more information, visit www.sethmnookin.com.

ABOUT THE TYPE

The text of this book was set in Janson, a misnamed typeface designed in about 1690 by Nicholas Kis, a Hungarian in Amsterdam. In 1919 the matrices became the property of the Stempel Foundry in Frankfurt. It is an old-style book face of excellent clarity and sharpness. Janson serifs are concave and splayed; the contrast between thick and thin strokes is marked.